Essays in Persuasion

by

John Maynard Keynes

WWW.ClassicHouseBooks.COM

Published by Classic House Books

First Printing 2009
Printed in the United States of America.
10 9 8 7 6 5 4 3 2 1

If this is a work of fiction, it is not meant to depict, portray or represent any particular real persons. All the characters, incidents and dialogues are the products of the author's imagination and are not to be construed as real. Any references or similarities to actual events, entities, real people, living or dead, or to real locales are intended to give the novel a sense of reality. Any similarity in other names, characters, entities, places and incidents is entirely coincidental.

Classic House Books
New York, New York
www.ClassicHouseBooks.com

TABLE OF CONTENTS

III.

After the Suspension of Gold (Sept. 28,1931)

IV.

V.

PREFACE

HERE are collected the croakings of twelve years --the croakings of a Cassandra who could never influence the course of events in time. The volume might have been entitled "Essays in Prophecy and Persuasion", for the Prophecy, unfortunately, has been more successful than the Persuasion. But it was in a spirit of persuasion that most of these essays were written, in an attempt to influence opinion. They were regarded at the time, many of them, as extreme and reckless utterances. But I think that the reader, looking through them to-day, will admit that this was because they often ran directly counter to the overwhelming weight of contemporary sentiment and opinion, and not because of their character in themselves. On the contrary, I feel--reading them again, though I am a prejudiced witness--that they contain more understatement than overstatement, as judged by after-events. That this should be their tendency, is a natural consequence of the circumstances in which they were written. For I wrote many of these essays painfully conscious that a cloud of witnesses would rise up against me and very few in my support, and that I must, therefore, be at great pains to say nothing which I could not substantiate. I was constantly on my guard--as I well remember, looking back --to be as moderate as my convictions and the argument would permit.

All this applies to the first three of the five books into which these essays naturally group themselves, rather than to the last two; that is to say, to the three great controversies of the past decade, into which I plunged myself without reserve,--the Treaty of Peace and the War Debts, the Policy of Deflation, and the Return to the Gold Standard, 1 of which the last two, and indeed in some respects all three, were closely interconnected. In these essays the author was in a hurry, desperately anxious to convince his audience in time. But in the last two books time's chariots make a less disturbing noise. The author is looking into the more distant future, and is ruminating matters which need a slow course of evolution to determine them. He is more free to be leisurely and philosophical. And here emerges more clearly what is in truth his central thesis throughout,--the profound conviction that the Economic Problem, as one may call it for short, the problem of want and poverty and the economic struggle between classes and nations, is nothing but a frightful muddle, a transitory and an unnecessary muddle. For the Western World already has the resources and the technique, if we could create the organisation to use them, capable of reducing the Economic Problem, which now absorbs our moral and material energies, to a position of secondary importance.

Thus the author of these essays, for all his croakings, still hopes and believes that the day is not far off when the Economic Problem will take the back seat where it belongs, and that the arena of the heart and head will be occupied, or re-occupied, by our real problems--the problems of life and of human relations, of creation and behaviour and religion. And it happens that there is a subtle reason drawn from economic analysis why, in this case, faith may work. For if we consistently act on the optimistic hypothesis, this hypothesis will tend to be realised; whilst by acting on the pessimistic hypothesis we can keep ourselves for ever in the pit of want.

The essays have been taken out of the author's printed writings, whether books or pamphlets or newspaper and magazine articles, indiscriminately. The method has been to omit freely (without special indications in the text) anything which appeared to be redundant or unnecessary to the main line of the argument or to have lost interest with the passage of events; but to alter nothing in the text which has been retained. New explanatory footnotes, which have been added in this volume, have been placed between square brackets. The author has endeavoured to secure that the omissions shall not be such as to make the balance of argument to appear in any way different from what it was in the original context. But for the curious inquirer, if there be any, there is provided on the last page of the book a table of references showing the source from which each essay has been taken, and where it can be found in its complete contemporary setting.

I have thought it convenient to choose this date of publication, because we are standing at a point of transition. It is called a National Crisis. But that is not correct--for Great Britain the main crisis is over. There is a lull in our affairs. We are, in the autumn of 1931, resting ourselves in a quiet pool between two waterfalls. The main point is that we have regained our freedom of choice. Scarcely any one in England now believes in the Treaty of Versailles or in the pre-war Gold Standard or in the Policy of Deflation. These battles have been won--mainly by the irresistible pressure of events and only secondarily by the slow undermining of old prejudices. But most of us have, as yet, only a vague idea of what we are going to do next, of how we are going to use our regained freedom of choice. So I should like to clinch the past, as it were, by reminding the reader of what we have been through, and how it appeared at the time, and the nature of the mistakes we made.

J. M. KEYNES

November 8, 1931

I

THE TREATY OF PEACE

1. PARIS (1919)

THE power to become habituated to his surroundings is a marked characteristic of mankind. Very few of us realise with conviction the intensely unusual, unstable, complicated, unreliable, temporary nature of the economic organisation by which Western Europe has lived for the last half-century. We assume some of the most peculiar and temporary of our late advantages as natural, permanent, and to be depended on, and we lay our plans accordingly. On this sandy and false foundation we scheme for social improvement and dress our political platforms, pursue our animosities and particular ambitions, and feel ourselves with enough margin in hand to foster, not assuage, civil conflict in the European family. Moved by insane delusion and reckless self-regard, the German people overturned the foundations on which we all lived and built. But the spokesmen of the French and British people have run the risk of completing the ruin, which Germany began, by a Peace which, if it is carried into effect, must impair yet further, when it might have restored, the delicate, complicated organisation, already shaken and broken by war, through which alone the European peoples can employ themselves and live.

In England the outward aspect of life does not yet teach us to feel or realise in the least that an age is over. We are busy picking up the threads of our life where we dropped them, with this difference only, that many of us seem a good deal richer than we were before. Where we spent millions before the war, we have now learnt that we can spend hundreds of millions and apparently not suffer for it. Evidently we did not exploit to the utmost the possibilities of our economic life. We look, therefore, not only to a return to the comforts of 1914, but to an immense broadening and intensification of them. All classes alike thus build their plans, the rich to spend more and save less, the poor to spend more and work less.

But perhaps it is only in England (and America) that it is possible to be so unconscious. In continental Europe the earth heaves and no one but is aware of the rumblings. There it is not just a matter of extravagance or "labour troubles"; but of life and death, of starvation and existence, and of the fearful convulsions of a dying civilisation.

For one who spent in Paris the greater part of the six months which succeeded the Armistice, an occasional visit to London was a strange experience. England still stands outside Europe. Europe's voiceless tremors do not reach her. Europe is apart and England is not of her flesh and body. But Europe is solid with herself. France, Germany, Italy, Austria, and Holland, Russia and Roumania and Poland, throb together, and their structure and civilisation are essentially one. They flourished together, they have rocked together in a war, which we, in spite of our enormous contributions and sacrifices, (like though in a less degree than America) economically stood outside, and they may fall together. In this lies the destructive significance of the Peace of Paris. If the European Civil War is to end with France and Italy abusing their momentary victorious power to destroy Germany and Austria-Hungary now prostrate, they invite their own destruction also, being so deeply and inextricably intertwined with their victims by hidden psychic and economic bonds. At any rate an Englishman who took part in the Conference of Paris and was during those months a member of the Supreme Economic Council of the Allied Powers, was bound to become, for him a new experience, a European in his cares and outlook. There, at the nerve centre of the European system, his British preoccupations must largely fall away and he must be haunted by other and more dreadful spectres. Paris was a nightmare, and every one there was morbid. A sense of impending catastrophe overhung the frivolous scene; the futility and smallness of man before the great events confronting him; the mingled significance and unreality of the decisions; levity, blindness, insolence, confused cries from without,--all the elements of ancient tragedy were there. Seated indeed amid the theatrical trappings of the French Saloons of State, one could wonder if the extraordinary visages of Wilson and of Clemenceau, with their fixed hue and unchanging characterisation, were really faces at all and not the tragic-comic masks of some strange drama or puppet-show.

The proceedings of Paris all had this air of extraordinary importance and unimportance at the same time. The decisions seemed charged with consequences to the future of human society; yet the air whispered that the word was not flesh, that it was futile, insignificant, of no effect, dissociated from events; and one felt most strongly the impression, described by Tolstoy in War and Peace or by Hardy in The Dynasts, of events marching on to their fated conclusion uninfluenced and unaffected by the cerebrations of Statesmen in Council:

SPIRIT OF THE YEARS Observe that all wide sight and self-command Desert these throngs now driven to demonry By the Immanent Unrecking. Nought remains But vindictiveness here amid the strong, And there amid the weak an impotent rage.

SPIRIT OF THE PITIES Why prompts the Will so senseless-shaped a doing?

SPIRIT OF THE YEARS I have told thee that It works unwittingly, As one possessed, not judging

2. THE CAPACITY OF GERMANY TO PAY REPARATIONS

(1919) It is evident that Germany's pre-war capacity to pay an annual foreign tribute has not been unaffected by the almost total loss of her colonies, her overseas connections, her mercantile marine, and her foreign properties, by the cession of ten per cent of her territory and population, of one-third of her coal and of three-quarters of her iron ore, by two million casualties amongst men in the prime of life, by the starvation of her people for four years, by the burden of a vast war debt, by the depreciation of her currency to less than one-seventh its former value, by the disruption of her allies and their territories, by Revolution at home and Bolshevism on her borders, and by all the unmeasured ruin in strength and hope of four years of all-swallowing war and final defeat.

All this, one would have supposed, is evident. Yet most estimates of a great indemnity from Germany depend on the assumption that she is in a position to conduct in the future a vastly greater trade than ever she has had in the past. For the purpose of arriving at a figure it is of no great consequence whether payment takes the form of cash (or rather of foreign exchange) or is partly effected in kind (coal, dyes, timber, etc.), as contemplated by the Treaty. In any event, it is only by the export of specific commodities that Germany can pay, and the method of turning the value of these exports to account for Reparation purposes is, comparatively, a matter of detail.

We shall lose ourselves in mere hypothesis unless we return in some degree to first principles, and, whenever we can, to such statistics as there are. It is certain that an annual payment can only be made by Germany over a series of years by diminishing her imports and increasing her exports, thus enlarging the balance in her favour which is available for effecting payments abroad. Germany can pay in the long run in goods, and in goods only, whether these goods are furnished direct to the Allies, or whether they are sold to neutrals and the neutral credits so arising are then made over to the Allies. The most solid basis for estimating the extent to which this process can be carried is to be found, therefore, in an analysis of her trade returns before the war. Only on the basis of such an analysis, supplemented by some general data as to the aggregate wealthproducing capacity of the country, can a rational guess be made as to the maximum degree to which the exports of Germany could be brought to exceed her imports.

In the year 1913 Germany's imports amounted to £538,000,000 and her exports to £505,000,000, exclusive of transit trade and bullion. That is to say, imports exceeded exports by about £33,000,000. On the average of the five years ending 1913, however, her imports exceeded her exports by a substantially larger amount, namely, £74,000,000. It follows, therefore, that more than the whole of Germany's pre-war balance for new foreign investment was derived from the interest on her existing foreign securities, and from the profits of her shipping, foreign banking, etc. As her foreign properties and her mercantile marine are now to be taken from her, and as her foreign banking and other miscellaneous sources of revenue from abroad have been largely destroyed, it appears that, on the prewar basis of exports and imports, Germany, so far from having a surplus wherewith to make a foreign payment, would be not nearly selfsupporting. Her first task, therefore, must be to effect a readjustment of consumption and production to cover this deficit. Any further economy she can effect in the use of imported commodities, and any further stimulation of exports will then be available for Reparation.

Let us run over the chief items of export: (1) Iron goods. In view of Germany's loss of resources, an increased net export seems impossible and a large decrease probable. (2) Machinery. Some increase is possible. (3) Coal and coke. The value of Germany's net export before the war was £22,000,000; the Allies have agreed that for the time being 20,000,000 tons is the maximum possible export with a problematic (and in fact) impossible increase to 40,000,000 tons at some future time; even on the basis of 20,000,000 tons we have virtually no increase of value, measured in pre-war prices; whilst, if this amount is exacted, there must be a decrease of far greater value in the export of manufactured articles requiring coal for their production. (4) Woollen goods. An increase is impossible without the raw wool, and, having regard to the other claims on supplies of raw wool, a decrease is likely. (5) Cotton goods. The same considerations apply as to wool. (6) Cereals. There never was and never can be a net export. (7) Leather goods. The same considerations apply as to wool.

We have now covered nearly half of Germany's pre-war exports, and there is no other commodity which formerly represented as much as 3 per cent of her exports. In what commodity is she to pay? Dyes?--their total value in 1913 was £10,000,000. Toys? Potash?--1913 exports were worth £3,000,000. And even if the commodities could be specified, in what markets are they to be sold?-- remembering that we have in mind goods to the value not of tens of millions annually, but of hundreds of millions.

On the side of imports, rather more is possible. By lowering the standard of life, an appreciable reduction of expenditure on imported commodities may be possible. But,as we have already seen, many large items are incapable of reduction without reacting on the volume of exports.

Let us put our guess as high as we can without being foolish, and suppose that after a time Germany will be able, in spite of the reduction of her resources, her facilities, her markets, and her productive power, to increase her exports and diminish her imports so as to improve her trade balance altogether by £100,000,000 annually, measured in prewar prices. This adjustment is first required to liquidate the adverse trade balance, which in the five years before the war averaged £74,000,000; but we will assume that after allowing for this, she is left with a favourable trade balance of £50,000,000 a year. Doubling this to allow for the rise in post-war prices, we have a figure of £100,000,000. Having regard to the political, social, and human factors, as well as to the purely economic, I doubt if Germany could be made to pay this sum annually over a period of 30 years; but it would not be foolish to assert or to hope that she could.

Such a figure, allowing 5 per cent for interest, and 1 per cent for repayment of capital, represents a capital sum having a present value of about £1700 million.

I reach, therefore, the final conclusion that, including all methods of payment--immediately transferable wealth, ceded property, and an annual tribute--£2,000,000,000 is a safe maximum figure of Germany's capacity to pay. In all the actual circumstances, I do not believe that she can pay as much.

There is only one head under which I see a possibility of adding to the figure reached on the line of argument adopted above; that is, if German labour is actually transported to the devastated areas and there engaged in the work of reconstruction. I have heard that a limited scheme of this kind is actually in view. The additional contribution thus obtainable depends on the number of labourers which the German Government could contrive to maintain in this way and also on the number which, over a period of years, the Belgian and French inhabitants would tolerate in their midst. In any case, it would seem very difficult to employ on the actual work of reconstruction, even over a number of years, imported labour having a net present value exceeding (say) £250,000,000; and even this would not prove in practice a net addition to the annual contributions obtainable in other ways.

A capacity of £8,000,000,000 or even of £5,000,000,000 is, therefore, not within the limits of reasonable possibility. It is for those who believe that Germany can make an annual payment amounting to hundreds of millions sterling to say in what specific commodities they intend this payment to be made, and in what markets the goods are to be sold. Until they proceed to some degree of detail, and are able to produce some tangible argument in favour of their conclusions, they do not deserve to be believed.

I make three provisos only, none of which affect the force of my argument for immediate practical purposes.

First: If the Allies were to "nurse" the trade and industry of Germany for a period of five or ten years, supplying her with large loans, and with ample shipping, food, and raw materials during that period, building up markets for her, and deliberately applying all their resources and goodwill to making her the greatest industrial nation in Europe, if not in the world, a substantially larger sum could probably be extracted thereafter; for Germany is capable of very great productivity.

Second: Whilst I estimate in terms of money, I assume that there is no revolutionary change in the purchasing power of our unit of value. If the value of gold were to sink to a half or a tenth of its present value, the real burden of a payment fixed in terms of gold would be reduced proportionately. If a gold sovereign comes to be worth what a shilling is worth now, then, of course, Germany can pay a larger sum than I have named, measured in gold sovereigns.

Third: I assume that there is no revolutionary change in the yield of Nature and material to man's labour. It is not impossible that the progress of science should bring within our reach methods and devices by which the whole standard of life would be raised immeasurably, and a given volume of products would represent but a portion of the human effort which it represents now. In this case all standards of "capacity" would be changed everywhere. But the fact that all things are possible is no excuse for talking foolishly.

It is true that in 1870 no man could have predicted Germany's capacity in 1910. We cannot expect to legislate for a generation or more. The secular changes in man's economic condition and the liability of human forecast to error are as likely to lead to mistake in one direction as in another. We cannot as reasonable men do better than base our policy on the evidence we have and adapt it to the five or ten years over which we may suppose ourselves to have some measure of prevision; and we are not at fault if we leave on one side the extreme chances of human existence and of revolutionary changes in the order of Nature or of man's relations to her. The fact that we have no adequate knowledge of Germany's capacity to pay over a long period of years is no justification (as I have heard some people claim that it is) for the statement that she can pay ten thousand million pounds.

Why has the world been so credulous of the unveracities of politicians? If an explanation is needed, I attribute this particular credulity to the following influences in part.

In the first place, the vast expenditures of the war, the inflation of prices, and the depreciation of currency, leading up to a complete instability of the unit of value, have made us lose all sense of number and magnitude in matters of finance. What we believed to be the limits of possibility have been so enormously exceeded, and those who founded their expectations on the past have been so often wrong, that the man in the street is now prepared to believe anything which is told him with some show of authority, and the larger the figure the more readily he swallows it.

But those who look into the matter more deeply are sometimes misled by a fallacy, much more plausible to reasonable persons. Such a one might base his conclusions on Germany's total surplus of annual productivity as distinct from her export surplus. Helfferich's estimate of Germany's annual increment of wealth in 1913 was £400,000,000 to £425,000,000 (exclusive of increased money value of existing land and property). Before the war, Germany spent between £50,000,000 and £100,000,000 on armaments, with which she can now dispense. Why, therefore, should she not pay over to the Allies an annual sum of £500,000,000? This puts the crude argument in its strongest and most plausible form.

But there are two errors in it. First of all, Germany's annual savings, after what she has suffered in the war and by the Peace, will fall far short of what they were before, and, if they are taken from her year by year in future, they cannot again reach their previous level. The loss of Alsace-Lorraine, Poland, and Upper Silesia could not be assessed in terms of surplus productivity at less than £50,000,000 annually. Germany is supposed to have profited about £100,000,000 per annum from her ships, her foreign investments, and her foreign banking and connections, all of which have now been taken from her. Her saving on armaments is far more than balanced by her annual charge for pensions now estimated at £250,000,000, 1 which represents a real loss of productive capacity. And even if we put on one side the burden of the internal debt, which amounts to 240 milliards of marks, as being a question of internal distribution rather than of productivity, we must still allow for the foreign debt incurred by Germany during the war, the exhaustion of her stock of raw materials, the depletion of her livestock, the impaired productivity of her soil from lack of manures and of labour, and the diminution in her wealth from the failure to keep up many repairs and renewals over a period of nearly five years. Germany is not as rich as she was before the war, and the diminution in her future savings for these reasons, quite apart from the factors previously allowed for, could hardly be put at less than ten per cent, that is £40,000,000 annually.

These factors have already reduced Germany's annual surplus to less than the £100,000,000 at which we arrived on other grounds as the maximum of her annual payments. But even if the rejoinder be made, that we have not yet allowed for the lowering of the standard of life and comfort in Germany which may reasonably be imposed on a defeated enemy, there is still a fundamental fallacy in the method of calculation. An annual surplus available for home investment can only be converted into a surplus available for export abroad by a radical change in the kind of work performed. Labour, while it may be available and efficient for domestic services in Germany, may yet be able to find no outlet in foreign trade. We are back on the same question which faced us in our examination of the export trade--in what export trade is German labour going to find a greatly increased outlet? Labour can only be diverted into new channels with loss of efficiency, and a large expenditure of capital. The annual surplus which German labour can produce for capital improvements at home is no measure, either theoretically or practically, of the annual tribute which she can pay abroad.

I cannot leave this subject as though its just treatment wholly depended either on our own pledges or on economic facts. The policy of reducing Germany to servitude for a generation, of degrading the lives of millions of human beings, and of depriving a whole nation of happiness should be abhorrent and detestable, --abhorrent and detestable, even if it were possible, even if it enriched ourselves, even if it did not sow the decay of the whole civilised life of Europe. Some preach it in the name of Justice. In the great events of man's history, in the unwinding of the complex fates of nations Justice is not so simple. And if it were, nations are not authorised, by religion or by natural morals, to visit on the children of their enemies the misdoings of parents or of rulers.

3. PROPOSALS FOR THE RECONSTRUCTION OF EUROPE (1919)

(i) The Revision of the Treaty

Are any constitutional means open to us for altering the Treaty? President Wilson and General Smuts, who believe that to have secured the Covenant of the League of Nations outweighs much evil in the rest of the Treaty, have indicated that we must look to the League for the gradual evolution of a more tolerable life for Europe. "There are territorial settlements," General Smuts wrote in his statement on signing the Peace Treaty, "which will need revision. There are guarantees laid down which we all hope will soon be found out of harmony with the new peaceful temper and unarmed state of our former enemies. There are punishments foreshadowed over most of which a calmer mood may yet prefer to pass the sponge of oblivion. There are indemnities stipulated which cannot be exacted without grave injury to the industrial revival of Europe, and which it will be in the interests of all to render more tolerable and moderate. . . . I am confident that the League of Nations will yet prove the path of escape for Europe out of the ruin brought about by this war." Without the League, President Wilson informed the Senate when he presented the Treaty to them early in July 1919, ". . . long-continued supervision of the task of reparation which Germany was to undertake to complete within the next generation might entirely break down; the reconsideration and revision of administrative arrangements and restrictions which the Treaty prescribed, but which it recognised might not provide lasting advantage or be entirely fair if too long enforced, would be impracticable."

Can we look forward with fair hopes to securing from the operation of the League those benefits which two of its principal begetters thus encourage us to expect from it? The relevant passage is to be found in Article XIX. of the Covenant, which runs as follows:

The Assembly may from time to time advise the reconsideration by Members of the League of treaties which have become inapplicable and the consideration of international conditions whose continuance might endanger the peace of the world.

But alas! Article V. provides that "Except where otherwise expressly provided in this Covenant or by the terms of the present Treaty, decisions at any meeting of the Assembly or of the Council shall require the agreement of all the Members of the League represented at the meeting." Does not this provision reduce the League, so far as concerns an early reconsideration of any of the terms of the Peace Treaty, into a body merely for wasting time? If all the parties to the Treaty are unanimously of opinion that it requires alteration in a particular sense, it does not need a League and a Covenant to put the business through. Even when the Assembly of the League is unanimous it can only "advise" reconsideration by the members specially affected.

But the League will operate, say its supporters, by its influence on the public opinion of the world, and the view of the majority will carry decisive weight in practice, even though constitutionally it is of no effect. Let us pray that this be so. Yet the League in the hands of the trained European diplomatist may become an unequalled instrument for obstruction and delay. The revision of Treaties is entrusted primarily, not to the Council, which meets frequently, but to the Assembly, which will meet more rarely and must become, as any one with an experience of large Inter-Ally Conferences must know, an unwieldy polyglot debating society in which the greatest resolution and the best management may fail altogether to bring issues to a head against an opposition in favour of thestatus quo. There are indeed two disastrous blots on the Covenant,--Article V., which prescribes unanimity, and the much-criticised Article X., by which "The Members of the League undertake to respect and preserve as against external aggression the territorial integrity and existing political independence of all Members of the League." These two Articles together go some way to destroy the conception of the League as an instrument of progress, and to equip it from the outset with an almost fatal bias towards the status quo. It is these Articles which have reconciled to the League some of its original opponents, who now hope to make of it another Holy Alliance for the perpetuation of the economic ruin of their enemies and the Balance of Power in their own interests which they believe themselves to have established by the Peace.

But while it would be wrong and foolish to conceal from ourselves in the interests of "idealism" the real difficulties of the position in the special matter of revising treaties, that is no reason for any of us to decry the League, which the wisdom of the world may yet transform into a powerful instrument of peace, and which in Articles XI.-XVII. 1 has already accomplished a great and beneficent achievement. I agree, therefore, that our first efforts for the Revision of the Treaty must be made through the League rather than in any other way, in the hope that the force of general opinion, and if necessary, the use of financial pressure and financial inducements, may be enough to prevent a recalcitrant minority from exercising their right of veto. We must trust the new Governments, whose existence I premise in the principal Allied countries, to show a profounder wisdom and a greater magnanimity than their predecessors.I do not intend to enter here into details, or to attempt a revision of the Treaty clause by clause. I limit myself to three great changes which are necessary for the economic life of Europe, relating to Reparation, to Coal and Iron, and to Tariffs. Reparation.--If the sum demanded for Reparation is less than what the Allies are entitled to on a strict interpretation of their engagements, it is unnecessary to particularise the items it represents or to hear arguments about its compilation. I suggest, therefore, the following settlement:

1. The amount of the payment to be made by Germany in respect of Reparation and the costs of the Armies of Occupation might be fixed at £2000 million.

2. The surrender of merchant ships and submarine cables under the Treaty, of war material under the Armistice, of State property in ceded territory, of claims against such territory in respect of public debt, and of Germany's claims against her former Allies, should be reckoned as worth the lump sum of £500 million, without any attempt being made to evaluate them item by item.

3. The balance of £1500 million should not carry interest pending its repayment, and should be paid by Germany in thirty annual instalments of £50 million, beginning in 1923.

4. The Reparation Commission should be dissolved, or, if any duties remain for it to perform, it should become an appanage of the League of Nations and should include representatives of Germany and of the neutral States.

5. Germany would be left to meet the annual instalments in such manner as she might see fit, any complaint against her for non-fulfilment of her obligations being lodged with the League of Nations. That is to say, there would be no further expropriation of German private property abroad, except so far as is required to meet private German obligations out of the proceeds of such property already liquidated or in the hands of Public Trustees and EnemyProperty Custodians in the Allied countries and in the United States; and, in particular, Article 260 (which provides for the expropriation of German interests in public utility enterprises) would be abrogated.

6. No attempt should be made to extract Reparation payments from Austria.

Coal and Iron.--(1) The Allies' options on coal under Annex V. should be abandoned, but Germany's obligation to make good France's loss of coal through the destruction of her mines should remain. This obligation should lapse, nevertheless, in the event of the coal districts of Upper Silesia being taken from Germany in the final settlement consequent on the plebiscite.

(2) The arrangement as to the Saar should hold good, except that, on the one hand, Germany should receive no credit for the mines, and, on the other should receive back both the mines and the territory without payment and unconditionally after ten years. But this should be conditional on France's entering into an agreement for the same period to supply Germany from Lorraine with at least 50 per cent of the iron ore which was carried from Lorraine into Germany proper before the war, in return for an undertaking from Germany to supply Lorraine with an amount of coal equal to the whole amount formerly sent to Lorraine from Germany proper, after allowing for the output of the Saar.

(3) The arrangement as to Upper Silesia should hold good. That is to say, a plebiscite should be held, and in coming to a final decision "regard will be paid (by the principal Allied and Associated Powers) to the wishes of the inhabitants as shown by the vote, and to the geographical and economic conditions of the locality." But the Allies should declare that in their judgement "economic condi-

tions" require the inclusion of the coal districts in Germany unless the wishes of the inhabitants are decidedly to the contrary.

Tariffs.--A Free Trade Union should be established under the auspices of the League of Nations of countries undertaking to impose no protectionist tariffs 1 whatever against the produce of other members of the Union. Germany, Poland, the new States which formerly composed the Austro-Hungarian and Turkish Empires, and the Mandated States should be compelled to adhere to this Union for ten years, after which time adherence would be voluntary. The adherence of other States would be voluntary from the outset. But it is to be hoped that the United Kingdom, at any rate, would become an original member.

By fixing the Reparation payments well within Germany's capacity to pay, we make possible the renewal of hope and enterprise within her territory, we avoid the perpetual friction and opportunity of improper pressure arising out of Treaty clauses which are impossible of fulfilment, and we render unnecessary the intolerable powers of the Reparation Commission.

By a moderation of the clauses relating directly or indirectly to coal, and by the exchange of iron ore, we permit the continuance of Germany's industrial life, and put limits on the loss of productivity which would be brought about otherwise by the interference of political frontiers with the natural localisation of the iron and steel industry.

By the proposed Free Trade Union some part of the loss of organisation and economic efficiency may be retrieved, which must otherwise result from the innumerable new political frontiers now created between greedy, jealous, immature, and economically incomplete, nationalist States. Economic frontiers were tolerable so long as an immense territory was included in a few great Empires; but they will not be tolerable when the Empires of Germany, AustriaHungary, Russia, and Turkey have been partitioned between some twenty independent authorities. A Free Trade Union, comprising the whole of Central, Eastern, and SouthEastern Europe, Siberia, Turkey, and (I should hope) the United Kingdom, Egypt, and India, might do as much for the peace and prosperity of the world as the League of Nations itself. Belgium, Holland, Scandinavia, and Switzerland might be expected to adhere to it shortly. And it would be greatly to be desired by their friends that France and Italy also should see their way to adhesion.

It would be objected, I suppose, by some critics that such an arrangement might go some way in effect towards realising the former German dream of Mittel-Europa. If other countries were so foolish as to remain outside the Union and to leave to Germany all its advantages, there might be some truth in this. But an economic system, to which every one had the opportunity of belonging and which gave special privilege to none, is surely absolutely free from the objections of a privileged and avowedly imperialistic scheme of exclusion and discrimination. Our attitude to these criticisms must be determined by our whole moral and emotional reaction to the future of international relations and the Peace of the World. If we take the view that for at least a generation to come Germany cannot be trusted with even a modicum of prosperity, that while all our recent Allies are angels of light, all our recent enemies, Germans, Austrians, Hungarians, and the rest, are children of the devil, that year by year Germany must be kept impoverished and her children starved and crippled, and that she must be ringed round by enemies; then we shall reject all the proposals of this chapter, and particularly those which may assist Germany to regain a part of her former material prosperity and find a means of livelihood for the industrial population of her towns. But if this view of nations and of their relation to one another is adopted by the democracies of Western Europe, and is financed by the United States, heaven help us all. If we aim deliberately at the impoverishment of Central Europe, vengeance, I dare predict, will not limp. Nothing can then delay for very long that final civil war between the forces of Reaction and the despairing convulsions of Revolution, before which the horrors of the late German war will fade into nothing, and which will destroy, whoever is victor, the civilisation and the progress of our generation. Even though the result disappoint us, must we not base our actions on better expectations, and believe that the prosperity and happiness of one country promotes that of others, that the solidarity of man is not a fiction, and that nations can still afford to treat other nations as fellow-creatures?

Such changes as I have proposed above might do something appreciable to enable the industrial populations of Europe to continue to earn a livelihood. But they would not be enough by themselves. In particular, France would be a loser on paper (on paper only, for she will never secure the actual fulfilment of her present claims), and an escape from her embarrassments must be shown her in some other direction. I proceed, therefore, to proposals, first, for the adjustment of the claims of America and the Allies amongst themselves; and second, for the provision of sufficient credit to enable Europe to re-create her stock of circulating capital.

(ii) The Settlement of Inter-Ally Indebtedness In proposing a modification of the Reparation terms, I have considered them so far only in relation to Germany. But fairness requires that so great a reduction in the amount should be accompanied by a readjustment of its apportionment between the Allies themselves. The professions which our statesmen made on every platform during the war, as well as other considerations, surely require that the areas damaged by the enemy's invasion should receive a priority of compensation. While this was one of the ultimate objects for which we said we were fighting, we never included the recovery of separation allowances amongst our war aims. I suggest, therefore, that we should by our acts prove ourselves sincere and trustworthy, and that accordingly Great Britain should waive altogether her claims for cash payment, in favour of Belgium, Serbia, and France. The whole of the payments made by Germany would then be subject to the prior charge of repairing the material injury done to those countries and provinces which suffered actual invasion by the enemy; and I believe that the sum of £1,500,000,000 thus available would be adequate to cover entirely the actual costs of restoration. Further, it is only by a complete subordination of her own claims for cash compensation that Great Britain can ask with clean hands for a revision of the Treaty and clear her honour from the breach of faith for which she bears the main responsibility, as a result of the policy to which the General Election of 1918 pledged her representatives.

With the Reparation problem thus cleared up it would be possible to bring forward with a better grace and more hope of success two other financial proposals, each of which involves an appeal to the generosity of the United States. The first is for the entire cancellation of Inter-Ally indebtedness (that is to say, indebtedness between the Governments of the Allied and Associated countries) incurred for the purposes of the war. This proposal, which has been put forward already in certain quarters, is one which I believe to be absolutely essential to the future prosperity of the world. It would be an act of far-seeing statesmanship for the United Kingdom and the United States, the two Powers chiefly concerned, to adopt it. The sums of money which are involved are shown approximately in the following table:

Loans to	By United States.	By United Kingdom.	By France.	Total.
	£	£	£	£
United Kingdom	842,000,000	. . . .		842,000,000
France	550,000,000	508,000,000	. .	1,058,000,000
Italy	325,000,000	467,000,000	35,000,000	827,000,000
Russia	38,000,000	568,000,000	160,000,000	766,000,000
Belgium	80,000,000	98,000,000	90,000,000	268,000,000
Serbia and Jugo-Slavia	20,000,000	20,000,000	20,000,000	60,000,000
Other Allies	35,000,000	79,000,000	50,000,000	164,000,000
Total	1,900,000,000	1, 1740,000,000	355,000,000	3,995,000,000

Thus the total volume of Inter-Ally indebtedness, assuming that loans from one Ally are not set off against loans to another, is nearly £4,000,000,000. The United States is a lender only. The United Kingdom has lent about twice as much as she has borrowed. France has borrowed about three times as much as she has lent. The other Allies have been borrowers only.

If all the above Inter-Ally indebtedness were mutually forgiven, the net result on paper (i.e. assuming all the loans to be good) would be a surrender by the United States of about £2,000,000,000 and by the United Kingdom of about £900,000,000. France would gain about £700,000,000 and Italy about £800,000,000. But these figures overstate the loss to the United Kingdom and understate the gain to France; for a large part of the loans made by both these countries has been to Russia and cannot, by any stretch of imagination, be considered good. If the loans which the United Kingdom has made to her Allies are reckoned to be worth 50 per cent of their full value (an arbitrary but convenient assumption which the Chancellor of the Exchequer has adopted on more than one occasion as being as good as any other for the purposes of an approximate national balance sheet), the operation would involve her neither in loss nor in gain. But in whatever way the net result is calculated on paper, the relief in anxiety which such a liquidation of the position would carry with it would be very great. It is from the United States, therefore, that the proposal asks generosity.

Speaking with a very intimate knowledge of the relations throughout the war between the British, the American, and the other Allied Treasuries, I believe this to be an act of generosity for which Europe can fairly ask, provided Europe is making an honourable attempt in other directions, not to continue war, economic or otherwise, but to achieve the economic reconstitution of the whole Continent. The financial sacrifices of the United States have been, in proportion to her wealth, immensely less than those of the European States. This could hardly have been otherwise. It was a European quarrel, in which the United States Government could not have justified itself before its citizens in expending the whole national strength, as did the Europeans. After the United States came into the war her financial assistance was lavish and unstinted, and without this assistance the Allies could never have won the war, quite apart from the decisive influence of the arrival of the American troops.

But in speaking thus as we do of American financial assistance, we tacitly assume, and America, I believe, assumed it too when she gave the money, that it was not in the nature of an investment. If Europe is going to repay the £2,000,000,000 worth of financial assistance which she has had from the United States with compound interest at 5 per cent, the matter takes on quite a different complexion. If America's advances are to be regarded in this light, her relative financial sacrifice has been very slight indeed.

Failing such a settlement as is now proposed,   the war will have ended with a network of heavy tribute payable from one Ally to another. The total amount of this tribute is even likely to exceed the amount obtainable from the enemy; and the war will have ended with the intolerable result of the Allies paying indemnities to one another instead of receiving them from the enemy.

For this reason the question of Inter-Allied indebtedness is closely bound up with the intense popular feeling amongst the European Allies on the question of indemnities,--a feeling which is based, not on any reasonable calculation of what Germany can, in fact, pay, but on a well-founded appreciation of the unbearable financial situation in which these countries will find themselves unless she pays. Take Italy as an extreme example. If Italy can reasonably be expected to pay £800,000,000, surely Germany can and ought to pay an immeasurably higher figure. Or if it is decided (as it must be) that Austria can pay next to nothing, is it not an intolerable conclusion that Italy should be loaded with a crushing tribute, while Austria escapes? Or, to put it slightly differently, how can Italy be expected to submit to payment of this great sum and see CzechoSlovakia pay little or nothing? At the other end of the scale there is the United Kingdom. Here the financial position is different, since to ask us to pay £800,000,000 is a very different proposition from asking Italy to pay it. But the sentiment is much the same. If we have to be satisfied without full compensation from Germany, how bitter will be the protests against paying it to the United States. We, it will be said, have to be content with a claim against the bankrupt estates of Germany, France, Italy, and Russia, whereas the United States has secured a first mortgage upon us. The case of France is at least as overwhelming. She can barely secure from Germany the full measure of the destruction of her countryside. Yet victorious France must pay her friends and Allies more than four times the indemnity which in the defeat of 1870 she paid Germany. The hand of Bismarck was light compared with that of an Ally or of an Associate. A settlement of Inter-Ally indebtedness is, therefore, an indispensable preliminary to the peoples of the Allied countries facing, with other than a maddened and exasperated heart, the inevitable truth about the prospects of an indemnity from the enemy.

It might be an exaggeration to say that it is impossible for the European Allies to pay the capital and interest due from them on these debts, but to make them do so would certainly be to impose a crushing burden. They may be expected, therefore, to make constant attempts to evade or escape payment, and these attempts will be a constant source of international friction and ill-will for many years to come. A debtor nation does not love its creditor, and it is fruitless to expect feelings of goodwill from France, Italy, and Russia towards this country or towards America, if their future development is stifled for many years to come by the annual tribute which they must pay us. There will be a great incentive to them to seek their friends in other directions, and any future rupture of peaceable relations will always carry with it the enormous advantage of escaping the payment of external debts. If, on the other hand, these great debts are forgiven, a stimulus will be given to the solidarity and true friendliness of the nations lately associated.

The existence of the great war debts is a menace to financial stability everywhere. There is no European country in which repudiation may not soon become an important political issue. In the case of internal debt, however, there are interested parties on both sides, and the question is one of the internal distribution of wealth. With external debts this is not so, and the creditor nations may soon find their interest inconveniently bound up with the maintenance of a particular type of government or economic organisation in the debtor countries. Entangling alliances or entangling leagues are nothing to the entanglements of cash owing.

The final consideration influencing the reader's attitude to this proposal must, however, depend on his view as to the future place in the world's progress of the vast paper entanglements which are our legacy from war finance both at home and abroad. The war has ended with every one owing every one else immense sums of money. Germany owes a large sum to the Allies; the Allies owe a large sum to Great Britain; and Great Britain owes a large sum to the United States. The holders of war loan in every country are owed a large sum by the State; and the State in its turn is owed a large sum by these and other taxpayers. The whole position is in the highest degree artificial, misleading, and vexatious. We shall never be able to move again, unless we can free our limbs from these paper shackles. A general bonfire is so great a necessity that unless we can make of it an orderly and good-tempered affair in which no serious injustice is done to any one, it will, when it comes at last, grow into a conflagration that may destroy much else as well. As regards internal debt, I am one of those who believe that a capital levy for the extinction of debt is an absolute pre-requisite of sound finance in every one of the European belligerent countries. But the continuance on a huge scale of indebtedness between Governments has special dangers of its own.

Before the middle of the nineteenth century no nation owed payments to a foreign nation on any considerable scale, except such tributes as were exacted under the compulsion of actual occupation in force and, at one time, by absentee princes under the sanctions of feudalism. It is true that the need for European capitalism to find an outlet in the New World has led during the past fifty years, though even now on a relatively modest scale, to such countries as Argentine owing an annual sum to such countries as England. But the system is fragile; and it has only survived because its burden on the paying countries has not so far been oppressive, because this burden is represented by real assets and is bound up with the property system generally, and because the sums already lent are not unduly large in relation to those which it is still hoped to borrow. Bankers are used to this system, and believe it to be a necessary part of the permanent order of society. They are disposed to believe, therefore, by analogy with it, that a comparable system between Governments, on a far vaster and definitely oppressive scale, represented by no real assets, and less closely associated with the property system, is natural and reasonable and in conformity with human nature.

I doubt this view of the world. Even capitalism at home, which engages many local sympathies, which plays a real part in the daily process of production, and upon the security of which the present organisation of Society largely depends, is not very safe. But however this may be, will the discontented peoples of Europe be willing for a generation to come so to order their lives that an appreciable part of their daily produce may be available to meet a foreign payment, the reason of which, whether as between Europe and America, or as between Germany and the rest of Europe, does not spring compellingly from their sense of justice or duty?

On the one hand, Europe must depend in the long run on her own daily labour and not on the largesse of America; but, on the other hand, she will not pinch herself in order that the fruit of her daily labour may go elsewhere. In short, I do not believe that any of these tributes will continue to be paid, at the best, for more than a very few years. They do not square with human nature or agree with the spirit of the age.

If there is any force in this mode of thought, expediency and generosity agree together, and the policy which will best promote immediate friendship between nations will not conflict with the permanent interests of the benefactors.

(iii) An International Loan I pass to a second financial proposal. The requirements of Europe are immediate. The prospect of being relieved of oppressive interest payments to England and America over the whole life of the next two generations (and of receiving from Germany some assistance year by year to the costs of restoration) would free the future from excessive anxiety. But it would not meet the ills of the immediate present,--the excess of Europe's imports over her exports, the adverse exchange, and the disorder of the currency. It will be very difficult for European production to get started again without a temporary measure of external assistance. I am therefore a supporter of an international loan in some shape or form, such as has been advocated in many quarters in France, Germany, and England, and also in the United States. In whatever way the ultimate responsibility for repayment is distributed, the burden of finding the immediate resources must inevitably fall in major part upon the United States.

The chief objections to all the varieties of this species of project are, I suppose, the following. The United States is disinclined to entangle herself further (after recent experiences) in the affairs of Europe, and, anyhow, has for the time being no more capital to spare for export on a large scale. There is no guarantee that Europe will put financial assistance to proper use, or that she will not squander it and be in just as bad case two or three years hence as she is in now;--M. Klotz will use the money to put off the day of taxation a little longer, Italy and Jugo-Slavia will fight one another on the proceeds, Poland will devote it to fulfilling towards all her neighbours the military rôle which France has designed for her, the governing classes of Roumania will divide up the booty amongst themselves. In short, America would have postponed her own capital developments and raised her own cost of living in order that Europe might continue for another year or two the practices, the policy, and the men of the past nine months. And as for assistance to Germany, is it reasonable or at all tolerable that the European Allies, having stripped Germany of her last vestige of working capital, in opposition to the arguments and appeals of the American financial representatives at Paris, should then turn to the United States for funds to rehabilitate the victim in sufficient measure to allow the spoliation to recommence in a year or two?

There is no answer to these objections as matters are now. If I had influence at the United States Treasury, I would not lend a penny to a single one of the present Governments of Europe. They are not to be trusted with resources which they would devote to the furtherance of policies in repugnance to which, in spite of the President's failure to assert either the might or the ideals of the people of the United States, the Republican and the Democratic parties are probably united. But if, as we must pray they will, the souls of the European peoples turn away this winter from the false idols which have survived the war that created them, and substitute in their hearts for the hatred and the nationalism, which now possess them, thoughts and hopes of the happiness and solidarity of the European family,--then should natural piety and filial love impel the American people to put on one side all the smaller objections of private advantage and to complete the work that they began in saving Europe from the tyranny of organised force, by saving her from herself. And even if the conversion is not fully accomplished, and some parties only in each of the European countries have espoused a policy of reconciliation, America can still point the way and hold up the hands of the party of peace by having a plan and a condition on which she will give her aid to the work of renewing life.

The impulse which, we are told, is now strong in the mind of the United States to be quit of the turmoil, the complication, the violence, the expense, and, above all, the unintelligibility of the European problems, is easily understood. No one can feel more intensely than the writer how natural it is to retort to the folly and impracticability of the European statesmen,--Rot, then, in your own malice, and we will go our way--

Remote from Europe; from her blasted hopes; Her fields of carnage, and polluted air.

But if America recalls for a moment what Europe has meant to her and still means to her, what Europe, the mother of art and of knowledge, in spite of everything, still is and still will be, will she not reject these counsels of indifference and isolation, and interest herself in what may prove decisive issues for the progress and civilisation of all mankind?

Assuming then, if only to keep our hopes up, that America will be prepared to contribute to the process of building up the good forces of Europe, and will not, having completed the destruction of an enemy, leave us to our misfortunes,--what form should her aid take?

I do not propose to enter on details. But the main outlines of all schemes for an international loan are much the same. The countries in a position to lend assistance, the neutrals, the United Kingdom, and, for the greater portion of the sum required, the United States, must provide foreign purchasing credits for all the belligerent countries of continental Europe, allied and ex-enemy alike. The aggregate sum required might not be so large as is sometimes supposed. Much might be done, perhaps, with a fund of £200,000,000 in the first instance. This sum, even if a precedent of a different kind had been established by the cancellation of Inter-Ally War Debt, should be lent and should be borrowed with the unequivocal intention of its being repaid in full. With this object in view, the security for the loan should be the best obtainable, and the arrangements for its ultimate repayment as complete as possible. In particular, it should rank, both for payment of interest and discharge of capital, in front of all Reparation claims, all Inter-Ally War Debt, all internal war loans, and all other Government indebtedness of any other kind. Those borrowing countries who will be entitled to Reparation payments should be required to pledge all such receipts to repayment of the new loan. And all the borrowing countries should be required to place their customs duties on a gold basis and to pledge such receipts to its service.

Expenditure out of the loan should be subject to general, but not detailed, supervision by the lending countries. If, in addition to this loan for the purchase of food and materials, a guarantee fund were established up to an equal amount, namely £200,000,000 (of which it would probably prove necessary to find only a part in cash), to which all members of the League of Nations would contribute according to their means, it might be practicable to base upon it a general reorganisation of the currency.

In this manner Europe might be equipped with the minimum amount of liquid resources necessary to revive her hopes, to renew her economic organisation, and to enable her great intrinsic wealth to function for the benefit of her workers. It is useless at the present time to elaborate such schemes in further detail. A great change is necessary in public opinion before the proposals of this chapter can enter the region of practical politics, and we must await the progress of events as patiently as we can.

I see few signs of sudden or dramatic developments anywhere. Riots and revolutions there may be, but not such, at present, as to have fundamental significance. Against political tyranny and injustice Revolution is a weapon. But what counsels of hope can Revolution offer to sufferers from economic privation, which does not arise out of the injustices of distribution but is general? The only safeguard against revolution in Central Europe is indeed the fact that, even to the minds of men who are desperate, Revolution offers no prospect of improvement whatever. There may, therefore, be ahead of us a long, silent process of semistarvation, and of a gradual, steady lowering of the standards of life and comfort. The bankruptcy and decay of Europe, if we allow it to proceed, will affect every one in the longrun, but perhaps not in a way that is striking or immediate.

This has one fortunate side. We may still have time to reconsider our courses and to view the world with new eyes. For the immediate future events are taking charge, and the near destiny of Europe is no longer in the hands of any man. The events of the coming year will not be shaped by the deliberate acts of statesmen, but by the hidden currents, flowing continually beneath the surface of political history, of which no one can predict the outcome. In one way only can we influence these hidden currents,--by setting in motion those forces of instruction and imagination which change opinion. The assertion of truth, the unveiling of illusion, the dissipation of hate, the enlargement and instruction of men's hearts and minds, must be the means.

4. THE CHANGE OF OPINION (1921) It is the method of modern statesmen to talk as much folly as the public demand and to practise no more of it than is compatible with what they have said, trusting that such folly in action as must wait on folly in word will soon disclose itself as such, and furnish an opportunity for slipping back into wisdom, --the Montessori system for the child, the Public. He who contradicts this child will soon give place to other tutors. Praise, therefore, the beauty of the flames he wishes to touch, the music of the breaking toy; even urge him forward; yet waiting with vigilant care, the wise and kindly saviour of Society, for the right moment to snatch him back, just singed and now attentive.

I can conceive for this terrifying statesmanship a plausible defence. Mr. Lloyd George took the responsibility for a Treaty of Peace, which was not wise, which was partly impossible, and which endangered the life of Europe. He may defend himself by saying that he knew that it was not wise and was partly impossible and endangered the life of Europe; but that public passions and public ignorance play a part in the world of which he who aspires to lead a democracy must take account; that the Peace of Versailles was the best momentary settlement which the demands of the mob and the characters of the chief actors conjoined to permit; and for the life of Europe, that he has spent his skill and strength for two years in avoiding or moderating the dangers.

Such claims would be partly true and cannot be brushed away. The private history of the Peace Conference, as it has been disclosed by French and American participators, displays Mr. Lloyd George in a partly favourable light, generally striving against the excesses of the Treaty and doing what he could, short of risking a personal defeat. The public history of the two years which have followed it exhibit him as protecting Europe from as many of the evil consequences of his own Treaty, as it lay in his power to prevent, with a craft few could have bettered, preserving the peace, though not the prosperity, of Europe, seldom expressing the truth, yet often acting under its influence. He would claim, therefore, that by devious paths, a faithful servant of the possible, he was serving Man.

He may judge rightly that this is the best of which a democracy is capable--to be jockeyed, humbugged, cajoled along the right road. A preference for truth or for sincerity as a method may be a prejudice based on some aesthetic or personal standard, inconsistent, in politics, with practical good.

We cannot yet tell. Even the public learns by experience. Will the charm work still, when the stock of statesmen's credibility, accumulated before these times, is getting exhausted?

In any event, private individuals are not under the same obligation as Cabinet Ministers to sacrifice veracity to the public weal. It is a permitted self-indulgence for a private person to speak and write freely. Perhaps it may even contribute one ingredient to the congeries of things which the wands of statesmen cause to work together, so marvellously, for our ultimate good.

For these reasons I do not admit error in having based The Economic Consequences of the Peace on a literal interpretation of the Treaty of Versailles, or in having examined the results of actually carrying it out. I argued that much of it was impossible; but I do not agree with many critics, who held that, for this very reason, it was also harmless. Inside opinion accepted from the beginning many of my main conclusions about the Treaty. But it was not therefore unimportant that outside opinion should accept them also.

For there are, in the present times, two opinions; not, as in former ages, the true and the false, but the outside and the inside; the opinion of the public voiced by the politicians and the newspapers, and the opinion of the politicians, the journalists and the civil servants, upstairs and backstairs and behindstairs, expressed in limited circles.

Those who live in the limited circles and share the inside opinion pay both too much and too little attention to the outside opinion; too much, because, ready in words and promises to concede to it everything, they regard open opposition as absurdly futile; too little, because they believe that these words and promises are so certainly destined to change in due season, that it is pedantic, tiresome, and inappropriate to analyse their literal meaning and exact consequences. They know all this nearly as well as the critic, who wastes, in their view, his time and his emotions in exciting himself too much over what, on his own showing, cannot possibly happen. Nevertheless, what is said before the world, is still of deeper consequence than the subterranean breathings and well-informed whisperings, knowledge of which allows inside opinion to feel superior to outside opinion, even at the moment of bowing to it.

But there is a further complication. In England (and perhaps elsewhere also) there are two outside opinions, that which is expressed in the newspapers and that which the mass of ordinary men privately suspect to be true. These two degrees of the outside opinion are much nearer to one another than they are to the inside, and under some aspects they are identical; yet there is under the surface a real difference between the dogmatism and definiteness of the press and the living, indefinite belief of the individual man. I fancy that even in 1919 the average Englishman never really believed in the indemnity; he took it always with a grain of salt, with a measure of intellectual doubt. But it seemed to him that for the time being there could be little practical harm in going on the idemnity tack, and also that, in relation to his feelings at that time, a belief in the possibility of boundless payments by Germany was in better sentiment, even if less true, than the contrary. Thus the recent modification in British outside opinion is only partly intellectual, and is due rather to changed conditions; for it is seen that perseverance with the indemnity does now involve practical harm, whilst the claims of sentiment are no longer so decisive. He is therefore prepared to attend to arguments, of which he had always been aware out of the corner of his eye.

Foreign observers are apt to heed too little these unspoken sensibilities, which the voice of the press is bound to express ultimately. Inside opinion gradually affects them by percolating to wider and wider circles; and they are susceptible in time to argument, common sense, or self-interest. It is the business of the modern politician to be accurately aware of all three degrees; he must have enough intellect to understand the inside opinion, enough sympathy to detect the inner outside opinion, and enough brass to express the outer outside opinion.

Whether this account is true or fanciful, there can be no doubt as to the immense change in public sentiment over the past two years. The desire for a quiet life, for reduced commitments, for comfortable terms with our neighbours is now paramount. The megalomania of war has passed away, and every one wishes to conform himself with the facts. For these reasons the Reparation Chapter of the Treaty of Versailles is crumbling. There is little prospect now of the disastrous consequences of its fulfilment.

5. WAR DEBTS AND THE UNITED STATES (i) Cancellation (1921) Who believes that the Allies will, over a period of one or two generations, exert adequate force over the German Government, or that the German Government can exert adequate authority over its subjects, to extract continuing fruits on a vast scale from forced labour? No one believes it in his heart; no one at all. There is not the faintest possibility of our persisting with this affair to the end. But if this is so, then, most certainly, it will not be worth our while to disorder our export trades and disturb the equilibrium of our industry for two or three years; much less to endanger the peace of Europe.

The same principles apply with one modification to the United States and to the exaction by her of the debts which the Allied Governments owe. The industries of the United States would suffer, not so much from the competition of cheap goods from the Allies in their endeavours to pay their debts, as from the inability of the Allies to purchase from America their usual proportion of her exports. The Allies would have to find the money to pay America, not so much by selling more as by buying less. The farmers of the United States would suffer more than the manufacturers; if only because increased imports can be kept out by a tariff, whilst there is no such easy way of stimulating diminished exports. It is, however, a curious fact that whilst Wall Street and the manufacturing East are prepared to consider a modification of the debts, the Middle West and South is reported (I write ignorantly) to be dead against it. For two years Germany was not required to pay cash to the Allies, and during that period the manufacturers of Great Britain were quite blind to what the consequences would be to themselves when the payments actually began. The Allies have not yet been required to begin to pay cash to the United States, and the farmers of the latter are still as blind as were the British manufacturers to the injuries they will suffer if the Allies ever try seriously to pay in full.

The decisive argument, however, for the United States, as for Great Britain, is not the damage to particular interests (which would diminish with time), but the unlikelihood of permanence in the exaction of the debts, even if they were paid for a short period. I say this, not only because I doubt the ability of the European Allies to pay, but because of the great difficulty of the problem which the United States has before her in any case in balancing her commercial account with the Old World.

American economists have examined some shy; what carefully the statistical measure of the change from the pre-war position. According to their estimates, America is now owed more interest on foreign investments than is due from her, quite apart from the interest on the debts of the Allied Governments; and her mercantile marine now earns from foreigners more than she owes them for similar services. Her excess of exports of commodities over imports approaches $ 3000 million a year; whilst, on the other side of the balance, payments, mainly to Europe, in respect of tourists and of immigrant remittances are estimated at not above $ 1000 million a year. Thus, in order to balance the account as it now stands, the United States must lend to the rest of the world, in one shape or another, not less than $ 2000 million a year, to which interest and sinking fund on the European Governmental War Debts would, if they were paid, add about $600 million.

Recently, therefore, the United States must have been lending to the rest of the world, mainly Europe, something like $2000 million a year. Fortunately for Europe, a fair proportion of this was by way of speculative purchases of depreciated paper currencies. From 1919 to 1921 the losses of American speculators fed Europe; but this source of income can scarcely be reckoned on permanently. For a time the policy of loans can meet the situation; but, as the interest on past loans mounts up, it must in the long run aggravate it.

Mercantile nations have always employed large funds in overseas trade. But the practice of foreign investment, as we know it now, is a very modern contrivance, a very unstable one, and only suited to peculiar circumstances. An old country can in this way develop a new one at a time when the latter could not possibly do so with its own resources alone; the arrangement may be mutually advantageous, and out of abundant profits the lender may hope to be repaid. But the position cannot be reversed. If European bonds are issued in America on the analogy of the American bonds issued in Europe during the nineteenth century, the analogy will be a false one; because, taken in the aggregate, there is no natural increase, no real sinking fund, out of which they can be repaid. The interest will be furnished out of new loans, so long as these are obtainable, and the financial structure will mount always higher, until it is not worth while to maintain any longer the illusion that it has foundations. The unwillingness of American investors to buy European bonds is based on common sense.

At the end of 1919 I advocated (in The Economic Consequences of the Peace) a reconstruction loan from America to Europe, conditioned, however, on Europe's putting her own house in order. In the past two years America, in spite of European complaints to the contrary, has, in fact, made very large loans, much larger than the sum I contemplated, though not mainly in the form of regular, dollar-bond issues. No particular conditions were attached to these loans, and much of the money has been lost. Though wasted in part, they have helped Europe through the critical days of the post-Armistice period. But a continuance of them cannot provide a solution for the existing dis-equilibrium in the balance of indebtedness.

In part the adjustment may be effected by the United States taking the place hitherto held by England, France, and (on a small scale) Germany in providing capital for those new parts of the world less developed than herself --the British Dominions and South America. The Russian Empire, too, in Europe and Asia, is to be regarded as virgin soil, which may at a later date provide a suitable outlet for foreign capital. The American investor will lend more wisely to these countries, on the lines on which British and French investors used to lend to them, than direct to the old countries of Europe. But it is not likely that the whole gap can be bridged thus. Ultimately, and probably soon, there must be a readjustment of the balance of exports and imports. America must buy more and sell less. This is the only alternative to her making to Europe an annual present. Either American prices must rise faster than European (which will be the case if the Federal Reserve Board allows the gold influx to produce its natural consequences), or, failing this, the same result must be brought about by a further depreciation of the European exchanges, until Europe, by inability to buy, has reduced her purchases to articles of necessity. At first the American exporter, unable to scrap all at once the processes of production for export, may meet the situation by lowering his prices; but when these have continued, say for two years, below his cost of production, he will be driven inevitably to curtail or abandon his business.

It is useless for the United States to suppose that an equilibrium position can be reached on the basis of her exporting at least as much as at present, and at the same time restricting her imports by a tariff. Just as the Allies demand vast payments from Germany, and then exercise their ingenuity to prevent her paying them, so the American Administration devises, with one hand, schemes for financing exports, and, with the other, tariffs which will make it as difficult as possible for such credits to be repaid. Great nations can often act with a degree of folly which we should not excuse in an individual.

By the shipment to the United States of all the bullion in the world, and the erection there of a sky-scraping golden calf, a short postponement may be gained. But a point may even come when the United States will refuse gold, yet still demand to be paid--a new Midas vainly asking more succulent fare than the barren metal of her own contract.

In any case the readjustment will be severe, and injurious to important interests. If, in addition, the United States exacts payment of the Allied debts, the position will be intolerable. If she persevered to the bitter end, scrapped her export industries and diverted to other uses the capital now employed in them, and if her former European associates decided to meet their obligations at whatever cost to themselves, I do not deny that the final result might be to America's material interest. But the project is utterly chimerical. It will not happen. Nothing is more certain than that America will not pursue such a policy to its conclusion; she will abandon it as soon as she experiences its first consequences. Nor, if she did, would the Allies pay the money. The position is exactly parallel to that of German Reparation. America will not carry through to a conclusion the collection of Allied debt, any more than the Allies will carry through the collection of their present Reparation demands. Neither, in the long run, is serious politics. Nearly all well-informed persons admit this in private conversation. But we live in a curious age when utterances in the press are deliberately designed to be in conformity with the worst-informed, instead of with the best-informed, opinion, because the former is the wider spread; so that for comparatively long periods there can be discrepancies, laughable or monstrous, between the written and the spoken word.

If this is so, it is not good business for America to embitter her relations with Europe, and to disorder her export industries for two years, in pursuance of a policy which she is certain to abandon before it has profited her.

For the benefit of any reader who enjoys an abstract statement, I summarise the argument thus. The equilibrium of international trade is based on a complicated balance between the agriculture and the industries of the different countries of the world, and on a specialisation by each in the employment of its labour and its capital. If one country is required to transfer to another without payment great quantities of goods, for which this equilibrium does not allow, the balance is destroyed. Since capital and labour are fixed and organised in certain employments and cannot flow freely into others, the disturbance of the balance is destructive to the utility of the capital and labour thus fixed. The organisation, on which the wealth of the modern world so largely depends, suffers injury. In course of time a new organisation and a new equilibrium can be established. But if the origin of the disturbance is of temporary duration, the losses from the injury done to organisation may outweigh the profit of receiving goods without paying for them. Moreover, since the losses will be concentrated on the capital and labour employed in particular industries, they will provoke an outcry out of proportion to the injury inflicted on the community as a whole.

Most Americans, with whom I have discussed this question, express themselves as personally favourable to the cancellation of the European debts, but add that so great a majority of their countrymen think otherwise that such a proposal is at present outside practical politics. They think, therefore, that it is premature to discuss it; for the present, America must pretend she is going to demand the money and Europe must pretend she is going to pay it. Indeed, the position is much the same as that of German Reparation in England in the middle of 1921. Doubtless my informants are right about this public opinion, the mysterious entity which is the same thing perhaps as Rousseau's General Will. Yet, all the same, I do not attach, to what they tell me, too much importance. Public opinion held that Hans Andersen's Emperor wore a fine suit; and in the United States especially, public opinion changes sometimes, as it were, en bloc.

If, indeed, public opinion were an unalterable thing, it would be a waste of time to discuss public affairs. And though it may be the chief business of newsmen and politicians to ascertain its momentary features, a writer ought to be concerned, rather, with what public opinion should be. I record these platitudes because many

Americans give their advice, as though it were actually immoral to make suggestions which public opinion does not now approve. In America, I gather, an act of this kind is considered so reckless that some improper motive is at once suspected, and criticism takes the form of an inquiry into the culprit's personal character and antecedents.

Let us inquire, however, a little more deeply into the sentiments and emotions which underlie the American attitude to the European debts. They want to be generous to Europe, both out of good feeling and because many of them now suspect that any other course would upset their own economic equilibrium. But they don't want to be "done." They do not want it to be said that once again the old cynics in Europe have been one too many for them. Times, too, have been bad and taxation oppressive; and many parts of America do not feel rich enough at the moment to favour a light abandonment of a possible asset. Moreover, these arrangements, between nations warring together, they liken much more closely than we do to ordinary business transactions between individuals. It is, they say, as though a bank having made an unsecured advance to a client, in whom they believe, at a difficult time when he would have gone under without it, this client were then to cry off paying. To permit such a thing would be to do an injury to the elementary principles of business honour.

The average American, I fancy, would like to see the European nations approaching him with a pathetic light in their eyes and the cash in their hands, saying, " America, we owe to you our liberty and our life; here we bring what we can in grateful thanks, money not wrung by grievous taxation from the widow and orphan, but saved, the best fruits of victory, out of the abolition of armaments, militarism, Empire, and internal strife, made possible by the help you freely gave us." And then the average American would reply: "I honour you for your integrity. It is what I expected. But I did not enter the war for profit or to invest my money well. I have had my reward in the words you have just uttered. The loans are forgiven. Return to your homes and use the resources I release to uplift the poor and the unfortunate." And it would be an essential part of the little scene that his reply should come as a complete and overwhelming surprise.

Alas for the wickedness of the world! It is not in international affairs that we can secure the sentimental satisfactions which we all love. For only individuals are good, and all nations are dishon-

ourable, cruel, and designing. And whilst the various Prime Ministers will telegraph something suitable, drafted by their private sec-
retaries, to the effect that America's action makes the moment of
writing the most important in the history of the world and proves
that Americans are the noblest creatures living, America must not
expect adequate or appropriate thanks.

(ii) The Balfour Note (1925) The Balfour Note insists that our
receipts from Germanyplus our receipts from our Allies must equal
our payments to the United States. When the Note was written,
its effect was indeterminate. We did not know how much it would
require France to pay, or the proportion that this would bear to
what Germany would be paying France. Now we can make limiting
estimates of both sums.

We have to pay the United States about £35,000,000 a year,
rising to £40,000,000. The Dawes Scheme will yield, if and when
it is in full operation, and after allowing for various prior charges,
about £100,000,000 a year. France's share of this will be about
£54,000,000, Italy's £24,000,000 (less at first), and ours £24,000,000.
(I neglect the minor Allies because they would complicate the calculation and hardly affect the result.) Thus the Balfour Note demands that France and Italy should pay Great Britain not less than
£16,000,000 a year. Since the aggregate debts of these two Powers
to ourselves and to the United States respectively are about equal
(our share of Italy's total debt is greater, and of France's less), we
must assume that the United States will not settle for a smaller
sum than what we receive. If the whole of Italy's share of Reparations is devoted to her debts, France is left, on these assumptions,
with £22,000,000 to pay. In this case the net result of the Debt Settlements and the Dawes Scheme would be that the receipts from
Germany would be distributed as follows:

United Kingdom	Nil.
Italy	Nil.
France	£32,000,000
United States	£58,000,000

Very improbable things are easier said than done. Who believes
that this will ever be done?

But we have not yet reached the gravamen of my criticism of

the Balfour Note. The above is what would happen if the Dawes Scheme is perfectly successful. If the Dawes Scheme is only partly successful, then, by the principle of the Balfour Note, France must make good the difference to ourselves and the United States. For example, if the Dawes Scheme produces half its maximum, which, in the opinion of many good judges, would be a considerable achievement, France will get less than nothing at all and more than the whole of Germany's payments will go to the United States. France would become, in fact, a deferred claimant on a third share of the Dawes Scheme, if the Scheme works very well, and a guarantor of Germany, if it works less well. Is not any one very silly who thinks that this can come to pass?

It is obvious that France will never agree to such a settlement. But suppose per impossibile that she did. In this case Great Britain and the United States have, theoretically, no further interest whatever in the operation or productivity of the Dawes Scheme. France becomes the only interested party,--interested not merely as a creditor but as a guarantor who must make deficiencies good.

This fatal objection is necessarily inherent in the Balfour Note. It is of the essence of the Note that the less Germany pays, the more France shall pay;--that is to say, the less France is in a position to pay, the more she shall pay. Diplomatically and financially alike, this is topsy-turvy. It would never bring us cash; yet it would destroy our diplomatic authority as a moderator between France and Germany. The Foreign Office would have sold its influence for a mess of pottage which the Treasury would never taste.

The Balfour Note, therefore, is bad in principle. There can be no working settlement except on the exactly opposite principle, namely that the less Germany pays, the less France shall pay. The amount of France's payment must vary in the same direction as Germany's, not in the opposite direction. This was the principle of the suggestion, which I offered recently, by which France's payment should be a proportion of her receipts from Germany. According to current report, France herself has put forward just this principle through the mouth of M. Clémentel. I suggested that the proportion be one-third. M. Clémentel's reported offer would amount, on the assumption that the United States got the same terms, to about half my figure. But it does not follow that he would not offer more to obtain a settlement on these lines.

Such a settlement would increase, instead of diminishing, the interest of ourselves and the United States in the Dawes Scheme.

We should have, between us, a bigger interest than France. We might, in this way, obtain a moderate contribution towards our American debt, corresponding to that part of it which we contracted, indirectly, on French account. We should certainly place ourselves in a strong moral and diplomatic position to claim a moderating and pacific influence in the FrancoGerman problems which still lie ahead.

(iii) Cancellation (1928) Let us remember the origin of the War Debts. Soon after the beginning of the war it was clear that certain of our Allies--Russia and Belgium in the first instance, but subsequently all of them--would require financial assistance. We might have given this in loans or in subsidies. Loans were preferred to subsidies, in order to preserve a greater sense of responsibility and economy in the spending of them. But though financial assistance took the form of loans, it is scarcely to be supposed that the lending countries regarded them at the time as being in the nature of ordinary investments. Indeed it would have been very illogical to do so. For we often gave assistance in the form of money, precisely because we were less able to assist with men or ships. For example, when we sent guns to Italy to help her after her first serious reverse, she had to pay for them by loans. But when matters got worse still, and we sent not only guns but gunners too to man them and to be killed, then we charged nothing. Yet in the former case Italy's contribution was the greater and in the latter ours. In particular, America's contribution for some time after she came into the war was mainly financial, because she was not yet ready to help in any other way. So long as America was sending materials and munitions to be used by Allied soldiers, she charged us for them, and these charges are the origin of what we now owe her. But when later on she sent men too, to use the munitions themselves, then we were charged nothing. Evidently there is not much logic in a system which causes us to owe money to America, not because she was able to help us so much, but because at first she was able to help us, so far at least as man power was concerned, so little.

This does not mean that the financial help which America gave us was not of the most extraordinary value to us. By the time that America came into the war our own resources as a lender were literally at an end. We were still at that time just about able to finance ourselves, but we had reached a point when we could no longer finance our Allies as well. America's financial assistance was therefore quite invaluable. From the moment she entered the war she undertook to lend whatever was required for the expenditure of ourselves and our Allies in the United States, including some contribution to support the Foreign Exchanges. But she was not prepared to make loans for use outside America. Great Britain had therefore to go on making loans to her Allies for such expenditure--with the result that we had to lend our Allies after America came into the war an amount almost equal to what we ourselves borrowed. More precisely, we borrowed from the United States, after she came into the war, £850,000,000 and lent to our Allies during the same period £750,000,000; so that in effect it was true--what the Americans have always been concerned to deny--that the loans she made to us were for the purpose of financing our Allies rather than for ourselves.

The result was that by the end of the war we were owed by our Allies about £1,600,000,000, whilst we, in our turn, owed to the United States £850,000,000.

Since the war, the question has been constantly debated whether these sums ought to be treated as investments, just like any other business transaction, or whether regard should be paid to their origin and to the circumstances in which they were made. It has been the British view that they were not made as business transactions and should not be treated as such. It has been the American view, on the other hand, that they should be taken at their face value, that is to say, as bonds due and payable, tempered only by considerations as to the capacity of the debtor to pay, and, in practice, by a willingness on the part of the United States to accept a low rate of interest.

During the Peace Conference the British Government urged that the Allied War Debts should be entirely cancelled. Mr. Lloyd George raised the matter again with President Wilson in August 1920. Finally, in August 1922, in the famous Note written by Lord Balfour, the considered British view, from which we have never gone back, was set forth. In this Note the British Government declared their willingness to cancel the whole of what their Allies owed them, and also to forgo their own claims on Germany in favour of the other Allies, if the United States in turn would relieve them of their debt. By such an arrangement Great Britain would have been giving up on paper more than twice what she gained. The offer still holds good.

This policy was not accepted by the United States, and a separate settlement has been made between each pair of countries in turn. The settlement made with Great Britain is equivalent to charging a rate of interest of 3·3 per cent on the whole amount due. The American settlement with France is equivalent to repayment at 1·6 per cent interest, and that with Italy to repayment at 0·4 per cent interest. Thus, the American settlement with Great Britain is twice as onerous as that with France and eight times as onerous as that with Italy. Great Britain, in her turn, has made arrangements with France and Italy, and has in both cases let them off lighter even than has the United States--the British settlement with France being 10 per cent easier and that with Italy 33 per cent easier than the corresponding American settlements. Thus, whilst the other Allies have been largely relieved this country is left with the task of repaying her whole burden, subject only to the mitigation that the rate of interest charged, namely, 3·3 per cent, is moderate.

The effect of this settlement is that Great Britain will have to pay to the United States a sum of about £33,000,000 annually up to 1933, rising to nearly £38,000,000 annually thereafter from that year until 1984, when the debt will have been discharged. The reality of the weight of this burden may be illustrated by certain calculations which I made in the summer of 1923 when the details of Mr. Baldwin's settlement with Washington were first made public. We shall be paying to the United States each year for sixty years a sum equivalent to two-thirds of the cost of our Navy, a sum nearly equal to our State expenditure on Education, a sum which exceeds the total burden of our pre-war debt. Looked at from another standpoint, it represents more than the total normal profits of our coal mines and our mercantile marine added together. With these sums we could endow and splendidly house every month for sixty years one new university, one new hospital, one new institute of research, etc. etc. With an equal sacrifice over an equal period we could abolish slums and re-house in comfort the half of our population which is now inadequately sheltered.

On the other hand, we are now receiving from our Allies and from Germany an important contribution as an offset to what we ourselves pay to the United States. It will be interesting to establish a rough balance-sheet.

In 1928 we shall receive from our Allies £12,800,000 and pay the United States £33,200,000; and by 1933 these figures will have risen to £17,700,000 and £37,800,000. Thus apart from our share of German Reparations, we shall be paying annually in respect of War Debts about £20,000,000 more than we receive. Now if the

Dawes Annuities are paid by Germany in full, we shall come out just about "all-square." For the normal Dawes Annuity when it has reached its full figure (less the service of German loans, etc.) will amount to £117,000,000, of which our share (excluding the receipts of other parts of the Empire) will be about £22,000,000. Mr. Churchill has estimated that in the current financial year, 1928-29, our payments out will be £32,845,000, and our total receipts nearly £32,000,000.

It is not probable that these receipts will be realised in full. But it will enable us to summarise the situation if we assume for the moment that they are so realised. In this case, each Ally would be able to pay the United States out of their receipts from Germany. When the Allied Debt payments to the United States have reached their maximum amount under the existing settlements, they will total £83,000,000 per annum (the average amount payable annually over the whole period works out at a total of £61,000,000). If we add to this the direct American share in German Reparations, the United States will be receiving £78,000,000 annually out of the £117,000,000 receivable by the Allies from Germany, or 67 per cent, plus £10,000,000 from Italy not covered by Reparations; or if we take the average payments, in lieu of the maximum, the United States will be receiving £66,000,000 out £117,000,000 or 57 per cent. In either case Great Britain would receive, on balance, nothing.

It follows from the above that if the maximum Dawes Annuities were to be reduced by one-third--which, in the opinion of many of us, is highly probable--the United States will, by the time that the Allied payments to her have reached their full figure, be the sole beneficiary. In this event the net result of all War Debt settlements would be to leave the United States--on balance and off-setting receipts against payments -- receiving from Germany £78,000,000 per annum, and no one else getting anything.

I have put the calculation in this form because it renders it very clear why, in the minds of the Allies, the question of further relief to Germany is intimately bound up with the question of their own obligations to the United States. The official American attitude that there is no connection between the two, is a very hollow pretence. The resettlement of the Dawes Scheme is one to which the United States must be, in one way or another, a party. But-let me add--any concession she may make will go entirely to the relief of Germany and the European Allies, Great Britain adhering to her principle of receiving nothing on balance.

If all, or nearly all, of what Germany pays for Reparations has to be used, not to repair the damage done, but to repay the United States for the financial part which she played in the common struggle, many will feel that this is not an outcome tolerable to the sentiments of mankind or in reasonable accord with the spoken professions of Americans when they entered the war or afterwards. Yet it is a delicate matter, however keenly the public may feel, for any Englishman in authority to take the initiative in saying such things in an official way. Obviously, we must pay what we have covenanted to pay, and any proposal, if there is to be one, must come from the United States. It fell to my lot during the war to be the official draftsman in the British Treasury of all the financial agreements with the Allies and with the United States out of which this situation has arisen. I was intimately familiar, day by day, with the reasons and motives which governed the character of the financial arrangements which were made. In the light of the memories of those days, I continue to hope that in due course, and in her own time, America will tell us that she has not spoken her last word.

II

INFLATION AND DEFLATION

1. INFLATION (1919) LENIN is said to have declared that the best way to destroy the Capitalist System was to debauch the currency. By a continuing process of inflation, Governments can confiscate, secretly and unobserved, an important part of the wealth of their citizens. By this method they not only confiscate, but they confiscate arbitrarily; and, while the process impoverishes many, it actually enriches some. The sight of this arbitrary rearrangement of riches strikes not only at security, but at confidence in the equity of the existing distribution of wealth. Those to whom the system brings windfalls, beyond their deserts and even beyond their expectations or desires, become "profiteers," who are the object of the hatred of the bourgeoisie, whom the inflationism has impoverished, not less than of the proletariat. As the inflation proceeds and the real value of the currency fluctuates wildly from month to month, all permanent relations between debtors and creditors, which form the ultimate foundation of capitalism, become so utterly disordered as to be almost meaningless; and the process of wealth-getting degenerates into a gamble and a lottery.

Lenin was certainly right. There is no subtler, no surer means of overturning the existing basis of Society than to debauch the currency. The process engages all the hidden forces of economic law on the side of destruction, and does it in a manner which not one man in a million is able to diagnose.

In the latter stages of the war all the belligerent Governments practised, from necessity or incompetence, what a Bolshevist might have done from design. Even now, when the war is over, most of them continue out of weakness the same malpractices. But further, the Governments of Europe, being many of them at this moment reckless in their methods as well as weak, seek to direct on to a class known as "profiteers" the popular indignation against the more obvious consequences of their vicious methods. These "profiteers" are, broadly speaking, the entrepreneur class of capitalists, that is to say, the active and constructive element in the whole capitalist society, who in a period of rapidly rising prices cannot but get rich quick whether they wish it or desire it or not. If prices are continually rising, every trader who has purchased for stock or

owns property and plant inevitably makes profits. By directing hatred against this class, therefore, the European Governments are
carrying a step further the fatal process which the subtle mind of
Lenin had consciously conceived. The profiteers are a consequence
and not a cause of rising prices. By combining a popular hatred of
the class of entrepreneurs with the blow already given to social
security by the violent and arbitrary disturbance of contract and
of the established equilibrium of wealth which is the inevitable result of inflation, these Governments are fast rendering impossible
a continuance of the social and economic order of the nineteenth
century. But they have no plan for replacing it.

2. SOCIAL CONSEQUENCES OF CHANGES IN THE VAL-
UE OF MONEY (1923) Money is only important for what it will
procure. Thus a change in the monetary unit, which is uniform
in its operation and affects all transactions equally, has no consequences. If, by a change in the established standard of value, a
man received and owned twice as much money as he did before in
payment for all rights and for all efforts, and if he also paid out
twice as much money for all acquisitions and for all satisfactions,
he would be wholly unaffected.

It follows, therefore, that a change in the value of money, that
is to say in the level of prices, is important to Society only in so
far as its incidence is unequal. Such changes have produced in the
past, and are producing now, the vastest social consequences, because, as we all know, when the value of money changes, it does
not change equally for all persons or for all purposes. A man's receipts and his outgoings are not all modified in one uniform proportion. Thus a change in prices and rewards, as measured in money,
generally affects different classes unequally, transfers wealth from
one to another, bestows affluence here and embarrassment there,
and redistributes Fortune's favours so as to frustrate design and
disappoint expectation.

The fluctuations in the value of money since 1914 have been
on a scale so great as to constitute, with all that they involve, one
of the most significant events in the economic history of the modern world. The fluctuation of the standard, whether gold, silver, or
paper, has not only been of unprecedented violence, but has been
visited on a society of which the economic organisation is more dependent than that of any earlier epoch on the assumption that the
standard of value would be moderately stable.

During the Napoleonic Wars and the period immediately succeeding them the extreme fluctuation of English prices within a single year was 22 per cent; and the highest price level reached during the first quarter of the nineteenth century, which we used to reckon the most disturbed period of our currency history, was less than double the lowest and with an interval of thirteen years. Compare with this the extraordinary movements of the past nine years. From 1914 to 1920 all countries experienced an expansion in the supply of money to spend relatively to the supply of things to purchase, that is to say Inflation. Since 1920 those countries which have regained control of their financial situation, not content with bringing the Inflation to an end, have contracted their supply of money and have experienced the fruits of Deflation. Others have followed inflationary courses more riotously than before.

Each process, Inflation and Deflation alike, has inflicted great injuries. Each has an effect in altering the distribution of wealth between different classes, Inflation in this respect being the worse of the two. Each has also an effect in overstimulating or retarding the production of wealth, though here Deflation is the more injurious. The division of our subject thus indicated is the most convenient for us to follow,--examining first the effect of changes in the value of money on the distribution of wealth with most of our attention on Inflation, and next their effect on the production of wealth with most of our attention on Deflation.

(A) CHANGES IN THE VALUE OF MONEY, AS AFFECTING DISTRIBUTION (i) The Investing Class Of the various purposes which money serves, some essentially depend upon the assumption that its real value is nearly constant over a period of time. The chief of these are those connected, in a wide sense, with contracts for the investment of money. Such contracts--namely, those which provide for the payment of fixed sums of money over a long period of time--are the characteristic of what it is convenient to call the Investment System, as distinct from the property system generally.

Under this phase of capitalism, as developed during the nineteenth century, many arrangements were devised for separating the management of property from its ownership. These arrangements were of three leading types: (1) Those in which the proprietor, while parting with the management of his property, retained his ownership of it--i.e. of the actual land, buildings, and machinery, or of whatever else it consisted in, this mode of tenure being typified by a holding of ordinary shares in a joint-stock company; (2)

those in which he parted with the property temporarily, receiving a fixed sum of money annually in the meantime, but regained his property eventually, as typified by a lease; and (3) those in which he parted with his real property permanently, in return either for a perpetual annuity fixed in terms of money, or for a terminable annuity and the repayment of the principal in money at the end of the term, as typified by mortgages, bonds, debentures, and preference shares. This third type represents the full development of Investment.

Contracts to receive fixed sums of money at future dates (made without provision for possible changes in the real value of money at those dates) must have existed as long as money has been lent and borrowed. In the form of leases and mortgages, and also of permanent loans to Governments and to a few private bodies, such as the East India Company, they were already frequent in the eighteenth century. But during the nineteenth century they developed a new and increased importance, and had, by the beginning of the twentieth, divided the propertied classes into two groups --the "business men" and the "investors"-with partly divergent interests. The division was not sharp as between individuals; for business men might be investors also, and investors might hold ordinary shares; but the division was nevertheless real, and not the less important because it was seldom noticed.

By this system the active business class could call to the aid of their enterprises not only their own wealth but the savings of the whole community; and the professional and propertied classes, on the other hand, could find an employment for their resources, which involved them in little trouble, no responsibility, and (it was believed) small risk.

For a hundred years the system worked, throughout Europe, with an extraordinary success and facilitated the growth of wealth on an unprecedented scale. To save and to invest became at once the duty and the delight of a large class. The savings were seldom drawn on, and, accumulating at compound interest, made possible the material triumphs which we now all take for granted. The morals, the politics, the literature, and the religion of the age joined in a grand conspiracy for the promotion of saving. God and Mammon were reconciled. Peace on earth to men of good means. A rich man could, after all, enter into the Kingdom of Heaven--if only he saved. A new harmony sounded from the celestial spheres. "It is curious to observe how, through the wise and beneficent arrangement of

Providence, men thus do the greatest service to the public, when they are thinking of nothing but their own gain"; 1 so sang the angels.

The atmosphere thus created well harmonised the demands of expanding business and the needs of an expanding population with the growth of a comfortable non-business class. But amidst the general enjoyment of ease and progress, the extent to which the system depended on the stability of the money to which the investing classes had committed their fortunes, was generally overlooked; and an unquestioning confidence was apparently felt that this matter would look after itself. Investments spread and multiplied, until, for the middle classes of the world, the gilt-edged bonds came to typify all that was most permanent and most secure. So rooted in our day has been the conventional belief in the stability and safety of a money contract that, according to English law, trustees have been encouraged to embark their trust funds exclusively in such transactions, and are indeed forbidden, except in the case of real estate (an exception which is itself a survival of the conditions of an earlier age), to employ them otherwise. 1

As in other respects, so also in this, the nineteenth century relied on the future permanence of its own happy experiences and disregarded the warning of past misfortunes. It chose to forget that there is no historical warrant for expecting money to be represented even by a constant quantity of a particular metal, far less by a constant purchasing power. Yet Money is simply that which the State declares from time to time to be a good legal discharge of money contracts. In 1914 gold had not been the English standard for a century or the sole standard of any other country for half a century. There is no record of a prolonged war or a great social upheaval which has not been accompanied by a change in the legal tender, but an almost unbroken chronicle in every country which has a history, back to the earliest dawn of economic record, of a progressive deterioration in the real value of the successive legal tenders which have represented money.

Moreover, this progressive deterioration in the value of money through history is not an accident, and has had behind it two great driving forces--the impecuniosity of Governments and the superior political influence of the debtor class.

The power of taxation by currency depreciation is one which has been inherent in the State since Rome discovered it. The creation of legal tender has been and is a Government's ultimate reserve; and no State or Government is likely to decree its own bank-ruptcy or its own downfall so long as this instrument still lies at hand unused.

Besides this, as we shall see below, the benefits of a depreciat-ing currency are not restricted to the Government. Farmers and debtors and all persons liable to pay fixed money dues share in the advantage. As now in the persons of business men, so also in former ages these classes constituted the active and constructive elements in the economic scheme. Those secular changes, therefore, which in the past have depreciated money, assisted the new men and eman-cipated them from the dead hand; they benefited new wealth at the expense of old, and armed enterprise against accumulation. The tendency of money to depreciate has been in past times a weighty counterpoise against the cumulative results of compound interest and the inheritance of fortunes. It has been a loosening influence against the rigid distribution of old-won wealth and the separation of ownership from activity. By this means each generation can dis-inherit in part its predecessors' heirs; and the project of founding a perpetual fortune must be disappointed in this way, unless the community with conscious deliberation provides against it in some other way, more equitable and more expedient.

At any rate, under the influence of these two forces--the fi-nancial necessities of Governments and the political influence of the debtor class-sometimes the one and sometimes the other, the progress of inflation has been continuous, if we consider long pe-riods, ever since money was first devised in the sixth century B.C. Sometimes the standard of value has depreciated of itself; failing this, debasements have done the work.

Nevertheless it is easy at all times, as a result of the way we use money in daily life, to forget all this and to look on money as itself the absolute standard of value; and when, besides, the actual events of a hundred years have not disturbed his illusions, the av-erage man regards what has been normal for three generations as a part of the permanent social fabric.

The course of events during the nineteenth century favoured such ideas. During its first quarter, the very high prices of the Na-poleonic Wars were followed by a somewhat rapid improvement in the value of money. For the next seventy years, with some tem-porary fluctuations, the tendency of prices continued to be down-wards, the lowest point being reached in 1896. But while this was the tendency as regards direction, the remarkable feature of this long period was the relative stability of the price level. Approximately the same level of price ruled in or about the years 1826, 1841, 1855, 1862, 1867, 1871, and 1915. Prices were also level in the years 1844, 1881, and 1914. If we call the index number of these latter years 100, we find that, for the period of close on a century from 1826 to the outbreak of war, the maximum fluctuation in either direction was 30 points, the index number never rising above 130 and never falling below 70. No wonder that we came to believe in the stability of money contracts over a long period. The metal gold might not possess all the theoretical advantages of an artificially regulated standard, but it could not be tampered with and had proved reliable in practice.

At the same time, the investor in Consols in the early part of the century had done very well in three different ways. The "security" of his investment had come to be considered as near absolute perfection as was possible. Its capital value had uniformly appreciated, partly for the reason just stated, but chiefly because the steady fall in the rate of interest increased the number of years' purchase of the annual income which represented the capital. 1 And the annual money income had a purchasing power which on the whole was increasing. If, for example, we consider the seventy years from 1826 to 1896 (and ignore the great improvement immediately after Waterloo), we find that the capital value of Consols rose steadily, with only temporary set-backs, from 79 to 109 (in spite of Goschen's conversion from a 3 per cent rate to a 2 ¾ per cent rate in 1889 and a 2 ½ per cent rate effective in 1903), while the purchasing power of the annual dividends, even after allowing for the reduced rates of interest, had increased 50 per cent. But Consols, too, had added the virtue of stability to that of improvement. Except in years of crisis Consols never fell below 90 during the reign of Queen Victoria; and even in '48, when thrones were crumbling, the mean price of the year fell but 5 points. Ninety when she ascended the throne, they reached their maximum with her in the year of Diamond Jubilee. What wonder that our parents thought Consols a good investment!

Thus there grew up during the nineteenth century a large, powerful, and greatly respected class of persons, well-to-do individually and very wealthy in the aggregate, who owned neither buildings, nor land, nor businesses, nor precious metals, but titles to an annual income in legaltender money. In particular, that peculiar creation and pride of the nineteenth century, the savings of the middle class, had been mainly thus embarked. Custom and favourable experience had acquired for such investments an unimpeachable reputation for security.

Before the war these medium fortunes had already begun to suffer some loss (as compared with the summit of their prosperity in the middle 'nineties) from the rise in prices and also in the rate of interest. But the monetary events which have accompanied and have followed the war have taken from them about one-half of their real value in England, seven-eighths in France, eleven-twelfths in Italy, and virtually the whole in Germany and in the succession states of Austria-Hungary and Russia.

Thus the effect of the war, and of the monetary policy which has accompanied and followed it, has been to take away a large part of the real value of the possessions of the investing class. The loss has been so rapid and so intermixed in the time of its occurrence with other worse losses that its full measure is not yet separately apprehended. But it has effected, nevertheless, a far-reaching change in the relative position of different classes. Throughout the Continent the pre-war savings of the middle class, so far as they were invested in bonds, mortgages, or bank deposits, have been largely or entirely wiped out. Nor can it be doubted that this experience must modify social psychology towards the practice of saving and investment. What was deemed most secure has proved least so. He who neither spent nor "speculated," who made "proper provision for his family," who sang hymns to security and observed most straitly the morals of the edified and the respectable injunctions of the worldly-wise,--he, indeed, who gave fewest pledges to Fortune has yet suffered her heaviest visitations.

What moral for our present purpose should we draw from this? Chiefly, I think, that it is not safe or fair to combine the social organisation developed during the nineteenth century (and still retained) with a laisser-faire policy towards the value of money. It is not true that our former arrangements have worked well. If we are to continue to draw the voluntary savings of the community into "investments," we must make it a prime object of deliberate State policy that the standard of value, in terms of which they are expressed, should be kept stable; adjusting in other ways (calculated to touch all forms of wealth equally and not concentrated on the relatively helpless "investors") the redistribution of the national wealth, if, in course of time, the laws of inheritance and the rate of accumulation have drained too great a proportion of the income of the active classes into the spending control of the inactive.

(ii) The Business Class It has long been recognised, by the business world and by economists alike, that a period of rising prices acts as a stimulus to enterprise and is beneficial to business men.

In the first place there is the advantage which is the counterpart of the loss to the investing class which we have just examined. When the value of money falls, it is evident that those persons who have engaged to pay fixed sums of money yearly out of the profits of active business must benefit, since their fixed money outgoings will bear a smaller proportion than formerly to their money turnover. This benefit persists not only during the transitional period of change, but also, so far as old loans are concerned, when prices have settled down at their new and higher level. For example, the farmers throughout Europe, who had raised by mortgage the funds to purchase the land they farmed, now find themselves almost freed from the burden at the expense of the mortgagees.

But during the period of change, while prices are rising month by month, the business man has a further and greater source of windfall. Whether he is a merchant or a manufacturer, he will generally buy before he sells, and on at least a part of his stock he will run the risk of price changes. If, therefore, month after month his stock appreciates on his hands, he is always selling at a better price than he expected and securing a windfall profit upon which he had not calculated. In such a period the business of trade becomes unduly easy. Any one who can borrow money and is not exceptionally unlucky must make a profit, which he may have done little to deserve. Thus, when prices are rising, the business man who borrows money is able to repay the lender with what, in terms of real value, not only represents no interest, but is even less than the capital originally advanced.

But if the depreciation of money is a source of gain to the business man, it is also the occasion of opprobrium. To the consumer the business man's exceptional profits appear as the cause (instead of the consequence) of the hated rise of prices. Amidst the rapid fluctuations of his fortunes he himself loses his conservative instincts, and begins to think more of the large gains of the moment than of the lesser, but permanent, profits of normal business. The welfare of his enterprise in the relatively distant future weighs less with him than before, and thoughts are excited of a quick fortune and clearing out. His excessive gains have come to him unsought and without fault or design on his part, but once acquired he does not lightly surrender them, and will struggle to retain his booty.

With such impulses and so placed, the business man is himself not free from a suppressed uneasiness. In his heart he loses his former self-confidence in his relation to Society, in his utility and necessity in the economic scheme. He fears the future of his business and his class, and the less secure he feels his fortune to be the tighter he clings to it. The business man, the prop of Society and the builder of the future, to whose activities and rewards there had been accorded, not long ago, an almost religious sanction, he of all men and classes most respectable, praiseworthy, and necessary, with whom interference was not only disastrous but almost impious, was now to suffer sidelong glances, to feel himself suspected and attacked, the victim of unjust and injurious laws, -- to become, and know himself half guilty, a profiteer.

No man of spirit will consent to remain poor if he believes his betters to have gained their goods by lucky gambling. To convert the business man into the profiteer is to strike a blow at capitalism, because it destroys the psychological equilibrium which permits the perpetuance of unequal rewards. The economic doctrine of normal profits, vaguely apprehended by every one, is a necessary condition for the justification of capitalism. The business man is only tolerable so long as his gains can be held to bear some relation to what, roughly and in some sense, his activities have contributed to Society.

This, then, is the second disturbance to the existing economic order for which the depreciation of money is responsible. If the fall in the value of money discourages investment, it also discredits enterprise.

Not that the business man was allowed, even during the period of boom, to retain the whole of his exceptional profits. A host of popular remedies vainly attempted to cure the evils of the day; which remedies themselves -- subsidies, price and rent fixing, profiteer hunting, and excess profits duties--eventually became not the least part of the evils.

In due course came the depression, with falling prices, which operate on those who hold stocks in a manner exactly opposite to rising prices. Excessive losses, bearing no relation to the efficiency of the business, took the place of windfall gains; and the effort of every one to hold as small stocks as possible brought industry to a standstill, just as previously their efforts to accumulate stocks had over-stimulated it. Unemployment succeeded Profiteering as the problem of the hour.

(iii) The Earner It has been a commonplace of economic textbooks that wages tend to lag behind prices, with the result that the real earnings of the wage-earner are diminished during a period of rising prices. This has often been true in the past, and may be true even now of certain classes of labour which are ill-placed or illorganised for improving their position. But in Great Britain, at any rate, and in the United States also, some important sections of labour were able to take advantage of the situation not only to obtain money wages equivalent in purchasing power to what they had before, but to secure a real improvement, to combine this with a diminution in their hours of work (and, so far, of the work done), and to accomplish this (in the case of Great Britain) at a time when the total wealth of the community as a whole had suffered a decrease. This reversal of the usual course has not been due to an accident and is traceable to definite causes.

The organisation of certain classes of labour --railwaymen, miners, dockers, and others-for the purpose of securing wage increases is better than it was. Life in the army, perhaps for the first time in the history of wars, raised in many respects the conventional standard of requirements,--the soldier was better clothed, better shod, and often better fed than the labourer, and his wife, adding in war time a separation allowance to new opportunities to earn, had also enlarged her ideas.

But these influences, while they would have supplied the motive, might have lacked the means to the result if it had not been for another factor--the windfalls of the profiteer. The fact that the business man had been gaining, and gaining notoriously, considerable windfall profits in excess of the normal profits of trade, laid him open to pressure, not only from his employees but from public opinion generally; and enabled him to meet this pressure without financial difficulty. In fact, it was worth his while to pay ransom, and to share with his workmen the good fortune of the day.

Thus the working classes improved their relative position in the years following the war, as against all other classes except that of the "profiteers." In some important cases they improved their absolute position--that is to say, account being taken of shorter hours, increased money wages, and higher prices, some sections of the working classes secured for themselves a higher real remuneration for each unit of effort or work done. But we cannot estimate the stability of this state of affairs, as contrasted with its desirability, unless we know the source from which the increased reward of the working classes was drawn. Was it due to a permanent modification of the economic factors which determine the distribution of the national product between different classes? Or was it due to some temporary and exhaustible influence connected with Inflation and with the resulting disturbance in the standard of value?

The period of depression has exacted its penalty from the working classes more in the form of unemployment than by a lowering of real wages, and State assistance to the unemployed has greatly moderated even this penalty. Money wages have followed prices downwards. But the depression of 1921-22 did not reverse or even greatly diminish the relative advantage gained by the working classes over the middle class during the previous years. In 1923 British wage rates stood at an appreciably higher level above the pre-war rates than did the cost of living, if allowance is made for the shorter hours worked.

(B) CHANGES IN THE VALUE OF MONEY, AS AFFECTING PRODUCTION If, for any reason right or wrong, the business world expects that prices will fall, the processes of production tend to be inhibited; and if it expects that prices will rise, they tend to be overstimulated. A fluctuation in the measuringrod of value does not alter in the least the wealth of the world, the needs of the world, or the productive capacity of the world. It ought not, therefore, to affect the character or the volume of what is produced. A movement of relative prices, that is to say of the comparative prices of different commodities, ought to influence the character of production, because it is an indication that various commodities are not being produced in the exactly right proportions. But this is not true of a change, as such, in the general price level.

The fact that the expectation of changes in the general price level affects the processes of production, is deeply rooted in the peculiarities of the existing economic organisation of society. We have already seen that a change in the general level of prices, that is to say a change in the measuring-rod, which fixes the obligation of the borrowers of money (who make the decisions which set production in motion) to the lenders (who are inactive once they have lent their money), effects a redistribution of real wealth between the two groups. Furthermore, the active group can, if they foresee such a change, alter their action in advance in such a way as to minimise their losses to the other group or to increase their gains from it, if and when the expected change in the value of money occurs. If they expect a fall, it may pay them, as a group, to damp production down, although such enforced idleness impoverishes Society as a whole. If they expect a rise, it may pay them to increase their borrowings and to swell production beyond the point where the real return is just sufficient to recompense Society as a whole for the effort made. Sometimes, of course, a change in the measuring-rod, especially if it is unforeseen, may benefit one group at the expense of the other disproportionately to any influence it exerts on the volume of production; but the tendency, in so far as the active group anticipate a change, will be as I have described it. This is simply to say that the intensity of production is largely governed in existing conditions by the anticipated real profit of the entrepreneur. Yet this criterion is the right one for the community as a whole only when the delicate adjustment of interests is not upset by fluctuations in the standard of value.

There is also a considerable risk directly arising out of instability in the value of money. During the lengthy process of production the business world is incurring outgoings in terms of money--paying out in money for wages and other expenses of production--in the expectation of recouping this outlay by disposing of the product for money at a later date. That is to say, the business world as a whole must always be in a position where it stands to gain by a rise of price and to lose by a fall of price. Whether it likes it or not, the technique of production under a régime of money-contract forces the business world always to carry a big speculative position; and if it is reluctant to carry this position, the productive process must be slackened. The argument is not affected by the fact that there is some degree of specialisation of function within the business world, in so far as the professional speculator comes to the assistance of the producer proper by taking over from him a part of his risk.

Now it follows from this, not merely that the actual occurrence of price changes profits some classes and injures others (which has been the theme of the first section of this chapter), but that a general fear of falling prices may inhibit the productive process altogether. For if prices are expected to fall, not enough risktakers can be found who are willing to carry a speculative "bull" position, and this means that entrepreneurs will be reluctant to embark on lengthy productive processes involving a money outlay long in advance of money recoupment,--whence unemployment. The fact of falling prices injures entrepreneurs; consequently the fear of falling prices causes them to protect themselves by curtailing their operations; yet it is upon the aggregate of their individual estimations of the risk, and their willingness to run the risk, that the activity of production and of employment mainly depends. There is a further aggravation of the case, in that an expectation about the course of prices tends, if it is widely held, to be cumulative in its results up to a certain point. If prices are expected to rise and the business world acts on this expectation, that very fact causes them to rise for a time and, by verifying the expectation, reinforces it; and similarly, if it expects them to fall. Thus a comparatively weak initial impetus may be adequate to produce a considerable fluctuation.

The best way to cure this mortal disease of individualism must be to provide that there shall never exist any confident expectation either that prices generally are going to fall or that they are going to rise; and also that there shall be no serious risk that a movement, if it does occur, will be a big one. If, unexpectedly and accidentally, a moderate movement were to occur, wealth, though it might be redistributed, would not be diminished thereby.

To procure this result by removing all possible influences towards an initial movement would seem to be a hopeless enterprise. The remedy would lie, rather, in so controlling the standard of value that whenever something occurred which, left to itself, would create an expectation of a change in the general level of prices, the controlling authority should take steps to counteract this expectation by setting in motion some factor of a contrary tendency. Even if such a policy were not wholly successful, either in counteracting expectations or in avoiding actual movements, it would be an improvement on the policy of sitting quietly by whilst a standard of value, governed by chance causes and deliberately removed from central control, produces expectations which paralyse or intoxicate the government of production.

We see, therefore, that rising prices and falling prices each have their characteristic disadvantage. The Inflation which causes the former means Injustice to individuals and to classes,--particularly to rentiers; and is therefore unfavourable to saving. The Deflation which causes falling prices means Impoverishment to labour and to enterprise by leading entrepreneurs to restrict production, in their endeavour to avoid loss to themselves; and is therefore disastrous to employment. The counterparts are, of course, also true,-- namely that Deflation means Injustice to borrowers, and that Inflation leads to the over-stimulation of industrial activity. But these results are not so marked as those emphasised above, because borrowers are in a better position to protect themselves from the worst effects of Deflation than lenders are to protect themselves from those of Inflation, and because labour is in a better position to protect itself from overexertion in good times than from underemployment in bad times.

Thus Inflation is unjust and Deflation is inexpedient. Of the two perhaps Deflation is, if we rule out exaggerated inflations such as that of Germany, the worse; because it is worse, in an impoverished world, to provoke unemployment than to disappoint the rentier. But it is not necessary that we should weigh one evil against the other. It is easier to agree that both are evils to be shunned. The Individualistic Capitalism of to-day, precisely because it entrusts saving to the individual investor and production to the individual employer, presumes a stable measuring-rod of value, and cannot be efficient --perhaps cannot survive--without one.

For these grave causes we must free ourselves from the deep distrust which exists against allowing the regulation of the standard of value to be the subject of deliberate decision. We can no longer afford to leave it in the category of which the distinguishing characteristics are possessed in different degrees by the weather, the birth-rate, and the Constitution,--matters which are settled by natural causes, or are the resultant of the separate action of many individuals acting independently, or require a Revolution to change them.

3. THE FRENCH FRANC (i) An open letter to the French Minister of Finance (whoever he is or may be) (Jan. 1926) MONSIEUR,- -When I read in my daily paper the daily projects of yourself and your predecessors to draft new budgets and to fund old debts, I get the impression that Paris discusses very little what seems to me in London to be the technical analysis of your problem. May I, therefore, divert your attention for a moment from your Sisyphean task of rolling budgets up Parliament Hill back to certain fundamental calculations?

I have written about the French franc many times in recent years, and I do not find that I have changed my mind. More than two years ago I wrote: "The level of the franc is going to be settled in the long run, not by speculation or the balance of trade, or even the outcome of the Ruhr adventure, but by the proportion of his earned income which the French taxpayer will permit to be taken from him to pay the claims of the French rentier." I still think that this is the root idea from which your plans ought to develop.

Now it is obvious that there are two methods of attaining the desired equilibrium. You can increase the burdens on the taxpayer, or you can diminish the claims of the rentier. If you choose the first alternative, taxation will absorb nearly a quarter of the national income of France. Is this feasible? If it is ever safe to speak about the political atmosphere of another country, I should judge from recent indications that the French public will certainly refuse to submit to the imposition of a burden of additional taxation sufficient to satisfy the claims of the rentier at their present level. And even if such taxation were politically possible, it would probably, break down administratively. The pressing task of the French Treasury is not to devise additional taxes, but to construct an administrative machine capable of collecting, those which exist. If, therefore, I were in your place, I should not, as a politician, give another minute's thought to new taxes, but would concentrate, so far as concerned the fiscal part of my office, on consolidating and administering the taxes already voted.

Since this by itself is not enough, your next business--provided you accept my conclusion as to the mind of the French public--is to consider coolly how best to reduce the claims of the rentier. Three methods offer themselves: first, a general capital levy; second, a forced reduction of the rate of interest on the public debt; third, a rise of prices which would reduce the real value of the rentier's money claims. Unquestionably, the first is preferable on grounds of virtue, justice, and theory. For Britain in a similar fix I should advocate it. But I think it so probable that such a project would be defeated in France to-day by the same political and administrative difficulties which stand in the way of further taxation, that I should not lose my time on it. The second method is attractive, if only because it offers no administrative difficulties. I believe that some authorities in France have favoured it. Nevertheless, I should decline this expedient also, if I were in your place, because, unlike a general capital levy or a depreciation of money, this species of discrimination is truly named Repudiation, and Repudiation of the National Debt is a departure from financial virtue so extreme and so dangerous as not to be undertaken but in the last emergency.

We are left, therefore, by a process of the exclusion of alternatives, with one Exit only-a rise of internal prices; which leads us away from the fiscal field to the price level, the foreign exchanges, the gold in the Bank of France, the volume of foreign investment, and the balance of trade. Here I must invite your particular attention to an interesting paradox.

Successive Finance Ministers have, in fact, done their utmost to find an escape through the Exit I indicate. They have inflated magnificently, and they have brought down the gold value of the franc by progressive stages with only temporary set-backs. What more could they have done?

I will tell you. The great army of your predecessors have failed, in spite of all their efforts, to depreciate adequately the internal purchasing power of the franc. Your present difficulties are due, not to the inflation of the notes or to the fall of the exchange (for these events are tending all the time to help you out of your troubles), but to the failure of these factors to diminish proportionately the internal purchasing power of the rentier's money claims.

The following figures present the essence of your problem. In December 1925, the gold value of the franc on the foreign exchanges was 19 per cent of its pre-war parity; world gold prices were about 158 per cent of their pre-war level; therefore on the pre-war basis a note circulation and a franc price level amounting to 830 per cent (for $158 \div 19 = 8.3$) of their pre-war figures would be justified. Now the note circulation, being about 1000 per cent of its pre-war figure, roughly corresponds to the level of the foreign exchange--though, allowing for increased territory and the loss of gold and silver coin from the circulation, it is probably still too low in relation to the exchange, rather than too high, on a pre-war comparison.

When we come to the internal franc price level, on the other hand, we find an entirely different story. Imported raw materials have inevitably risen to their international parity. But the classes of goods such as food and other articles entering into the cost-of-living index number, which are dominated by home production, are far below their equilibrium value. Wholesale food prices in November 1925 were 490 per cent of pre-war, retail prices in Paris (thirteen items) were 433 per cent, and in the third quarter of 1925 the cost-of-living index for Paris stood at 401 per cent. These figures may understate the real rise of prices, but it certainly seems that French domestic costs are not above five times their pre-war figure. This means that the prices of purely home produce, converted at the present rate of exchange, are not much more than half world prices, and are actually below their pre-war level in terms of gold. Thus the Inflation of the currency has produced its full effect on the exchanges, and consequently on the prices of imported commodities, but has largely failed to do so on the prices of home produce.

Now the burden of the rentier on the taxpayer is measured by the internal purchasing power of the francs which have to be taken from the latter to be handed to the former. Thus if internal prices had risen as fast as the exchange has fallen, the real burden of the national debt service would be reduced by at least a third. I suggest to you, therefore, that, whilst the solution of your fiscal difficulties can come about in no other way than by a rise in the internal price level, it is not so clear that this need be accompanied either by further Inflation or by a further fall in the exchange.

It is for you to decide in your own mind at what level of internal prices you can hope to balance your budget. Your next step must be to bring about this rise in as orderly and scientific a way as you are able. Looking from outside, it appears to me that an internal price level between eight and nine times pre-war might be high enough. In this case there is no justification for any considerable further Inflation or fall in the franc exchange. All you have to do is to stabilise the note circulation and the franc exchange at near their present level and to allow time for internal prices to rise correspondingly.

What are the explanations of the present low level of franc prices? I think that they are: (1) the time element--internal prices move slowly, but will move as they should in time; (2) the hoarding of bank-notes on an even greater scale than formerly, leading to a sluggish circulation of the available currency; (3) excessive foreign investment by Frenchmen, due to lack of confidence, which drives the exchange down below the figure appropriate to the trading position; and (4) the legal restrictions on rents, etc.

These influences should be remediable as regards (1) by the mere lapse of time, and as regards (2) and (3) by the restoration of internal confidence. The right strategy, therefore, is to restore confidence and then just wait. And the way to restore confidence is, surely, not to heap up taxes, but to stabilise the franc exchange beyond doubt or criticism near its present level.

How to stabilise the franc exchange? Not so difficult as it is supposed to be. The balance of trade is strongly in favour of France. The present level of internal prices encourages exports and discourages imports. The metallic reserve of the Bank of France is worth (at the present exchange) nearly 40 per cent of the note issue. Nothing is required, I expect, but that the Bank of France should declare that for two years at least it will furnish dollar exchange against francs in unlimited amounts on terms not worse than some stated rate between dollars and francs, and that the Bank should be prepared, if necessary, to use its gold for the purpose. The rate selected should probably lie somewhere between 1 dollar for 25 francs and 1 dollar for 30 francs, and it would be safer to choose the latter ratio at first, with just a hope that the former might be achieved in the end. 1 The success of the scheme requires no more than that the Bank's undertaking should be believed. With this background of stability you will be able to borrow enough to carry you through the transitional period without further Inflation.

For the rest you can trust time. As the internal price level gradually rises to an equilibrium with the exchange and as the machinery for collecting the taxes is gradually improved, your budget receipts will grow month by month until they balance the expenses. Those taxes which are fixed in francs and are not ad valorem should, of course, be raised pari passu with the rise in prices.

There are two matters on which the Government of France needs to exercise an iron resolve --to fix the franc exchange at a minimum figure even if it costs gold to do so, and to collect the taxes in full. These are the indispensable measures. Heroic efforts to increase the rates of taxation are, at this stage, efforts in a wrong direction, and will not be successful.

What are the arguments against these courses? They are entirely political. A policy which will not be successful unless it raises prices by a heavy percentage will be open to the universal unpopularity of la vie chère. A policy of bringing about an equilibrium between internal and external prices must be injurious to the export interests which flourish on their disequilibrium. It may not be sufficient to reply that the first must happen in any case unless the taxpayer will sacrifice himself to the rentier, and that the second must happen some day unless the franc is to fall for ever.

But there are political considerations of some weight to set on the other side. A rise in the prices of agricultural produce will not be unpopular with farmers and peasant producers who have been selling their output much too cheap. Further, the Government must make it clear that wage-earners and officials are not intended to suffer, and will, if it is wise, pass a law providing for automatic quarterly increases of all wages and salaries throughout the next two years corresponding to every increase in the cost of living.Well, I offer these reflections for what they are worth. Whether or not they commend themselves to your judgement, I am sure that the following questions are those which you need to ponder:--

1. Would a rise in the level of internal prices solve your difficulties?

2. Can you solve your difficulties without a rise of prices?

3. Is it not impossible anyhow to prevent a rise in the long run?

4. If so, will you not be judicious to facilitate an orderly rise and to play for time meanwhile?

5. Whether you choose this course or another, is there any sufficient objection to using the gold in the Bank of France to anchor the franc exchange?

Your obedient servant,

J. M. KEYNES

(ii) The Stabilisation of the Franc (1928) One blames politicians, not for inconsistency, but for obstinacy. They are the interpreters, not the masters, of our fate. It is their job, in short, to register the fait accompli. In this spirit we all applaud M. Poincaré for not allowing himself to be hampered by a regard for consistency. After declaring for years that it would be an act of national bankruptcy and shame to devalue the franc, he has fixed it at about onefifth of its pre-war gold value, and has retorted with threats of resignation against anyone who would hinder him in so good a deed.

The figure finally chosen seems about right. There are high authorities in France who argue that one-sixth of pre-war (150 francs to the £) would be better and safer. But about onefifth (124.21 francs to the £) has the great advantage of conforming to the rate which has actually existed for some eighteen months. None of the relevant statistics suggests that M. Poincaré has made the mistake of stabilising at a figure which involves Deflation. No lower value for the franc (in terms of gold) than that now chosen has ever existed except during the hectic twelve months from December 1925 to November 1926, when internal prices had no time to adjust themselves to the furious fluctuations of the exchanges. Moreover, the Budget balances with the burden of the rentes on the taxpayer bearable at the present level. I see no sufficient reason, therefore, to choose a lower figure.

Is the value too low? For that is the line of criticism in France itself. There are two chief tests. Is it lower than the figure to which internal prices are adjusted? Does it demand too great a sacrifice from the rentier? The official Index Numbers, if taken at their face-value, suggest that prices are in line with a gold value of the franc nearer to one quarter (100 francs to the £) than to one-fifth of the pre-war value. But the French Index Numbers are very crude affairs subject to a wide margin of error, and the two and a half years which has elapsed since the franc was worth more than the figure now fixed, is a fair time to allow for an adjustment of prices upward--a much quicker business than a downward adjustment can be. House rents doubtless must rise, but it is probable that other prices will trend only a little upward if at all, compared with gold prices abroad. As for the rentier, a very drastic capital levy having been brought about de facto and the awkward consequences surmounted, it is asking too much to undo gratuitously what is already done. Three other arguments, however, of a practical order are probably those which have convinced M. Poincaré. To choose a higher value for the franc might disturb the equilibrium of the Budget which has been so painfully achieved. It would upset the industrialist exporters--who have their means of exerting political influence. And--most tangible of all--it would involve the Bank of France in a loss on the foreign exchange, said to amount to some £300,000,000, which, as an agent of the Government, it has bought up at the present rate. To fix 100 francs to the £, for example, might cost the Bank of France £60,000,000, of which no mean proportion might accrue to foreigners. This is just the sort of argument which M. Poincaré and every other Frenchman is able to understand.

The deed, therefore, is done. Since it removes an element of uncertainty from the Money Markets and Stock Exchanges of the world, and since French importers and manufacturers need hesitate no longer, a good deal of purchasing power, which has been lying idle, may be returned to active employment. M. Poincaré has, therefore, done something--perhaps for the first time in his career--to make the rest of us feel more cheerful.

It is interesting to compare the several fortunes of France and Great Britain over the post-war period. In Great Britain our authorities have never talked such rubbish as their French colleagues or offended so grossly against all sound principles of finance. But Great Britain has come out of the transitional period with the weight of her war debt aggravated, her obligations to the United States unabated, and deflationary finance still in the ascendant; with the heavy burden of taxes appropriate to the former and a million unemployed as the outcome of the latter. France, on the other hand, has written down her internal war debt by fourfifths, and has persuaded her Allies to let her off more than half of her external debt; and now she is avoiding the sacrifices of Deflation. Yet she has contrived to do this without the slightest loss of reputation for conservative finance and capitalist principles. The Bank of France emerges much stronger than the Bank of England; and everyone still feels that France is the last stronghold of tenacious saving and the rentier mentality. Assuredly it does not pay to be good.

Perhaps we deserve what we have got. France has abandoned principle and consistency alike, but she has always refused sacrifices which were avoidable and has obeyed in the end the teachings of experience. We in England have not submitted either to the warnings of theory or to the pressure of facts, obstinately obedient to conventions.

4. A PROGRAMME OF EXPANSION (GENERAL ELECTION, MAY 1929)

I. Except for a brief recovery in 1924 before the return to the gold standard, one-tenth or more of the working population of this country have been unemployed for eight years--a fact unprecedented in our history. The number of insured persons counted by the Ministry of Labour as out of work has never been less than one million since the initiation of their statistics in 1923. To-day (April 1929) 1,140,000 workpeople are unemployed.

This level of unemployment is costing us out of the Unemployment Fund a cash disbursement of about £50,000,000 a year. This does not include poor relief. Since 1921 we have paid out to the unemployed in cash a sum of about £500,000,000--and have got literally nothing for it. This sum would have built a million houses; it is nearly double the whole of the accumulated savings of the Post Office Savings Bank; it would build a third of all the roads in the country; it far exceeds the total value of all the mines, of every description, which we possess; it would be enough to revolutionise the industrial equipment of the country; or to proceed from what is heavy to what is lighter, it would provide every third family in the country with a motor car or would furnish a fund enough to allow the whole population to attend cinemas for nothing to the end of time.

But this is not nearly all the waste. There is the far greater loss to the unemployed themselves, represented by the difference between the dole and a full working wage, and by the loss of strength and morale. There is the loss in profits to employers and in taxation to the Chancellor of the Exchequer. There is the incalculable loss of retarding for a decade the economic progress of the whole country.

The Census of Production of 1924 calculated that the average value of the net annual output of a British working man when employed is about £220. On this basis the waste through unemployment since 1921 has mounted up to approximately £2,000,000,000, a sum which would be nearly sufficient to build all the railways in the country twice over. It would pay off our debt to America twice over. It is more than the total sum that the Allies are asking from Germany for Reparations.

It is important to know and appreciate these figures because they put the possible cost of Mr. Lloyd George's schemes into its true perspective. He calculates that a development programme of £100,000,000 a year will bring back 500,000 men into employment. This expenditure is not large in proportion to the waste and loss accruing year by year through unemployment, as can be seen by comparing it with the figures quoted above. It only represents 5 per cent of the loss already accumulated on account of unemployment since 1921. It is equal to about 2 1/2 per cent of the national income. If the experiment were to be continued at the rate of £100,000,000 per annum for three years, and if the whole of it were to be entirely wasted, the annual interest payable on it hereafter would increase the Budget by less than 2 per cent. In short, it is a very modest programme. The idea that it represents a desperate risk to cure a moderate evil is the reverse of the truth. It is a negligible risk to cure a monstrous anomaly.

Nothing has been included in the programme which cannot be justified as worth doing for its own sake. Yet even if half of it were to be wasted, we should still be better off. Was there ever a stronger case for a little boldness, for taking a risk if there be one?

It may seem very wise to sit back and wag the head. But while we wait, the unused labour of the workless is not piling up to our credit in a bank, ready to be used at some later date. It is running irrevocably to waste; it is irretrievably lost. Every puff of Mr. Baldwin's pipe costs us thousands of pounds.

The objection, which is raised more frequently, perhaps, than any other, is that money raised by the State for financing productive schemes must diminish pro tanto the supply of capital available for ordinary industry. If this is true, a policy of national development will not really increase employment. It will merely substitute employment on State schemes for ordinary employment. Either that, or (so the argument often runs) it must mean Inflation. There is, therefore, little or nothing that the Government can usefully do. The case is hopeless, and we must just drift along.

This was the contention of the Chancellor of the Exchequer in his Budget speech. "It is the orthodox Treasury dogma, steadfastly held," he told the House of Commons, "that whatever might be the political or social advantages, very little additional employment and no permanent additional employment can, in fact, and as a general rule, be created by State borrowing and State expenditure." Some State expenditure, he concluded, is inevitable, and even wise and right for its own sake, but not as a cure for unemployment.

In relation to the actual facts of to-day, this argument is, we believe, quite without foundation.

In the first place, there is nothing in the argument which limits its applicability to Statepromoted undertakings. If it is valid at all, it must apply equally to a new works started by Morris, or Courtaulds, to any new business enterprise entailing capital expenditure. If it were announced that some of our leading captains of industry had decided to launch out boldly, and were about to sink capital in new industrial plant to the tune, between them, of £100 millions, we should all expect to see a great improvement in employment. And, of course, we should be right. But, if the argument we are dealing with were sound, we should be wrong. We should have to conclude that these enterprising business men were merely diverting capital from other uses, and that no real gain to employment could result. Indeed, we should be driven to a still more remarkable conclusion. We should have to conclude that it was virtually out of the question to absorb our unemployed workpeople by any means whatsoever (other than the unthinkable Inflation), and that the obstacle which barred the path was no other than an insufficiency of capital. This, if you please, in Great Britain, who has surplus savings which she is accustomed to lend abroad on the scale of more than a hundred millions a year.

The argument is certainly not derived from common sense. No ordinary man, left to himself, is able to believe that, if there had been no housing schemes in recent years, there would, nevertheless, have been just as much employment. And, accordingly, most ordinary men are easily persuaded by Mr. Lloyd George that, if his schemes for employment are adopted, more men will be employed.

But the argument is not only unplausible. It is also untrue. There are three resources which can enable new investment to provide a net addition to the amount of employment.

The first source of supply comes out of the savings which we are now disbursing to pay the unemployed.

The second source of supply comes from the savings which now run to waste through lack of adequate credit.

The third source of supply comes from a reduction in the net amount of foreign lending.

Let us consider these in turn, beginning with the first source. Individual saving means that some individuals are producing more than they are consuming. This surplus may, and should, be used to increase capital equipment. But, unfortunately, this is not the only way in which it can be used. It can also be used to enable other individuals to consume more than they produce.

This is what happens when there is unemployment. We are using our savings to pay for unemployment instead of using them to equip the country. The savings which Mr. Lloyd George's schemes will employ will be diverted not from financing other capital equipment, but partly from financing unemployment. From the Unemployment Fund alone we are now paying out £50,000,000 a year; and this is not the whole of the cost of supporting the unemployed.

In the second place, the savings of individuals do not necessarily materialise in investments. The amount of investment in capital improvements depends, on the one hand, on the amount of credit created by the Bank of England; and, on the other hand, on the eagerness of entrepreneurs to invest, of whom the Government itself is nowadays the most important. So far from the total of investment, as determined by these factors, being necessarily equal to the total of saving, disequilibrium between the two is at the root of many of our troubles.

When investment runs ahead of saving we have a boom, intense employment, and a tendency to Inflation. When investment lags behind, we have a slump and abnormal unemployment, as at present.

It is commonly objected to this that an expansion of credit necessarily means Inflation. But not all credit-creation means Inflation. Inflation only results when we endeavour, as we did in the war and afterwards, to expand our activities still further after everyone is already employed and our savings are being used up to the hilt.

The suggestion that a policy of capital expenditure, if it does not take capital away from ordinary industry, will spell Inflation, would be true enough if we were dealing with boom conditions. And it would become true if the policy of capital expenditure were pushed unduly far, so that the demand for savings began to exceed the supply. But we are far, indeed, from such a position at the present time. A large amount of deflationary slack has first to be taken up before there can be the smallest danger of a development policy leading to Inflation. To bring up the bogy of Inflation as an objection to capital expenditure at the present time is like warning a patient who is wasting away from emaciation of the dangers of excessive corpulence.

The real difficulty hitherto in the way of an easier credit policy by the Bank of England has been the fear that an expansion of credit might lead to a loss of gold which the Bank could not afford.

Now if the Bank were to try to increase the volume of credit at a time when, on account of the depression of home enterprise, no reliance could be placed on the additional credit being absorbed at home at the existing rate of interest, this might quite well be true. Since market rates of interest would fall, a considerable part of the new credit might find its way to foreign borrowers, with the result of a drain of gold out of the Bank. Thus it is not safe for the Bank to expand credit unless it is certain beforehand that there are home borrowers standing ready to absorb it at the existing rates of interest.

This is the reason why the Liberal plan is exactly suited to the fundamentals of the present position. It provides the necessary condition for an expansion of credit to be safe.

It is, of course, essential that the Bank of England should loyally co-operate with the Government's programme of capital development, and do its best to make it a success. For, unfortunately, it would lie within the power of the Bank, provided it were to pursue a deflationary policy aimed at preventing any expansion in bank-credit, to defeat the best-laid plans and to ensure that the expenditure financed by the Treasury was at the expense of other business enterprise.

Thus we accept Mr. McKenna's contention that an expansion of credit is the key to the situation. But if we were simply to increase credit without providing a specific use for it at home, we should be nervous that too much of this extra credit would be lent to foreigners and taken away in gold. We conclude, therefore, that, whilst an increased volume of bank-credit is probably a sine qua non of increased employment, a programme of home investment which will absorb this increase is a sine qua non of the safe expansion of credit.

The third source of the funds required for the Liberal policy will be found by a net reduction of foreign lending.

An important part of our savings is now finding its outlet in foreign issues. Granted that a big policy of national development could not be financed wholly out of the existing expenditure on unemployment and out of the savings which are at present running to waste, granted that, to meet the borrowing demands of the State other borrowers must go without, why should we assume that these other borrowers must be British business men? The technique of the capital market makes it far more probable that they would be some of the overseas Governments or municipalities which London at present finances on so large a scale.

It is the bond market that would be principally affected by a British Government loan.

Now anything which served to diminish the volume of foreign issues would be welcomed by the Bank of England at the present time for its own sake. The exchange position is uncomfortable and precarious; the recent rise in bankrate is proof of that. A diminution of foreign investment would ease the strain on the exchanges. Why, it is only a year or two since the Bank of England, with this end in view, was maintaining a semi-official embargo on foreign issues. The embargo was a crude instrument, suitable only for temporary use, and we do not suggest its renewal. But the need which that embargo was designed to supply still remains, if in a less acute degree. In relation to our less favourable balance of foreign trade, we are investing abroad dangerously much; and we are investing abroad to this dangerous extent partly because there are insufficient outlets for our savings at home.

It follows, therefore, that a policy of capital expenditure, in so far as it might go beyond the mere absorption of deflationary slack, would serve mainly to divert to home development savings which now find their way abroad, and that this would be a welcome result in the interests of the Bank of England.

It has been objected that if we lend less abroad, our exports will fall off. We see no reason to anticipate this. Immediately, as we have said, the reduction in net foreign lending will relieve the pressure on the Bank of England's stock of gold. But, ultimately, its main effect will be realised, not in a reduction of exports, but in an increase of imports. For the new schemes will require a certain amount of imported raw materials, whilst those who are now unemployed will consume more imported food when they are once again earning decent wages.

Here, then, is our answer. The savings which Mr. Lloyd George's schemes will employ will be diverted, not from financing other capital equipment, but partly from financing unemployment. A further part will come from the savings which now run to waste through lack of adequate credit. Something will be provided by the very prosperity which the new policy will foster. And the balance will be found by a reduction of foreign lending.

The whole of the labour of the unemployed is available to increase the national wealth. It is crazy to believe that we shall ruin ourselves financially by trying to find means for using it and that "Safety First" lies in continuing to maintain men in idleness.

It is precisely with our unemployed productive resources that we shall make the new investments.

We are left with a broad, simple, and surely incontestable proposition. Whatever real difficulties there may be in the way of absorbing our unemployed labour in productive work, an inevitable diversion of resources from other forms of employment is not one of them.

II. Our whole economic policy during recent years has been dominated by the preoccupation of the Treasury with their departmental problem of debt conversion. The less the Government borrows, the better, they argue, are the chances of converting the

National Debt into loans carrying a lower rate of interest. In the interests of conversion, therefore, they have exerted themselves to curtail, as far as they can, all public borrowing, all capital expenditure by the State, no matter how productive and desirable in itself. We doubt if the general public has any idea how powerful, persistent, and farreaching this influence has been.

To all well-laid schemes of progress and enterprise, they have (whenever they could) barred the door with, No! Now, it is quite true, that curtailing capital expenditure exerts some tendency towards lower interest rates for Government loans. But it is no less true that it makes for increased unemployment and that it leaves the country with a pre-war outfit.

Even from the Budget point of view, it is a question whether the game is worth the candle. It is difficult to believe that, if this question were considered squarely on its merits, any intelligent person could return an affirmative answer. The capital market is an international market. All sorts of influences which are outside our control go to determine the gilt-edged rate of interest; and the effect which the British Government can exert on it by curtailing or expanding its capital programme is limited. Suppose, which is putting the case extremely high, that the effect might be as much as 1/4 per cent. This, applied to the £2000 millions of War Loan, which are ripe for conversion, would represent a difference in the annual debt charge of £5 millions annually. Compare this with the expenditure of the Unemployment Fund--over £50 millions last year.

Moreover, in the course of (say) ten years it is not unlikely that a situation will arise--as used to happen from time to time before the war--when for world reasons the rate of interest will be abnormally low--much lower than we could possibly hope for by Treasury contrivances in the exceptionally unfavourable environment of abnormally high world rates. This will be the moment for a successful conversion scheme. Even, therefore, if the Treasury could convert to-day at a saving of 1/4 per cent or 1/2 per cent, it might be extremely improvident to do so. A premature conversion for an inconsiderable saving would be a grave blunder. We must have the patience to wait for the ideal conjuncture of conditions, and then the Chancellor of the Exchequer of the day will be able to pull off something big.

But apart from budgetary advantages and disadvantages, there is a deep-seated confusion of thought in hindering on these grounds the capital development of the country. The rate of interest can fall for either of two opposite reasons. It may fall on account of an abundant supply of savings, i.e. of money available to be spent on investments; or it may fall on account of a deficient supply of investments, i.e. on desirable purposes on which to spend the savings. Now a fall in the rate of interest for the first reason is, obviously, very much in the national interest. But a fall for the second reason, if it follows from a deliberate restriction of outlets for investment, is simply a disastrous method of impoverishing ourselves.

A country is enriched not by the mere negative act of an individual not spending all his income on current consumption. It is enriched by the positive act of using these savings to augment the capital equipment of the country. It is not the miser who gets rich; but he who lays out his money in fruitful investment.

The object of urging people to save is in order to be able to build houses and roads and the like. Therefore a policy of trying to lower the rate of interest by suspending new capital improvements and so stopping up the outlets and purposes of our savings is simply suicidal. No one, perhaps, would uphold such a policy expressed in so many words. But this, in fact, is what the Treasury has been doing for several years. In some cases, the pressure of public opinion or of other Government Departments or Local Authorities has been too much for them. But whenever it has been within their power to choke something off, they have done so.

The futility of their policy and the want of sound reasoning behind it have been finally demonstrated by its failure even to secure a fall in the rate of interest. For, as we have seen above, if outlets for investment at home are stopped up, savings flow abroad on a scale disproportionate to our favourable balance of trade, with the result that the Bank of England tends to lose gold. To counteract this position, the bankrate has to be raised.

So in the end we have the worst of all worlds. The country is backward in its equipment, instead of being thoroughly up to date. Business profits are poor, with the result that the yield of the income tax disappoints the Chancellor of the Exchequer, and he is unable either to relieve the taxpayer or to push forward with schemes of social reform. Unemployment is rampant. This want of prosperity actually diminishes the rate of saving and thus defeats even the original object of a lower rate of interest. So rates of interest are, after all, high.

It is not an accident that the Conservative Government have landed us in the mess where we find ourselves. It is the natural outcome of their philosophy:

"You must not press on with telephones or electricity, because this will raise the rate of interest."

"You must not hasten with roads or housing, because this will use up opportunities for employment which we may need in later years." "You must not try to employ every one, because this will cause inflation."

"You must not invest, because how can you know that it will pay?"

"You must not do anything, because this will only mean that you can't do something else."

"Safety First! The policy of maintaining a million unemployed has now been pursued for eight years without disaster. Why risk a change?"

"We will not promise more than we can perform. We, therefore, promise nothing."

This is what we are being fed with.

They are slogans of depression and decay-the timidities and obstructions and stupidities of a sinking administrative vitality.

Negation, Restriction, Inactivity--these are the Government's watchwords. Under their leadership we have been forced to button up our waistcoats and compress our lungs. Fears and doubts and hypochondriac precautions are keeping us muffled up indoors. But we are not tottering to our graves. We are healthy children. We need the breath of life. There is nothing to be afraid of. On the contrary. The future holds in store for us far more wealth and economic freedom and possibilities of personal life than the past has ever offered.

There is no reason why we should not feel ourselves free to be bold, to be open, to experiment, to take action, to try the possibilities of things. And over against us, standing in the path, there is nothing but a few old gentlemen tightly buttoned-up in their frock coats, who only need to be treated with a little friendly disrespect and bowled over like ninepins.

Quite likely they will enjoy it themselves, when once they have got over the shock.

5. THE GREAT SLUMP OF 1930 (1930)

I. The world has been slow to realise that we are living this year in the shadow of one of the greatest economic catastrophes of modern history. But now that the man in the street has become aware of what is happening, he, not knowing the why and wherefore, is as full to-day of what may prove excessive fears as, previously, when the trouble was first coming on, he was lacking in what would have been a reasonable anxiety. He begins to doubt the future. Is he now awakening from a pleasant dream to face the darkness of facts? Or dropping off into a nightmare which will pass away?

He need not be doubtful. The other was not a dream. This is a nightmare, which will pass away with the morning. For the resources of Nature and men's devices are just as fertile and productive as they were. The rate of our progress towards solving the material problems of life is not less rapid. We are as capable as before of affording for every one a high standard of life -- high, I mean, compared with, say, twenty years ago--and will soon learn to afford a standard higher still. We were not previously deceived. But to-day we have involved ourselves in a colossal muddle, having blundered in the control of a delicate machine, the working of which we do not understand. The result is that our possibilities of wealth may run to waste for a time--perhaps for a long time.

I doubt whether I can hope to bring what is in my mind into fully effective touch with the mind of the reader. I shall be saying too much for the layman, too little for the expert. For-though no one will believe it--economics is a technical and difficult subject. It is even becoming a science. However, I will do my best --at the cost of leaving out, because it is too complicated, much that is necessary to a complete understanding of contemporary events. First of all, the extreme violence of the slump is to be noticed. In the three leading industrial countries of the world--the United States, Great Britain, and Germany -- 10,000,000 workers stand idle. There is scarcely an important industry anywhere earning enough profit to make it expand--which is the test of progress. At the same time, in the countries of primary production the output of mining and of agriculture is selling, in the case of almost every important commodity, at a price which, for many or for the majority of producers, does not cover its cost. In 1921, when prices fell as heavily, the fall was from a boom level at which producers were making abnormal profits; and there is no example in modern history of so great and rapid a fall of prices from a normal figure as has occurred in the past year. Hence the magnitude of the catastrophe.

The time which elapses before production ceases and unemployment reaches its maximum is, for several reasons, much longer in the case of the primary products than in the case of manufacture. In most cases the productive units are smaller and less well organised amongst themselves for enforcing a process of orderly contraction; the length of the production period, especially in agriculture, is longer; the costs of a temporary shut-down are greater; men are more often their own employers and so submit more readily to a contraction of the income for which they are willing to work; the social problems of throwing men out of employment are greater in more primitive communities; and the financial problems of a cessation of production of primary output are more serious in countries where such primary output is almost the whole sustenance of the people. Nevertheless we are fast approaching the phase in which the output of primary producers will be restricted almost as much as that of manufacturers; and this will have a further adverse reaction on manufacturers, since the primary producers will have no purchasing power wherewith to buy manufactured goods; and so on, in a vicious circle.

In this quandary individual producers base illusory hopes on courses of action which would benefit an individual producer or class of producers so long as they were alone in pursuing them, but which benefit no one if every one pursues them. For example, to restrict the output of a particular primary commodity raises its price, so long as the output of the industries which use this commodity is unrestricted; but if output is restricted all round, then the demand for the primary commodity falls off by just as much as the supply, and no one is further forward. Or again, if a particular producer or a particular country cuts wages, then, so long as others do not follow suit, that producer or that country is able to get more of what trade is going. But if wages are cut all round, the purchasing power of the community as a whole is reduced by the same amount as the reduction of costs; and, again, no one is further forward.

Thus neither the restriction of output nor the reduction of wages serves in itself to restore equilibrium.

Moreover, even if we were to succeed eventually in re-establishing output at the lower level of money-wages appropriate to (say) the prewar level of prices, our troubles would not be at an end. For since 1914 an immense burden of bonded debt, both national and international, has been contracted, which is fixed in terms of money. Thus every fall of prices increases the burden of this debt, because it increases the value of the money in which it is fixed. For example, if we were to settle down to the prewar level of prices, the British National Debt would be nearly 40 per cent greater than it was in 1924 and double what it was in 1920; the Young Plan would weigh on Germany much more heavily than the Dawes Plan, which it was agreed she could not support; the indebtedness to the United States of her associates in the Great War would represent 40-50 per cent more goods and services than at the date when the settlements were made; the obligations of such debtor countries as those of South America and Australia would become insupportable without a reduction of their standard of life for the benefit of their creditors; agriculturists and householders throughout the world, who have borrowed on mortgage, would find themselves the victims of their creditors. In such a situation it must be doubtful whether the necessary adjustments could be made in time to prevent a series of bankruptcies, defaults, and repudiations which would shake the capitalist order to its foundations. Here would be a fertile soil for agitation, seditions, and revolution. It is so already in many quarters of the world. Yet, all the time, the resources of Nature and men's devices would be just as fertile and productive as they were. The machine would merely have been jammed as the result of a muddle. But because we have magneto trouble, we need not assume that we shall soon be back in a rumbling waggon and that motoring is over.

II. We have magneto trouble. How, then, can we start up again? Let us trace events backwards:--

1. Why are workers and plant unemployed? Because industrialists do not expect to be able to sell without loss what would be produced if they were employed.

2. Why cannot industrialists expect to sell without loss? Because prices have fallen more than costs have fallen--indeed, costs have fallen very little.

3. How can it be that prices have fallen more than costs? For costs are what a business man pays out for the production of his commodity, and prices determine what he gets back when he sells

it. It is easy to understand how for an individual business or an individual commodity these can be unequal. But surely for the community as a whole the business men get back the same amount as they pay out, since what the business men pay out in the course of production constitutes the incomes of the public which they pay back to the business men in exchange for the products of the latter? For this is what we understand by the normal circle of production, exchange, and consumption.

4. No! Unfortunately this is not so; and here is the root of the trouble. It is not true that what the business men pay out as costs of production necessarily comes back to them as the sale-proceeds of what they produce. It is the characteristic of a boom that their saleproceeds exceed their costs; and it is the characteristic of a slump that their costs exceed their sale-proceeds. Moreover, it is a delusion to suppose that they can necessarily restore equilibrium by reducing their total costs, whether it be by restricting their output or cutting rates of remuneration; for the reduction of their outgoings may, by reducing the purchasing power of the earners who are also their customers, diminish their sale-proceeds by a nearly equal amount.

2. How, then, can it be that the total costs of production for the world's business as a whole can be unequal to the total sale-proceeds? Upon what does the inequality depend? I think that I know the answer. But it is too complicated and unfamiliar for me to expound it here satisfactorily. (Elsewhere I have tried to expound it accurately. 1) So I must be somewhat perfunctory.

Let us take, first of all, the consumptiongoods which come on to the market for sale. Upon what do the profits (or losses) of the producers of such goods depend? The total costs of production, which are the same thing as the community's total earnings looked at from another point of view, are divided in a certain proportion between the cost of consumption-goods and the cost of capital-goods. The incomes of the public, which are again the same thing as the community's total earnings, are also divided in a certain proportion between expenditure on the purchase of consumption-goods and savings. Now if the first proportion is larger than the second, producers of consumption-goods will lose money; for their sale proceeds, which are equal to the expenditure of the public on consumption-goods, will be less (as a little thought will show) than what these goods have cost them to produce. If, on the other hand, the second proportion is larger than the first, then the producers of consumptiongoods will make exceptional gains. It follows that the profits of the producers of consumptiongoods can only be restored, either by the public spending a larger proportion of their incomes on such goods (which means saving less), or by a larger proportion of production taking the form of capital-goods (since this means a smaller proportionate output of consumptiongoods).

But capital-goods will not be produced on a larger scale unless the producers of such goods are making a profit. So we come to our second question--upon what do the profits of the producers of capital-goods depend? They depend on whether the public prefer to keep their savings liquid in the shape of money or its equivalent or to use them to buy capital-goods or the equivalent. If the public are reluctant to buy the latter, then the producers of capitalgoods will make a loss; consequently less capital-goods will be produced; with the result that, for the reasons given above, producers of consumption-goods will also make a loss. In other words, all classes of producers will tend to make a loss; and general unemployment will ensue. By this time a vicious circle will be set up, and, as the result of a series of actions and reactions, matters will get worse and worse until something happens to turn the tide.

This is an unduly simplified picture of a complicated phenomenon. But I believe that it contains the essential truth. Many variations and fugal embroideries and orchestrations can be superimposed; but this is the tune.

If, then, I am right, the fundamental cause of the trouble is the lack of new enterprise due to an unsatisfactory market for capital investment. Since trade is international, an insufficient output of new capital-goods in the world as a whole affects the prices of commodities everywhere and hence the profits of producers in all countries alike.

Why is there an insufficient output of new capital-goods in the world as a whole? It is due, in my opinion, to a conjunction of several causes. In the first instance, it was due to the attitude of lenders--for new capital-goods are produced to a large extent with borrowed money. Now it is due to the attitude of borrowers, just as much as to that of lenders.

For several reasons lenders were, and are, asking higher terms for loans than new enterprise can afford. First, the fact, that enterprise could afford high rates for some time after the war whilst war wastage was being made good, accustomed lenders to expect much higher rates than before the war. Second, the existence of political borrowers to meet Treaty obligations, of banking borrowers to support newly restored gold standards, of speculative borrowers to take part in Stock Exchange booms, and, latterly, of distress borrowers to meet the losses which they have incurred through the fall of prices, all of whom were ready if necessary to pay almost any terms, have hitherto enabled lenders to secure from these various classes of borrowers higher rates than it is possible for genuine new enterprise to support. Third, the unsettled state of the world and national investment habits have restricted the countries in which many lenders are prepared to invest on any reasonable terms at all. A large proportion of the globe is, for one reason or another, distrusted by lenders, so that they exact a premium for risk so great as to strangle new enterprise altogether. For the last two years, two out of the three principal creditor nations of the world, namely, France and the United States, have largely withdrawn their resources from the international market for long-term loans.

Meanwhile, the reluctant attitude of lenders has become matched by a hardly less reluctant attitude on the part of borrowers. For the fall of prices has been disastrous to those who have borrowed, and any one who has postponed new enterprise has gained by his delay. Moreover, the risks that frighten lenders frighten borrowers too. Finally, in the United States, the vast scale on which new capital enterprise has been undertaken in the last five years has somewhat exhausted for the time being--at any rate so long as the atmosphere of business depression continues--the profitable opportunities for yet further enterprise. By the middle of 1929 new capital undertakings were already on an inadequate scale in the world as a whole, outside the United States. The culminating blow has been the collapse of new investment inside the United States, which to-day is probably 20 to 30 per cent less than it was in 1928. Thus in certain countries the opportunity for new profitable investment is more limited than it was; whilst in others it is more risky.

A wide gulf, therefore, is set between the ideas of lenders and the ideas of borrowers for the purpose of genuine new capital investment; with the result that the savings of the lenders are being used up in financing business losses and distress borrowers, instead of financing new capital works.

At this moment the slump is probably a little overdone for psychological reasons. A modest upward reaction, therefore, may be due at any time. But there cannot be a real recovery, in my judgement, until the ideas of lenders and the ideas of productive borrowers are brought together again; partly by lenders becoming ready to lend on easier terms and over a wider geographical field, partly by borrowers recovering their good spirits and so becoming readier to borrow.

Seldom in modern history has the gap between the two been so wide and so difficult to bridge. Unless we bend our wills and our intelligences, energised by a conviction that this diagnosis is right, to find a solution along these lines, then, if the diagnosis is right, the slump may pass over into a depression, accompanied by a sagging price level, which might last for years, with untold damage to the material wealth and to the social stability of every country alike. Only if we seriously seek a solution, will the optimism of my opening sentences be confirmed--at least for the nearer future.

It is beyond the scope of this essay to indicate lines of future policy. But no one can take the first step except the central banking authorities of the chief creditor countries; nor can any one Central Bank do enough acting in isolation. Resolute action by the Federal Reserve Banks of the United States, the Bank of France, and the Bank of England might do much more than most people, mistaking symptoms or aggravating circumstances for the disease itself, will readily believe. In every way the most effective remedy would be that the Central Banks of these three great creditor nations should join together in a bold scheme to restore confidence to the international long-term loan market; which would serve to revive enterprise and activity everywhere, and to restore prices and profits, so that in due course the wheels of the world's commerce would go round again. And even if France, hugging the supposed security of gold, prefers to stand aside from the adventure of creating new wealth, I am convinced that Great Britain and the United States, likeminded and acting together, could start the machine again within a reasonable time; if, that is to say, they were energised by a confident conviction as to what was wrong. For it is chiefly the lack of this conviction which to-day is paralysing the hands of authority on both sides of the Channel and of the Atlantic.

6. ECONOMY (1931)

(i) Saving and Spending (Jan. 1931)

The slump in trade and employment and the business losses which are being incurred are as bad as the worst which have ever occurred in the modern history of the world. No country is exempt.

The privation and--what is sometimes worse--the anxiety which exist to-day in millions of homes all over the world is extreme. In the three chief industrial countries of the world, Great Britain, Germany, and the United States, I estimate that probably 12,000,000 industrial workers stand idle. But I am not sure that there is not even more human misery to-day in the great agricultural countries of the world --Canada, Australia, and South America, where millions of small farmers see themselves ruined by the fall in the prices of their products, so that their receipts after harvest bring them in much less than the crops have cost them to produce. For the fall in the prices of the great staple products of the world such as wheat, wool, sugar, cotton, and indeed most other commodities has been simply catastrophic. Most of these prices are now below their pre-war level; yet costs, as we all know, remain far above their pre-war level. A week or two ago, it is said, wheat in Liverpool sold at the lowest price recorded since the reign of Charles II. more than 250 years ago. How is it possible for farmers to live in such conditions? Of course it is impossible.

You might suppose--and some austere individuals do in fact believe--that cheapness must be an advantage. For what the producer loses, the consumer gains. But it is not so. For those of us who work--and we are in the great majority--can only consume so long as we produce. So that anything which interferes with the processes of production necessarily interferes also with those of consumption.

The reason for this is that there are all kinds of obstacles to the costs and prices of everything falling equally. For example, the wages-costs of most manufacturers are practically the same as they were. See how the vicious process works out. The prices of wool and wheat fall. Good for the British consumer of wheat and woollen garments--so one might suppose. But the producers of wool and wheat, since they receive too little for their products, cannot make their usual purchases of British goods. Consequently those British consumers who are at the same time workers who make these goods find themselves out of work. What is the use of cheapness when incomes are falling?

When Dr. Johnson, visiting the Island of Skye, was told that twenty eggs might be bought for a penny, he said, "Sir, I don't gather from this that eggs are plenty in your miserable Island, but that pence are few."

Cheapness which is due to increased efficiency and skill in the arts of production is indeed a benefit. But cheapness which means the ruin of the producer is one of the greatest economic disasters which can possibly occur.

It would not be true to say that we are not taking a grave view of the case. Yet I doubt whether we are taking a grave enough view. In the enforced idleness of millions, enough potential wealth is running to waste to work wonders. Many million pounds' worth of goods could be produced each day by the workers and the plants which stand idle--and the workers would be the happier and the better for it. We ought to sit down to mend matters, in the mood of grave determination and the spirit of action at all costs, which we should have in a war. Yet a vast inertia seems to weigh us down. The peculiarity of the position to-day--to my mind --is that there is something to be said for nearly all the remedies that any one has proposed, though some, of course, are better than others. All the rival policies have something to offer. Yet we adopt none of them.

The worst of it is that we have one excellent excuse for doing nothing. To a large extent the cure lies outside our own power. The problem is an international one, and for a country which depends on foreign trade as much as we do there are narrow limits to what we can achieve by ourselves. But this is not the only reason why we are inactive. Nor is it a sufficient reason. For something we can do by ourselves. The other principal reason, in my opinion, is a serious misunderstanding as to what kind of action is useful and what kind is not. There are to-day many well-wishers of their country who believe that the most useful thing which they and their neighbours can do to mend the situation is to save more than usual. If they refrain from spending a larger proportion of their incomes than usual they believe that they will have helped employment. If they are members of Town or County Councils they believe that their right course at such a time as this is to oppose expenditure on new amenities or new public works.

Now, in certain circumstances all this would be quite right, but in present circumstances, unluckily, it is quite wrong. It is utterly harmful and misguided--the very opposite of the truth. For the object of saving is to release labour for employment on producing capitalgoods such as houses, factories, roads, machines, and the like. But if there is a large unemployed surplus already available for such purposes, then the effect of saving is merely to add to this surplus and therefore to increase the number of the unemployed. Moreover, when a man is thrown out of work in this or any other way, his diminished spending power causes further unemployment amongst those who would have produced what he can no longer afford to buy.

And so the position gets worse and worse in a vicious circle.

The best guess I can make is that whenever you save five shillings, you put a man out of work for a day. Your saving that five shillings adds to unemployment to the extent of one man for one day--and so on in proportion. On the other hand, whenever you buy goods you increase employment--though they must be British, home-produced goods if you are to increase employment in this country. After all, this is only the plainest common sense. For if you buy goods, some one will have to make them. And if you do not buy goods, the shops will not clear their stocks, they will not give repeat orders, and some one will be thrown out of work.

Therefore, oh patriotic housewives, sally out to-morrow early into the streets and go to the wonderful sales which are everywhere advertised. You will do yourselves good--for never were things so cheap, cheap beyond your dreams. Lay in a stock of household linen, of sheets and blankets to satisfy all your needs. And have the added joy that you are increasing employment, adding to the wealth of the country because you are setting on foot useful activities, bringing a chance and a hope to Lancashire, Yorkshire, and Belfast.

These are only examples. Do whatever is necessary to satisfy the most sensible needs of yourself and your household, make improvements, build.

For what we need now is not to button up our waistcoats tight, but to be in a mood of expansion, of activity--to do things, to buy things, to make things. Surely all this is the most obvious common sense. For take the extreme case. Suppose we were to stop spending our incomes altogether, and were to save the lot. Why, every one would be out of work. And before long we should have no incomes to spend. No one would be a penny the richer, and the end would be that we should all starve to death-which would surely serve us right for refusing to buy things from one another, for refusing to take in one another's washing, since that is how we all live. The same is true, and even more so, of the work of a local authority. Now is the time for municipalities to be busy and active with all kinds of sensible improvements.

The patient does not need rest. He needs exercise. You cannot set men to work by holding back, by refusing to place orders, by inactivity. On the contrary, activity of one kind or another is the only possible means of making the wheels of economic progress and of the production of wealth go round again.

Nationally, too, I should like to see schemes of greatness and magnificence designed and carried through. I read a few days ago of a proposal to drive a great new road, a broad boulevard, parallel to the Strand, on the south side of the Thames, as a new thoroughfare joining Westminster to the City. That is the right sort of notion. But I should like to see something bigger still. For example, why not pull down the whole of South London from Westminster to Greenwich, and make a good job of it--housing on that convenient area near to their work a much greater population than at present, in far better buildings with all the conveniences of modern life, yet at the same time providing hundreds of acres of squares and avenues, parks and public spaces, having, when it was finished, something magnificent to the eye, yet useful and convenient to human life as a monument to our age. Would that employ men? Why, of course it would! Is it better that the men should stand idle and miserable, drawing the dole? Of course it is not.

These, then, are the chief observations which I want to leave with you now--first of all, to emphasise the extreme gravity of the situation, with about a quarter of our working population standing idle; next, that the trouble is a worldwide one which we cannot cure by ourselves; and, third, that we can all the same do something by ourselves and that something must take the form of activity, of doing things, of spending, of setting great enterprises afoot.

But I also have one final theme to put before you. I fancy that a reason why some people may be a little horrified at my suggestions is the fear that we are much too poor to be able to afford what they consider to be extravagance. They think that we are poor, much poorer than we were and that what we chiefly need is to cut our coat according to our cloth, by which they mean that we must curtail our consumption, reduce our standard of life, work harder and consume less; and that that is the way out of the wood. This view is not, in my judgement, in accordance with the facts. We have plenty of cloth and only lack the courage to cut it into coats. I want, therefore, to give you some cheerful facts to dispose you to take an ampler view of the economic strength of this country.

Let me first of all remind you of the obvious. The great mass of the population is living much better than it ever lived before. We are supporting in idleness, at a higher standard of life than is possible for those who are in work in most other countries, nearly a quarter of our employable population. Yet at the same time the national wealth is increasing year by year. After paying wages which are far higher than, for example, in France or in Germany, after supporting a quarter of our population in idleness, after adding to the country's equipment of houses and roads and electrical plant and so forth on a substantial scale, we still have a surplus available to be lent to foreign countries, which in 1929 was greater than the surplus for such purposes of any other country in the world, even of the United States.

How do we do it? If the pessimists were right who believe that we are terribly inefficient, overextravagant and getting poorer, obviously it would be impossible. We can only do it because the pessimists are quite wrong. We are not nearly so rich as we might be if we could manage our affairs better and not get them into such a muddle. But we are not inefficient, we are not poor, we are not living on our capital. Quite the contrary. Our labour and our plant are enormously more productive than they used to be. Our national income is going up quite quickly. That is how we do it.

Let me give you a few figures. As compared with so recent a date as 1924, our productive output per head has probably increased by 10 per cent. That is to say, we can produce the same amount of wealth with 10 per cent fewer men employed. As compared with pre-war the increase in output per head is probably as much as 20 per cent. Apart from changes in the value of money, the national income--even so recently as 1929 with a great mass of unemployment (it cannot, of course, be quite so good to-day) --was probably increasing by as much as £100,000,000 a year; and this has been going on year by year for a good many years. At the same time we have been quietly carrying through almost a revolution in the distribution of incomes in the direction of equality.

Be confident, therefore, that we are suffering from the growing pains of youth, not from the rheumatics of old age. We are failing to make full use of our opportunities, failing to find an outlet for the great increase in our productive powers and our productive energy. Therefore we must not draw in our horns; we must push them out. Activity and boldness and enterprise, both individually and nationally, must be the cure.

(ii) The Economy Report (Aug. 15, 1931) The Report of the

Economy Committee can be considered from several points of view. It is an exceedingly valuable document because it is a challenge to us to make up our minds one way or the other on certain vital matters of policy. In particular it invites us to decide whether it is our intention to make the Deflation effective by transmitting the reduction of international prices to British salaries and wages; though if this is our intention, it would be absurd to pretend that the process can stop with schoolteachers and policemen. The Committee's Report goes too far or not far enough. But this is not the question which I wish to discuss here. I would like to confine myself to what has been so far, as it seems to me, a neglected aspect of the Report.

The Committee show no evidence of having given a moment's thought to the possible repercussions of their programme, either on the volume of unemployment or on the receipts of taxation. They recommend a reduction of the purchasing power of British citizens partly by the reduction of incomes and partly by throwing out of work persons now employed. They give no reason for supposing that this reduction of purchasing power will be offset by increases in other directions; for their idea is that the Government should take advantage of the economies proposed, not to tax less, but to borrow less. Perhaps at the back of their heads they have some crude idea that there is a fixed Loan Fund, the whole of which is always lent, so that, if the Government borrows less, private enterprise necessarily borrows more. But they could not believe this on reflection, if they were to try to translate it into definite, concrete terms.

Their proposals do not even offer the possible advantages to our trade balance which might ensue on a reduction of industrial wages. For there is nothing in what they propose calculated to reduce the costs of production; indeed, on the contrary, they propose to increase them by raising the employers' insurance contribution.

Let us try, therefore, to write the missing paragraphs of the Report and to make some guesses as to the probable consequences of reducing purchasing power in the manner proposed.

Some part of this reduction of purchasing power may be expected to lead to a reduced buying of foreign goods, e.g. if the dole is cut down, the unemployed will have to tighten their belts and eat less imported food. To this extent the situation will be helped. Some part will be economised by saving less; e.g. if teachers' salaries are cut down, teachers will probably save less or even draw on their past savings, to maintain the standard of life to which they have become accustomed. But for the rest British producers will find the receipts reaching them from the expenditure of consumers (policemen, school-teachers, men on the dole, etc.) reduced by the balance of, say, £70,000,000. They cannot meet this loss without reducing their own expenditure or discharging some of their men, or both; i.e. they will have to follow the example of the Government, and this will again set moving the same series of consequences, and so on.

The net result would necessarily be a substantial increase in the number of unemployed drawing the dole and a decrease in the receipts of taxation as a result of the diminished incomes and profits. Indeed the immediate consequences of the Government's reducing its deficit are the exact inverse of the consequences of its financing additional capital works out of loans. One cannot predict with accuracy the exact quantitative consequences of either, but they are broadly the same. Several of the Committee's recommendations, e.g. those relating to Roads, to Housing, and to Afforestation, do indeed expressly imply that the whole theory underlying the principle of Public Works as a remedy for unemployment is mistaken, and they ask, in effect, for a reversal of the policies based on this principle. Yet they do not trouble to argue the case. I suppose that they are such very plain men that the advantages of not spending money seem obvious to them. They may even be so plain as to be unaware of the existence of the problem which I am now discussing. But they are flying in the face of a considerable weight of opinion. For the main opposition to the Public Works remedy is based on the practical difficulties of devising a reasonable programme, not on the principle. But a proposal to reverse measures already in force involves a denial of the principle as well as of the feasibility.I should like, though it is rash, to make, if only for purposes of illustration, a very rough guess as to the magnitudes of the more immediate consequences of the adoption of economies of £100,000,000, carried out on the lines of the Committee's recommendations. I should expect something like the following:

1. An increase of 250,000-400,000 in the number of the unemployed;

2. A decrease of, say, £20,000,000 in the excess of our imports over our exports;

3. A decrease of £10,000,000 to £15,000,000 in the savings of the general public;

4. A decrease of £20,000,000 to £30,000,000 in business profits;

5. A decrease of £10,000,000 to £15,000,000 in the personal expenditure of business men and others, who depend on business profits, as a result of these profits being less;

6. A decrease of £5,000,000 to £10,000,000 in the aggregate of capital construction and working capital and other investment at home entered upon by private enterprise, as a result of the lower level of business profits, after allowing for any favourable psychological effects on business "confidence" of the adoption of the Committee's recommendations:

7. A net reduction in the Government deficit not exceeding £50,000,000, as a result of the Budget economies of £100,000,000 being partly offset by the diminished yield of taxation and the cost of the increased unemployment.

The actual figures I have used are, of course, guess-work. But $(2) + (3) + (4) - (5) - (6) = (7)$, where (7) is the net reduction in the Government deficit, is a necessary truth--as necessary as $2 + 2 = 4$. There is nothing rational to dispute about except the size of the various items entering into this equation. It might be held by some, for example, that there would be an increase under (6), instead of a decrease; and if there were a large increase of this item-which, however, could not, in my judgement, be maintained with good reason--this would make all the difference in the world to the expediency of the policy proposed.

At the present time, all Governments have large deficits. For Government borrowing of one kind or another is nature's remedy, so to speak, for preventing business losses from being, in so severe a slump as the present one, so great as to bring production altogether to a standstill. It is much better in every way that the borrowing should be for the purpose of financing capital works, if these works are any use at all, than for the purpose of paying doles (or veterans' bonuses). But, so long as the slump lasts on the present scale, this is the only effective which we possess, and Government borrowing for the one purpose or the other (or a diminished Sinking Fund, which has the same effect) is practically inevitable. For this is a case, fortunately perhaps, where the weakness of human nature will, we can be sure, come to the rescue of human wrongheadedness.

This is not to say that there are not other ways in which we can help ourselves. I am not concerned here with the possible advantages--for example--of a Tariff or of Devaluation or of a National Treaty for the reduction of all money incomes. I am simply analysing the results to be expected from the recommendations of the Economy Committee adopted as a means of reducing the uncovered deficit of the Budget. And I should add, to prevent misunderstanding, that I should prefer some of their recommendations--for they have done their work in detail with ability and fair-mindedness--to most kinds of additional taxation other than a tariff.

My own policy for the Budget, so long as the slump lasts, would be to suspend the Sinking Fund, to continue to borrow for the Unemployment Fund, and to impose a Revenue Tariff. To get us out of the slump we must look to quite other expedients. When the slump is over, when the demands of private enterprise for new capital have recovered to normal and employment is good and the yield of taxation is increasing, then is the time to restore the Sinking Fund and to look critically at the less productive State enterprises.

(iii) The Economy Bill (Sept. 19, 1931) The Budget and the Economy Bill are replete with folly and injustice. It is a tragedy that the moral energies and enthusiasm of many truly self-sacrificing and well-wishing people should be so misdirected.

The objects of national policy, so as to meet the emergency, should be primarily to improve our balance of trade, and secondarily to equalise the yield of taxation with the normal recurrent expenditure of the Budget by methods which would increase, rather than diminish, output, and hence increase the national income and the yield of the revenue, whilst respecting the principles of social justice. The actual policy of the Government fails on each of these tests. It will have comparatively little effect on the balance of trade. It will largely increase unemployment and diminish the yield of the revenue. And it outrages the principles of justice to a degree which I should have thought inconceivable.

To begin with the last. The incomes of wellto-do people have been cut by 2½ to 3½ per cent. The school-teachers are cut 15 per cent, 1 in addition to the extra taxes which they have to pay. It is a monstrous thing to single out this class and discriminate against them, merely because they happen to be employees of the Government. It is particularly outrageous, because efforts have been made in recent years to attract into the profession teachers of higher qualifications by holding out to them certain expectations.

It is even proposed to take powers to dissolve existing contracts. That the school-teachers should have been singled out for sacrifice as an offering to the Moloch of finance is a sufficient proof of the state of hysteria and irresponsibility into which Cabinet Ministers have worked themselves. For it is impossible to represent this cut as one of unavoidable necessity. The money saved is £6,000,000. At the same time £32,000,000 is going to the Sinking Fund, whilst tea, sugar, and a tariff as sources of revenue are left untapped. The Prime Minister has offered no defence, except that some of his former colleagues, who have since recovered their heads, were temporarily frightened into considering something of the same kind.

The school-teachers are the most outstanding case of injustice. But the same considerations apply in varying degrees to all the attacks on the standards of Government employees. The principle of discriminating against persons in the service of the State, because they can be reached most easily, is not right. At least it would have been more decent in the circumstances if the phrase "equality of sacrifice" had not been used.

Moreover, the Government's programme is as foolish as it is wrong. Its direct effect on employment must be disastrous. It is safe to predict that it will increase the volume of unemployment by more than the 10 per cent by which the dole is to be cut. It represents a reckless reversal of all the partial attempts which have been made hitherto to mitigate the consequences of the collapse of private investment; and it is a triumph for the so-called "Treasury View" in its most extreme form. Not only is purchasing power to be curtailed, but road-building, housing, and the like are to be retrenched. Local authorities are to follow suit. If the theory which underlies all this is to be accepted, the end will be that no one can be employed, except those happy few who grow their own potatoes, as a result of each of us refusing, for reasons of economy, to buy the services of any one else. To raid the Road Fund in order to maintain the Sinking Fund is, in present circumstances, a policy of Bedlam.

Finally there is the problem of the Balance of Trade, which, after all, is the main point so far as concerns the emergency. Broadly speaking, the cost of production is left unchanged. Cutting the school-teachers' salaries will not help us to recapture the markets of the world. Those wages and the like which are within the Government's direct control happen to be just those which it is most useless to cut in the interests of the export trade. We are told that it is a wicked misrepresentation to say that all this is a preliminary to a general assault on wages. Yet it has less than no sense unless it is. But meanwhile the Government have noticed that there is just one point where their activities raise the cost of production, namely, the employers' insurance contribution, which is, in effect, a poll tax on employment. So, in order to prove for certain that they are quite mad, the Government have decided to increase it.

There are only two ways in which the Government plan can help the Balance of Trade. Whenever any one is thrown out of work or otherwise impoverished, he will perforce consume less. Most of this reduced consumption will merely cause business losses and unemployment to other Englishmen. Some part of it, however, perhaps a fifth, will be at the expense of imports; though even this would not help if those Free Traders are right who think that a reduction of imports leads to a corresponding reduction of exports. But it is a wasteful way of setting about the task of reducing imports. The other way is by increasing both the quantity of unemployment and also the pains of being unemployed, since this may slightly increase the chance of wage-reductions being accepted. Economy can have no other purpose or meaning except to release resources. A small proportion of what is thus released will relieve the Balance of Trade. The rest will be resources of domestic plant and labour, of which we already have a surplus out of use.

Thus the Government's scheme, for the sake of which we are asked to swallow so much, is in the main misdirected, and will not assist the solution of our twin problems of unemployment and an adverse balance of trade.

As regards the latter, which, unremedied, will at no distant date break the gold standard even if we cut school-teachers' salaries to nothing, the only remedies now open to us are Devaluation, a drastic restriction of imports by direct methods, a severe cut, not less than 30 per cent in my judgement, in wages and salaries, or a decisive change in the international position. An attack on wages would mean a severe industrial struggle which would drive us off gold-parity within a few weeks; so that this is not in practice an alternative to Devaluation. Thus there are only three lines of policy to which it is worth the Cabinet's while to direct their minds. The first and mildest is a plan for the restriction of imports. The second is a plan for getting off goldparity without allowing the slide to go too far. The third is a plan for an International Conference--one that means business of the most definite kind, quite different from any Conference ever held hitherto--for giving the goldstandard countries a last opportunity. All the rest is waste of time. The advantage of the last alternative is that this alone offers any chance, however slight, of an amelioration of the international position, without which we are faced with a disappearance of income from our foreign investments on a scale which neither a Tariff nor Devaluation could offset.

7. THE CONSEQUENCES TO THE BANKS OF THE COLLAPSE OF MONEY VALUES (Aug. 1931) A year ago it was the failure of agriculture, mining, manufactures, and transport to make normal profits, and the unemployment and waste of productive resources ensuing on this, which was the leading feature of the economic situation. To-day, in many parts of the world, it is the serious embarrassment of the banks which is the cause of our gravest concern. The shattering German crisis of July 1931, which took the world more by surprise than it should, was in its essence a banking crisis, though precipitated, no doubt, by political events and political fears. That the top-heavy position, which ultimately crumbled to the ground, should have been built up at all, was, in my judgement, a sin against the principles of sound banking. One watched its erection with amazement and terror. But the fact which was primarily responsible for bringing it down was a factor for which the individual bankers were not responsible and which very few people foresaw --namely, the enormous change in the value of gold money and consequently in the burden of indebtedness which debtors, in all countries adhering to the gold standard, had contracted to pay in terms of gold.

Let us begin at the beginning of the argument. There is a multitude of real assets in the world which constitute our capital wealth --buildings, stocks of commodities, goods in course of manufacture and of transport, and so forth. The nominal owners of these assets, however, have not infrequently borrowed money in order to become possessed of them. To a corresponding extent the actual owners of wealth have claims, not on real assets, but on money. A considerable part of this "financing" takes place through the banking system, which interposes its guarantee between its depositors who lend it money, and its borrowing customers to whom it loans money wherewith to finance the purchase of real assets. The interposition of this veil of money between the real asset and the wealth owner is a specially marked characteristic of the modern world. Partly as a result of the increasing confidence felt in recent years in the leading banking systems, the practice has grown to formidable dimensions. The bank - deposits of all kinds in the United States, for example, stand in round figures at $50,000,000,000; those of Great Britain at £2,000,000,000. In addition to this there is the great mass of bonded and mortgage indebtedness held by individuals.

All this is familiar enough in general terms. We are also familiar with the idea that a change in the value of money can gravely upset the relative positions of those who possess claims to money and those who owe money. For, of course, a fall in prices, which is the same thing as a rise in the value of claims on money, means that real wealth is transferred from the debtor in favour of the creditor, so that a larger proportion of the real asset is represented by the claims of the depositor, and a smaller proportion belongs to the nominal owner of the asset who has borrowed in order to buy it. This, we all know, is one of the reasons why changes in prices are upsetting.

But it is not to this familiar feature of falling prices that I wish to invite attention. It is to a further development which we can ordinarily afford to neglect but which leaps to importance when the change in the value of money is very large--when it exceeds a more or less determinate amount.

Modest fluctuations in the value of money, such as those which we have frequently experienced in the past, do not vitally concern the banks which have interposed their guarantee between the depositor and the debtor. For the banks allow beforehand for some measure offluctuation in the value both of particular assets and of real assets in general, by requiring from the borrower what is conveniently called a "margin." That is to say, they will only lend him money up to a certain proportion of the value of the asset which is the "security" offered by the borrower to the lender. Experience has led to the fixing of conventional percentages for the "margin" as being reasonably safe in all ordinary circumstances. The amount will, of course, vary in different cases within wide limits. But for marketable assets a "margin" of 20 per cent to 30 per cent is conventionally considered as adequate, and a "margin" of as much as 50 per cent as highly conservative. Thus provided the amount of the downward change in the money value of assets is well within these conventional figures, the direct interest of the banks is not excessive;-they owe money to their depositors on one side of their balance-sheet and are owed it on the other, and it is no vital concern of theirs just what the money is worth. But consider what happens when the downward change in the money value of assets within a brief period of time exceeds the amount of the conventional "margin" over a large part of the assets against which money has been borrowed. The horrible possibilities to the banks are immediately obvious. Fortunately, this is a very rare, indeed a unique event. For it had never occurred in the modern history of the world prior to the year 1931. There have been large upward movements in the money value of assets in those countries where inflation has proceeded to great lengths. But this, however disastrous in other ways, did nothing to jeopardise the position of the banks; for it increased the amount of their "margins." There was a large downward movement in the slump of 1921, but that was from an exceptionally high level of values which had ruled for only a few months or weeks, so that only a small proportion of the banks' loans had been based on such values and these values had not lasted long enough to be trusted. Never before has there been such a world-wide collapse over almost the whole field of the money values of real assets as we have experienced in the last two years. And, finally, during the last few months--so recently that the bankers themselves have, as yet, scarcely appreciated it--it has come to exceed in very many cases the amount of the conventional "margins." In the language of the market the "margins" have run off. The exact details of this are not likely to come to the notice of the outsider until some special event--perhaps some almost accidental event--occurs which brings the situation to a dangerous head. For, so long as a bank is in a position to wait quietly for better times and to ignore meanwhile the fact that the security against many of its loans is no longer as good as it was when the loans were first made, nothing appears on the surface and there is no cause for panic. Nevertheless, even at this stage the underlying position is likely to have a very adverse effect on new business. For the banks, being aware that many of their advances are in fact "frozen" and involve a larger latent risk than they would voluntarily carry, become particularly anxious that the remainder of their assets should be as liquid and as free from risk as it is possible to make them. This reacts in all sorts of silent and unobserved ways on new enterprise. For it means that the banks are less willing than they would normally be to finance any project which may involve a lock-up of their resources.

Now, in estimating the quantitative importance of the factor to which I am calling attention, we have to consider what has been happening to the prices of various types of property. There are, first of all, the principal raw materials and foodstuffs of international commerce. These are of great importance to the banks, because the stocks of these commodities, whether in warehouse or in transit or embodied in halffinished or unsold manufactured articles, are very largely financed through the banks. In the last eighteen months the prices of these commodities have fallen on the average by about 25 per cent. But this is an average, and banks cannot average the security of one customer with that of another. Many individual commodities of the greatest commercial importance have fallen in price by 40 to 50 per cent or even more.

Next come the ordinary or common shares of the great companies and corporations which are the market leaders in the Stock Exchanges of the world. In most countries the average fall amounts to 40 to 50 per cent; and, this again, is an average which means that individual shares, even amongst those which would have been considered of good quality two years ago, have fallen enormously more. Then there are the bonds and the fixed interest securities. Those of the very highest grade have, indeed, risen slightly, or, at the worst, not fallen by more than 5 per cent, which has been of material assistance in some quarters. But many other fixed interest securities, which, while not of the highest grade, were, and are, good securities, have fallen from 10 to 15 per cent; whilst foreign government bonds have, as is well known, suffered prodigious falls. These declines, even where they are more moderate, may be scarcely less serious, because such bonds (though not in Great Britain) are often owned by the banks themselves outright, so that there is no "margin" to protect them from loss.

The declines in the prices of commodities and of securities have, broadly speaking, affected most countries alike. When we come to the next category of property--and one of great quantitative importance--namely, real estate, the facts are more various as between one country and another. A great element of stability in Great Britain, and, I believe, in France also, has been the continued comparative firmness in real estate values:--no slump has been experienced in this quarter, with the result that mortgage business is sound and the multitude of loans granted on the security of real estate are unimpaired. But in many other countries the slump has affected this class of property also; and particularly, perhaps, in the United States, where farm values have suffered a great decline, and also city property of modern construction, much of which would not fetch to-day more than 60 to 70 per cent of its original cost of construction, and not infrequently much less. This is an immense aggravation of the problem, where it has occurred, both because of the very large sums involved and because such property is ordinarily regarded as relatively free from risk.

Finally, there are the loans and advances which banks have made to their customers for the purposes of their customers' business. These are, in many cases, in the worst condition of all. The security in these cases is primarily the profit, actual and prospective, of the business which is being financed; and in present circumstances for many classes of producers of raw materials, of farmers and of manufacturers, there are no profits and every prospect of insolvencies, if matters do not soon take a turn for the better.

To sum up, there is scarcely any class of property, except real estate, however useful and important to the welfare of the community, the current money value of which has not suffered an enormous and scarcely precedented decline. This has happened in a community which is so organised that a veil of money is, as I have said, interposed over a wide field between the actual asset and the wealth owner. The ostensible proprietor of the actual asset has financed it by borrowing money from the actual owner of wealth. Furthermore, it is largely through the banking system that all this has been arranged. That is to say, the banks have, for a consideration, interposed their guarantee. They stand between the real borrower and the real lender. They have given their guarantee to the real lender; and this guarantee is only good if the money value of the asset belonging to the real borrower is worth the money which has been advanced on it.

It is for this reason that a decline in money values so severe as that which we are now experiencing threatens the solidity of the whole financial structure. Banks and bankers are by nature blind. They have not seen what was coming. Some of them have even welcomed the fall of prices towards what, in their innocence, they have deemed the just and "natural" and inevitable level of pre-war, that is to say, to the level of prices to which their minds became accustomed in their formative years. In the United States some of them employ so-called "economists" who tell us even to-day that our troubles are due to the fact that the prices of some commodities and some services have not yet fallen enough, regardless of what should be the obvious fact that their cure, if it could be realised, would be a menace to the solvency of their institution. A "sound" banker, alas! is not one who foresees danger and avoids it, but one who, when he is ruined, is ruined in a conventional and orthodox way along with his fellows, so that no one can really blame him.

But to-day they are beginning at last to take notice. In many countries bankers are becoming unpleasantly aware of the fact that, when their customers' margins have run off, they are themselves "on margin." I believe that, if to - day a really conservative valuation were made of all doubtful assets, quite a significant proportion of the banks of the world would be found to be insolvent; and with the further progress of Deflation this proportion will grow rapidly. Fortunately our own domestic British Banks are probably at present -- for various reasons--among the strongest. But there is a degree of Deflation which no bank can stand. And over a great part of the world, and not least in the United States, the position of the banks, though partly concealed from the public eye, may be in fact the weakest element in the whole situation. It is obvious that the present trend of events cannot go much further without something breaking. If nothing is done, it will be amongst the world's banks that the really critical breakages will occur.

Modern capitalism is faced, in my belief, with the choice between finding some way to increase money values towards their former figure, or seeing widespread insolvencies and defaults and the collapse of a large part of the financial structure; -- after which we should all start again, not nearly so much poorer as we should expect, and much more cheerful perhaps, but having suffered a period of waste and disturbance and social injustice, and a general re-arrangement of private fortunes and the ownership of wealth. Individually many of us would be "ruined," even though collectively we were much as before. But under the pressure of hardship and excitement, we might have found out better ways of managing our affairs.

The present signs suggest that the bankers of the world are bent on suicide. At every stage they have been unwilling to adopt a sufficiently drastic remedy. And by now matters have been allowed to go so far that it has become extraordinarily difficult to find any way out.

It is necessarily part of the business of a banker to maintain appearances and to profess a conventional respectability which is more than human. Lifelong practices of this kind make them the most romantic and the least realistic of men. It is so much their stock-in-trade that their position should not be questioned, that they do not even question it themselves until it is too late. Like the honest citizens they are, they feel a proper indignation at the perils of the wicked world in which they live,--when the perils mature; but they do not foresee them. A Bankers' Conspiracy! The idea is absurd! I only wish there were one! So, if they are saved, it will be,

I expect, in their own despite.

III

THE RETURN TO THE GOLD STANDARD

1. AURI SACRA FAMES (Sept. 1930) THE choice of gold as a standard of value is chiefly based on tradition. In the days before the evolution of Representative Money, it was natural, for reasons which have been many times told, to choose one or more of the metals as the most suitable commodity for holding a store of value or a command of purchasing power.

Some four or five thousand years ago the civilised world settled down to the use of gold, silver, and copper for pounds, shillings, and pence, but with silver in the first place of importance and copper in the second. The Mycenaeans put gold in the first place. Next, under Celtic or Dorian influences, came a brief invasion of iron in place of copper over Europe and the northern shores of the Mediterranean. With the Achaemenid Persian Empire, which maintained a bimetallic standard of gold and silver at a fixed ratio (until Alexander overturned them), the world settled down again to gold, silver, and copper, with silver once more of predominant importance; and there followed silver's long hegemony (except for a certain revival of the influence of gold in Roman Constantinople), chequered by imperfectly successful attempts at gold-and-silver bimetallism, especially in the eighteenth century and the first half of the nineteenth, and only concluded by the final victory of gold during the fifty years before the war.

Dr. Freud relates that there are peculiar reasons deep in our subconsciousness why gold in particular should satisfy strong instincts and serve as a symbol. The magical properties, with which Egyptian priestcraft anciently imbued the yellow metal, it has never altogether lost. Yet, whilst gold as a store of value has always had devoted patrons, it is, as the sole standard of purchasing power, almost a parvenu. In 1914 gold had held this position in Great Britainde jure over less than a hundred years (though de facto for more than two hundred), and in most other countries over less than sixty. For except during rather brief intervals gold has been too scarce to serve the needs of the world's principal medium of currency. Gold is, and always has been, an extraordinarily scarce commodity. A modern liner could convey across the Atlantic in a single voyage all the gold which has been dredged or mined in seven thousand years. At intervals of five hundred or a thousand years a new source of supply has been discovered--the latter half of the nineteenth century was one of these epochs--and a temporary abundance has ensued. But as a rule, generally speaking, there has been not enough.

Of late years the auri sacra fames has sought to envelop itself in a garment of respectability as densely respectable as was ever met with, even in the realms of sex or religion. Whether this was first put on as a necessary armour to win the hard-won fight against bimetallism and is still worn, as the gold-advocates allege, because gold is the sole prophylactic against the plague of fiat moneys, or whether it is a furtive Freudian cloak, we need not be curious to inquire. But we may remind the reader of what he well knows--namely, that gold has become part of the apparatus of conservatism and is one of the matters which we cannot expect to see handled without prejudice.

One great change, nevertheless--probably, in the end, a fatal change--has been effected by our generation. During the war individuals threw their little stocks into the national melting-pots. Wars have sometimes served to disperse gold, as when Alexander scattered the temple hoards of Persia or Pizarro those of the Incas. But on this occasion war concentrated gold in the vaults of the Central Banks; and these Banks have not released it. Thus, almost throughout the world, gold has been withdrawn from circulation. It no longer passes from hand to hand, and the touch of the metal has been taken away from men's greedy palms. The little household gods, who dwelt in purses and stockings and tin boxes, have been swallowed by a single golden image in each country, which lives underground and is not seen. Gold is out of sight--gone back again into the soil. But when gods are no longer seen in a yellow panoply walking the earth, we begin to rationalise them; and it is not long before there is nothing left.

Thus the long age of Commodity Money has at last passed finally away before the age of Representative Money. Gold has ceased to be a coin, a hoard, a tangible claim to wealth, of which the value cannot slip away so long as the hand of the individual clutches the material stuff. It has become a much more abstract thing--just a standard of value; and it only keeps this nominal status by being handed round from time to time in quite small quantities amongst a group of Central Banks, on the occasions when one of them has been inflating or deflating its managed representative money in a different degree from what is appropriate to the behaviour of its neighbours. Even the handing round is becoming a little old-fashioned, being the occasion of unnecessary travelling expenses, and the most modern way, called "ear-marking," is to change the ownership without shifting the location. It is not a far step from this to the beginning of arrangements between Central Banks by which, without ever formally renouncing the rule of gold, the quantity of metal actually buried in their vaults may come to stand, by a modern alchemy, for what they please, and its value for what they choose. Thus gold, originally stationed in heaven with his consort silver, as Sun and Moon, having first doffed his sacred attributes and come to earth as an autocrat, may next descend to the sober status of a constitutional king with a cabinet of Banks; and it may never be necessary to proclaim a Republic. But this is not yet--the evolution may be quite otherwise. The friends of gold will have to be extremely wise and moderate if they are to avoid a Revolution.

2. ALTERNATIVE AIMS IN MONETARY POLICY (1923) The instability of money has been compounded, in most countries except the United States, of two elements: the failure of the national currencies to remain stable in terms of what was supposed to be the standard of value, namely gold; and the failure of gold itself to remain stable in terms of purchasing power. Attention has been mainly concentrated (e.g. by the Cunliffe Committee) on the first of these two factors. It is often assumed that the restoration of the gold standard, that is to say, of the convertibility of each national currency at a fixed rate in terms of gold, must be, in any case, our objective; and that the main question of controversy is whether national currencies should be restored to their pre-war gold value or to some lower value nearer to the present facts; in other words, the choice between Deflation and Devaluation.

This assumption is hasty. If we glance at the course of prices during the last five years, it is obvious that the United States, which has enjoyed a gold standard throughout, has suffered as severely as many other countries, that in the United Kingdom the instability of gold has been a larger factor than the instability of the exchange, that the same is true even of France, and that in Italy it has been nearly as large. On the other hand, in India, which has suffered violent exchange fluctuations, the standard of value has been more stable than in any other country.We should not, therefore, by fixing the exchanges get rid of our currency troubles. It is even possible that this step might weaken our control. The problem of stabilisation has several sides, which we must consider one by one:

1. Devaluation versus Deflation. Do we wish to fix the standard of value, whether or not it be gold, near the existing value? Or do we wish to restore it to the pre-war value?

2. Stability of Prices versus Stability of Exchange. Is it more important that the value of a national currency should be stable in terms of purchasing power, or stable in terms of the currency of certain foreign countries?

3. The Restoration of a Gold Standard. In the light of our answers to the first two questions, is a gold standard, however imperfect in theory, the best available method for attaining our ends in practice?

(i) Devaluation versus Deflation The policy of reducing the ratio between the volume of a country's currency and its requirements of purchasing power in the form of money, so as to increase the exchange value of the currency in terms of gold or of commodities, is conveniently called Deflation.

The alternative policy of stabilising the value of the currency somewhere near its present value, without regard to its pre-war value, is called Devaluation.

Up to the date of the Genoa Conference of April 1922, these two policies were not clearly distinguished by the public, and the sharp opposition between them has been only gradually appreciated. Even now (October 1923) there is scarcely any European country in which the authorities have made it clear whether their policy is to stabilise the value of their currency or to raise it. Stabilisation at the existing level has been recommended by International Conferences; and the actual value of many currencies tends to fall rather than to rise. But, to judge from other indications, the heart's desire of the State Banks of Europe, whether they pursue it successfully, as in CzechoSlovakia, or unsuccessfully, as in France, is to raise the value of their currencies.

The simple arguments against Deflation fall under two heads.

In the first place, Deflation is not desirable, because it effects, what is always harmful, a change in the existing Standard of Value, and redistributes wealth in a manner injurious, at the same time, to business and to social stability. Deflation, as we have already seen, involves a transference of wealth from the rest of the community to the rentier class and to all holders of titles to money; just as Inflation involves the opposite. In particular it involves a transference from all borrowers, that is to say from traders, manufacturers, and farmers, to lenders, from the active to the inactive.

But whilst the oppression of the taxpayer for the enrichment of the rentier is the chief lasting result, there is another, more violent, disturbance during the period of transition. The policy of gradually raising the value of a country's money to (say) 100 per cent above its present value in terms of goods amounts to giving notice to every merchant and every manufacturer, that for some time to come his stock and his raw materials will steadily depreciate on his hands, and to every one who finances his business with borrowed money that he will, sooner or later, lose 100 per cent on his liabilities (since he will have to pay back in terms of commodities twice as much as he has borrowed). Modern business, being carried on largely with borrowed money, must necessarily be brought to a standstill by such a process. It will be to the interest of everyone in business to go out of business for the time being; and of everyone who is contemplating expenditure to postpone his orders so long as he can. The wise man will be he who turns his assets into cash, withdraws from the risks and the exertions of activity, and awaits in country retirement the steady appreciation promised him in the value of his cash. A probable expectation of Deflation is bad enough; a certain expectation is disastrous. For the mechanism of the modern business world is even less adapted to fluctuations in the value of money upwards than it is to fluctuations downwards.

In the second place, in many countries, Deflation, even were it desirable, is not possible; that is to say, Deflation in sufficient degree to restore the currency to its pre-war parity. For the burden which it would throw on the taxpayer would be insupportable. This practical impossibility might have rendered the policy innocuous, if it were not that, by standing in the way of the alternative policy, it prolongs the period of uncertainty and severe seasonal fluctuation, and even, in some cases, can be carried into effect sufficiently to cause much interference with business. The fact, that the restoration of their currencies to the pre-war parity is still the declared official policy of the French and Italian Governments, is preventing, in those countries, any rational discussion of currency reform. All those--and in the financial world they are many --who have reasons for wishing to appear "correct," are compelled to talk foolishly. In Italy, where sound economic views have much influence and which may be nearly ripe for currency reform, Signor Mussolini has threatened to raise the lira to its former value. Fortunately for the Italian taxpayer and Italian business, the lira does not listen even to a dictator and cannot be given castor oil. But such talk can postpone positive reform; though it may be doubted if so good a politician would have propounded such a policy, even in bravado and exuberance, if he had understood that, expressed in other but equivalent words, it was as follows: "My policy is to halve wages, double the burden of the National Debt, and to reduce by 50 per cent the prices which Sicily can get for her exports of oranges and lemons."

If the restoration of many European currencies to their pre-war parity with gold is neither desirable nor possible, what are the forces or the arguments which have established this undesirable impossibility as the avowed policy of most of them? The following are the most important:

1. To leave the gold value of a country's currency at the low level to which war has driven it is an injustice to the rentier class and to others whose income is fixed in terms of currency, and practically a breach of contract; whilst to restore its value would meet a debt of honour.

The injury done to pre-war holders of fixed interest-bearing stocks is beyond dispute. Real justice, indeed, might require the restoration of the purchasing power, and not merely the gold value, of their money incomes, a measure which no one in fact proposes; whilst nominal justice has not been infringed, since these investments were not in gold bullion but in the legal tender of the realm. Nevertheless, if this class of investors could be dealt with separately, considerations of equity and the expedience of satisfying reasonable expectation would furnish a strong case.

But this is not the actual situation. The vast issues of War Loans have swamped the pre-war holdings of fixed interest-bearing stocks, and Society has largely adjusted itself to the new situation. To restore the value of pre-war holdings by Deflation means enhancing at the same time the value of war and post-war holdings, and thereby raising the total claims of the rentier class not only beyond what they are entitled to, but to an intolerable proportion of the total income of the community. Indeed justice, rightly weighed, comes down on the other side. Much the greater proportion of the money contracts still outstanding were entered into when money was worth more nearly what it is worth now than what it was worth in 1913. Thus, in order to do justice to a minority of creditors, a great injustice would be done to a great majority of debtors.

When, therefore, the depreciation of the currency has lasted long enough for Society to adjust itself to the new values, Deflation is even worse than Inflation. Both are "unjust" and disappoint reasonable expectation. But whereas Inflation, by easing the burden of national debt and stimulating enterprise, has a little to throw into the other side of the balance, Deflation has nothing.

2. The restoration of a currency to its pre-war gold value enhances a country's financial prestige and promotes future confidence.

Where a country can hope to restore its prewar parity at an early date, this argument cannot be neglected. This might be said of Great Britain, Holland, Sweden, Switzerland, and (perhaps) Spain, but of no other European country. The argument cannot be extended to those countries which, even if they could raise somewhat the value of their legal-tender money, could not possibly restore it to its old value. It is of the essence of the argument that the exact pre-war parity should be recovered. It would not make much difference to the financial prestige of Italy whether she stabilised the lira at 100 to the £ sterling or at 60; and it would be much better for her prestige to stabilise it definitely at 100 than to let it fluctuate between 60 and 100.

This argument is limited, therefore, to those countries the gold value of whose currencies is within (say) 5 or 10 per cent of their former value. Its force in these cases depends, I think, upon what answer we give to the problem discussed below, namely, whether we intend to pin ourselves in the future, as in the past, to an unqualified gold standard. If we still prefer such a standard to any available alternative, and if future "confidence" in our currency is to depend not on the stability of its purchasing power but on the fixity of its gold value, then it may be worth our while to stand the racket of Deflation to the extent of 5 or 10 per cent. This view is in accordance with that expressed by Ricardo in analogous circumstances a hundred years ago. If, on the other hand, we decide to aim for the future at stability of the price level rather than at a fixed parity with gold, in that case cadit quaestio.

value of a country's currency can be increased, labour will profit by a reduced cost of living, foreign goods will be obtainable cheaper, and foreign debts fixed in terms of gold (e.g. to the United States) will be discharged with less effort.

This argument, which is pure delusion, exercises quite as much influence as the other two. If the franc is worth more, wages, it is argued, which are paid in francs, will surely buy more, and French imports, which are paid for in francs, will be so much cheaper. No! If francs are worth more they will buy more labour as well as more goods,--that is to say, wages will fall; and the French exports, which pay for the imports, will, measured in francs, fall in value just as much as the imports. Nor will it make in the long run any difference whatever in the amount of goods the value of which England will have to transfer to America to pay her dollar debts whether in the end sterling settles down at four dollars to the pound or at its prewar parity. The burden of this debt depends on the value of gold, in terms of which it is fixed, not on the value of sterling. It is not easy, it seems, for men to apprehend that their money is a mere intermediary, without significance in itself, which flows from one hand to another, is received and is dispensed, and disappears when its work is done from the sum of a nation's wealth.

(ii) Stability of Prices versus Stability of Exchange Since, subject to certain qualifications, the rate of exchange of a country's currency with the currency of the rest of the world (assuming for the sake of simplicity that there is only one external currency) depends on the relation between the internal price level and the external price level, it follows that the exchange cannot be stable unless both internal and external price levels remain stable. If, therefore, the external price level lies outside our control, we must submit either to our own internal price level or to our exchange being pulled about by external influences. If the external price level is unstable, we cannot keep both our own price level and our exchanges stable. And we are compelled to choose.

In pre-war days, when almost the whole world was on a gold standard, we had all plumped for stability of exchange as against stability of prices, and we were ready to submit to the social consequences of a change of price level for causes quite outside our control, connected, for example, with the discovery of new gold mines in foreign countries or a change of banking policy abroad. But we submitted, partly because we did not dare trust ourselves to a less automatic (though more reasoned) policy, and partly because the price fluctuations experienced were in fact moderate. Nevertheless, there were powerful advocates of the other choice. In particular, the proposals of Professor Irving Fisher for a Compensated Dollar, amounted, unless all countries adopted the same plan, to putting into practice a preference for stability of internal price level over stability of external exchange.

The right choice is not necessarily the same for all countries. It must partly depend on the relative importance of foreign trade in the economic life of the country. Nevertheless, there does seem to be in almost every case a presumption in favour of the stability of prices, if only it can be achieved. Stability of exchange is in the nature of a convenience which adds to the efficiency and prosperity of those who are engaged in foreign trade. Stability of prices, on the other hand, is profoundly important for the avoidance of the various evils described above. Contracts and business expectations, which presume a stable exchange, must be far fewer, even in a trading country such as England, than those which presume a stable level of internal prices. The main argument to the contrary seems to be that exchange stability is an easier aim to attain, since it only requires that the same standard of value should be adopted at home and abroad; whereas an internal standard, so regulated as to maintain stability in an index number of prices, is a difficult scientific innovation, never yet put into practice.

At any rate the unthinking assumption, in favour of the restoration of a fixed exchange as the one thing to aim at, requires more examination than it sometimes receives. Especially is this the case if the prospect that a majority of countries will adopt the same standard is still remote. When by adopting the gold standard we could achieve stability of exchange with almost the whole world, whilst any other standard would have appeared as a solitary eccentricity, the solid advantages of certainty and convenience supported the conservative preference for gold. Nevertheless, even so, the convenience of traders and the primitive passion for solid metal might not, I think, have been adequate to preserve the dynasty of gold, if it had not been for another, half-accidental circumstance; namely, that for many years past gold had afforded not only a stable exchange but, on the whole, a stable price level also. In fact, the choice between stable exchanges and stable prices had not presented itself as an acute dilemma. And when, prior to the development of the South African mines, we seemed to be faced with a continu-

ously falling price level, the fierceness of the bimetallic controversy
testified to the discontent provoked as soon as the existing standard appeared seriously incompatible with the stability of prices.

Indeed, it is doubtful whether the pre-war system for regulating the international flow of gold would have been capable of dealing with such large or sudden divergencies between the price levels
of different countries as have occurred lately. The fault of the pre-
war régime, under which the rates of exchange between a country
and the outside world were fixed, and the internal price level had
to adjust itself thereto (i.e. was chiefly governed by external influences), was that it was too slow and insensitive in its mode of
operation. The fault of the post-war régime, under which the price
level mainly depends on internal influences (i.e. internal currency
and credit policy) and the rates of exchange with the outside world
have to adjust themselves thereto, is that it is too rapid in its effect and over-sensitive, with the result that it may act violently
for merely transitory causes. Nevertheless, when the fluctuations
are large and sudden, a quick reaction is necessary for the maintenance of equilibrium; and the necessity for quick reaction has been
one of the factors which have rendered the prewar method inapplicable to post-war conditions, and have made every one nervous
of proclaiming a final fixation of the exchange.

A fluctuating exchange means that relative prices can be
knocked about by the most fleeting influences of politics and of
sentiment, and by the periodic pressure of seasonal trades. But it
also means that this method is a most rapid and powerful correc-
tive of real disequilibria in the balance of international payments
arising from whatever causes, and a wonderful preventive in the
way of countries which are inclined to spend abroad beyond their
resources.

Thus when there are violent shocks to the pre-existing equilibrium between the internal and external price levels, the pre-war
method is likely to break down in practice, simply because it cannot bring about the readjustment of internal prices quick enough.
Theoretically, of course, the pre-war method must be able to make
itself effective sooner or later, provided the movement of gold is allowed to continue without restriction until the inflation or deflation
of prices has taken place to the necessary extent. But in practice
there is usually a limit to the rate and to the amount by which the
actual currency or the metallic backing for it can be allowed to
flow abroad. If the supply of money or credit is reduced faster than

social and business arrangements allow prices to fall, intolerable inconveniences result.

(iii) The Restoration of a Gold Standard Our conclusions up to this point are, therefore, that, when stability of the internal price level and stability of the external exchanges are incompatible, the former is generally preferable; and that on occasions when the dilemma is acute the preservation of the former at the expense of the latter is, fortunately perhaps, the line of least resistance.

The restoration of the gold standard (whether at the pre-war parity or at some other rate) certainly will not give us complete stability of internal prices, and can only give us complete stability of the external exchanges if all other countries also restore the gold standard. The advisability of restoring it depends, therefore, on whether, on the whole, it will give us the best working compromise obtainable between the two ideals.

The advocates of gold, as against a more scientific standard, base their cause on the double contention that in practice gold has provided and will provide a reasonably stable standard of value and that in practice, since governing authorities lack wisdom as often as not, a managed currency will, sooner or later, come to grief. Conservatism and scepticism join arms--as they often do. Perhaps superstition comes in too; for gold still enjoys the prestige of its smell and colour.

The considerable success with which gold maintained its stability of value in the changing world of the nineteenth century was certainly remarkable. After the discoveries of Australia and California it began to depreciate dangerously, and before the exploitation of South Africa it began to appreciate dangerously. Yet in each case it righted itself and retained its reputation.

But the conditions of the future are not those of the past. We have no sufficient ground for expecting the continuance of the special conditions which preserved a sort of balance before the war. For what are the underlying explanations of the good behaviour of gold during the nineteenth century?

In the first place, it happened that progress in the discovery of gold mines roughly kept pace with progress in other directions--a correspondence which was not altogether a matter of chance, because the progress of that period, since it was characterised by the gradual opening up and exploitation of the world's surface, not unnaturally brought to light pari passu the remoter deposits of gold. But this stage of history is now almost at an end. A quarter of a century has passed by since the discovery of an important deposit. Material progress is more dependent now on the growth of scientific and technical knowledge, of which the application to gold-mining may be intermittent. Years may elapse without great improvement in the methods of extracting gold; and then the genius of a chemist may realise past dreams and forgotten hoaxes, transmuting base into precious like Subtle, or extracting gold from sea-water as in the Bubble. Gold is liable to be either too dear or too cheap. In either case, it is too much to expect that a succession of accidents will keep the metal steady.

But there was another type of influence which used to aid stability. The value of gold has not depended on the policy or the decisions of a single body of men; and a sufficient proportion of the supply has been able to find its way, without any flooding of the market, into the Arts or into the hoards of Asia for its marginal value to be governed by a steady psychological estimation of the metal in relation to other things. This is what is meant by saying that gold has "intrinsic value" and is free from the dangers of a "managed" currency. The independent variety of the influences determining the value of gold has been in itself a steadying influence. The arbitrary and variable character of the proportion of gold reserves to liabilities maintained by many of the note-issuing banks of the world, so far from introducing an incalculable factor, was an element of stability. For when gold was relatively abundant and flowed towards them, it was absorbed by their allowing their ratio of gold reserves to rise slightly; and when it was relatively scarce, the fact that they had no intention of ever utilising their gold reserves for any practical purpose permitted most of them to view with equanimity a moderate weakening of their proportion. A great part of the flow of South African gold between the end of the Boer War and 1914 was able to find its way into the central gold reserves of European and other countries with the minimum effect on prices.

But the war has effected a great change. Gold itself has become a "managed" currency. The West, as well as the East, has learnt to hoard gold; but the motives of the United States are not those of India. Now that most countries have abandoned the gold standard, the supply of the metal would, if the chief user of it restricted its holdings to its real needs, prove largely redundant. The United States has not been able to let gold fall to its "natural" value, because it could not face the resulting depreciation of its standard. It has been driven, therefore, to the costly policy of burying in the vaults of Washington what the miners of the Rand have laboriously brought to the surface. Consequently gold now stands at an "artificial" value, the future course of which almost entirely depends on the policy of the Federal Reserve Board of the United States. The value of gold is no longer the resultant of the chance gifts of Nature and the judgement of numerous authorities and individuals acting independently. Even if other countries gradually return to a gold basis, the position will not be greatly changed. The tendency to employ some variant of the goldexchange standard and the probably permanent disappearance of gold from the pockets of the people are likely to mean that the strictly necessary gold reserves of the Central Banks of the gold-standard countries will fall considerably short of the available supplies. The actual value of gold will depend, therefore, on the policy of three or four of the most powerful Central Banks, whether they act independently or in unison. If, on the other hand, pre-war conventions about the use of gold in reserves and in circulation were to be restored--which is, in my opinion, the much less probable alternative--there might be, as Professor Cassel has predicted, a serious shortage of gold, leading to a progressive appreciation in its value.

Nor must we neglect the possibility of a partial demonetisation of gold by the United States through a closing of its mints to further receipts of gold. The present policy of the United States in accepting unlimited imports of gold can be justified, perhaps, as a temporary measure, intended to preserve tradition and to strengthen confidence through a transitional period. But, looked at as a permanent arrangement, it could hardly be judged otherwise than as a foolish expense. If the Federal Reserve Board intends to maintain the value of the dollar at a level which is irrespective of the inflow or outflow of gold, what object is there in continuing to accept at the mints gold which is not wanted, yet costs a heavy price? If the United States mints were to be closed to gold, everything, except the actual price of the metal, could continue precisely as before.

Confidence in the future stability of the value of gold depends therefore on the United States being foolish enough to go on accepting gold which it does not want, and wise enough, having accepted it, to maintain it at a fixed value. This double event might be realised through the collaboration of a public understanding nothing with a Federal Reserve Board understanding everything. But the position is precarious; and not very attractive to any country which is still in a position to choose what its future standard is to be.

This discussion of the prospects of the stability of gold has partly answered by anticipation the second principal argument in favour of the restoration of an unqualified gold standard, namely that this is the only way of avoiding the dangers of a "managed" currency.

It is natural, after what we have experienced, that prudent people should desiderate a standard of value which is independent of Finance Ministers and State Banks. The present state of affairs has allowed to the ignorance and frivolity of statesmen an ample opportunity of bringing about ruinous consequences in the economic field. It is felt that the general level of economic and financial education amongst statesmen and bankers is hardly such as to render innovations feasible or safe; that, in fact, a chief object of stabilising the exchanges is to strap down Ministers of Finance.

These are reasonable grounds of hesitation. But the experience on which they are based is by no means fair to the capacities of statesmen and bankers. The non-metallic standards of which we have experience have been anything rather than scientific experiments coolly carried out. They have been a last resort, involuntarily adopted, as a result of war or inflationary taxation, when the State finances were already broken or the situation out of hand. Naturally in these circumstances such practices have been the accompaniment and the prelude of disaster. But we cannot argue from this to what can be achieved in normal times. I do not see that the regulation of the standard of value is essentially more difficult than many other objects of less social necessity which we attain successfully.

If, indeed, a providence watched over gold, or if Nature had provided us with a stable standard ready-made, I would not, in an attempt after some slight improvement, hand over the management to the possible weakness or ignorance of Boards and Governments. But this is not the situation. We have no ready-made standard. Experience has shown that in emergencies Ministers of Finance cannot be strapped down. And--most important of all--in the modern world of paper currency and bank credit there is no escape from a "managed" currency, whether we wish it or not;-- convertibility into gold will not alter the fact that the value of gold itself depends on the policy of the Central Banks.

It is worth while to pause a moment over the last sentence. It differs significantly from the doctrine of gold reserves which we learnt and taught before the war. We used to assume that no Central Bank would be so extravagant as to keep more gold than it required or so imprudent as to keep less. From time to time gold would flow out into the circulation or for export abroad; experience showed that the quantity required on these occasions bore some rough proportion to the Central Bank's liabilities; a decidedly higher proportion than this would be fixed on to provide for contingencies and to inspire confidence; and the creation of credit would be regulated largely by reference to the maintenance of this proportion. The Bank of England, for example, would allow itself to be swayed by the tides of gold, permitting the inflowing and outflowing streams to produce their "natural" consequences unchecked by any ideas as to preventing the effect on prices. Already before the war the system was becoming precarious by reason of its artificiality. The "proportion" was by the lapse of time losing its relation to the facts and had become largely conventional. Some other figure, greater or less, would have done just as well. 1 The War broke down the convention; for the withdrawal of gold from actual circulation destroyed one of the elements of reality lying behind the convention, and the suspension of convertibility destroyed the other. It would have been absurd to regulate the bank-rate by reference to a "proportion" which had lost all its significance; and in the course of the past ten years a new policy has been evolved. The bankrate is now employed, however incompletely and experimentally, to regulate the expansion and deflation of credit in the interests of business stability and the steadiness of prices. In so far as it is employed to procure stability of the dollar exchange, where this is inconsistent with stability of internal prices, we have a relic of pre-war policy and a compromise between discrepant aims.

Those who advocate the return to a gold standard do not always appreciate along what different lines our actual practice has been drifting. If we restore the gold standard, are we to return also to the pre-war conceptions of bank-rate, allowing the tides of gold to play what tricks they like with the internal price level, and abandoning the attempt to moderate the disastrous influence of the credit-cycle on the stability of prices and employment? Or are we to continue and develop the experimental innovations of our present policy, ignoring the "bank ratio" and, if necessary, allowing unmoved a piling up of gold reserves far beyond our requirements or their depletion far below them?

In truth, the gold standard is already a barbarous relic. All of us, from the Governor of the Bank of England downwards, are now primarily interested in preserving the stability of business, prices, and employment, and are not likely, when the choice is forced on us, deliberately to sacrifice these to the outworn dogma, which had its value once, of £3:17:10½ per ounce. Advocates of the ancient standard do not observe how remote it now is from the spirit and the requirements of the age. A regulated non-metallic standard has slipped in unnoticed. It exists. Whilst the economists dozed, the academic dream of a hundred years, doffing its cap and gown, clad in paper rags, has crept into the real world by means of the bad fairies --always so much more potent than the good --the wicked Ministers of Finance.

For these reasons enlightened advocates of the restoration of gold, such as Mr. Hawtrey, do not welcome it as the return of a "natural" currency, and intend, quite decidedly, that it shall be a "managed" one. They allow gold back only as a constitutional monarch, shorn of his ancient despotic powers and compelled to accept the advice of a Parliament of Banks. The adoption of the ideas present in the minds of those who drafted the Genoa Resolutions on Currency is an essential condition of Mr. Hawtrey's adherence to gold. He contemplates "the practice of continuous co-operation among central banks of issue" (Res. 3), and an international convention, based on a gold exchange standard, and designed "with a view to preventing undue fluctuations in the purchasing power of gold" (Res. 11). 1 But he is not in favour of resuming the gold standard irrespective of "whether the difficulties in regard to the future purchasing power of gold have been provided against or not." "It is not easy," he admits, "to promote international action, and, should it fail, the wisest course for the time being might be to concentrate on the stabilisation of sterling in terms of commodities, rather than tie the pound to a metal the vagaries of which cannot be foreseen."

It is natural to ask, in face of advocacy of this kind, why it is necessary to drag in gold at all. Mr. Hawtrey lays no stress on the obvious support for his compromise, namely the force of sentiment and tradition, and the preference of Englishmen for shearing a monarch of his powers rather than of his head. But he adduces three other reasons: (1) that gold is required as a liquid reserve for the settlement of international balances of indebtedness; (2) that it enables an experiment to be made without cutting adrift from the old system; and (3) that the vested interests of gold producers must be considered. These objects, however, are so largely attained by my own suggestions in the following section that I need not dwell on them here.

On the other hand, I see grave objections to reinstating gold in the pious hope that international co-operation will keep it in order. With the existing distribution of the world's gold the reinstatement of the gold standard means, inevitably, that we surrender the regulation of our price level and the handling of the credit cycle to the Federal Reserve Board of the United States. Even if the most intimate and cordial co-operation is established between the Board and the Bank of England, the preponderance of power will still belong to the former. The Board will be in a position to disregard the Bank. But if the Bank disregard the Board, it will render itself liable to be flooded with, or depleted of, gold, as the case may be. Moreover, we can be confident beforehand that there will be much suspicion amongst Americans (for that is their disposition) of any supposed attempt on the part of the Bank of England to dictate their policy or to influence American discount rates in the interests of Great Britain. We must also be prepared to incur our share of the vain expense of bottling up the world's redundant gold.

It would be rash in present circumstances to surrender our freedom of action to the Federal Reserve Board of the United States. We do not yet possess sufficient experience of its capacity to act in times of stress with courage and independence. The Federal Reserve Board is striving to free itself from the pressure of sectional interests; but we are not yet certain that it will wholly succeed. It is still liable to be overwhelmed by the impetuosity of a cheap money campaign. A suspicion of British influence would, so far from strengthening the Board, greatly weaken its resistance to popular clamour. Nor is it certain, quite apart from weakness or mistakes, that the simultaneous application of the same policy will always be in the interests of both countries. The development of the credit cycle and the state of business may sometimes be widely different on the two sides of the Atlantic.

Therefore, since I regard the stability of prices, credit, and employment as of paramount importance, and since I feel no confidence that an old-fashioned gold standard will even give us the modicum of stability that it used to give, I reject the policy of restoring the gold standard on pre-war lines. At the same time, I doubt the wisdom of attempting a "managed" gold standard jointly with the United States, on the lines recommended by Mr. Hawtrey, because it retains too many of the disadvantages of the old system without its advantages, and because it would make us too dependent on the policy and on the wishes of the Federal Reserve Board.

3. POSITIVE SUGGESTIONS FOR THE FUTURE REGULATION OF MONEY (1923) A sound constructive scheme must provide:

I. A method for regulating the supply of currency and credit with a view to maintaining, so far as possible, the stability of the internal price level; and

II. A method for regulating the supply of foreign exchange so as to avoid purely temporary fluctuations caused by seasonal or other influences and not due to a lasting disturbance in the relation between the internal and the external price level.

I believe that in Great Britain the ideal system can be most nearly and most easily reached by an adaptation of the actual system which has grown up, half haphazard, since the war.

I. My first requirement in a good constructive scheme can be supplied merely by a development of our existing arrangements on more deliberate and self-conscious lines. Hitherto the Treasury and the Bank of England have looked forward to the stability of the dollar exchange (preferably at the pre-war parity) as their objective. It is not clear whether they   intend to stick to this irrespective of fluctuations in the value of the dollar (or of gold); whether, that is to say, they would sacrifice the stability of sterling prices to the stability of the dollar exchange in the event of the two proving to be incompatible. At any rate, my scheme would require that they should adopt the stability of sterling prices as their primary objective-though this would not prevent their aiming at exchange stability also as a secondary objective by co-operating with the Federal Reserve Board in a common policy. So long as the Federal Reserve Board was successful in keeping dollar prices steady the objective of keeping sterling prices steady would be identical with the objective of keeping the dollar sterling exchange steady. My recommendation does not involve more than a determination that, in the event of the Federal Reserve Board failing to keep dollar prices steady, sterling prices should not, if it could be helped, plunge with them merely for the sake of maintaining a fixed parity of exchange.

If the Bank of England, the Treasury, and the Big Five were to adopt this policy, to what criteria should they look respectively in regulating bank-rate, Government borrowing, and trade-advances? The first question is whether the criterion should be a precise, arithmetical formula or whether it should be sought in a general judgement of the situation based on all the available data. The pioneer of pricestability as against exchange-stability, Professor Irving Fisher, advocated the former in the shape of his "compensated dollar," which was to be automatically adjusted by reference to an index number of prices without any play of judgement or discretion. He may have been influenced, however, by the advantage of propounding a method which could be grafted as easily as possible on to the pre-war system of gold reserves and gold ratios. In any case, I doubt the wisdom and the practicability of a system so cut and dried. If we wait until a price movement is actually afoot before applying remedial measures, we may be too late. "It is not the past rise in prices but the future rise that has to be counteracted."

It is characteristic of the impetuosity of the credit cycle that price movements tend to be cumulative, each movement promoting, up to a certain point, a further movement in the same direction. Professor Fisher's method may be adapted to deal with long-period trends in the value of gold but not with the, often more injurious, short-period oscillations of the credit cycle. Nevertheless, whilst it would not be advisable to postpone action until it was called for by an actual movement of prices, it would promote confidence, and furnish an objective standard of value, if, an official index number having been compiled of such a character as to register the price of a standard composite commodity, the authorities were to adopt this composite commodity as their standard of value in the sense that they would employ all their resources to prevent a movement of its price by more than a certain percentage in either direction away from the normal, just as before the war they employed all their resources to prevent a movement in the price of gold by more than a certain percentage. The precise composition of the standard composite commodity could be modified from time to time in accordance with changes in the relative economic importance of its various components.

As regards the criteria, other than the actual trend of prices, which should determine the action of the controlling authority, it is beyond the scope of this essay to deal adequately with the diagnosis and analysis of the credit cycle. The more deeply our researches penetrate into this subject, the more accurately shall we understand the right time and method for controlling credit-expansion by bank-rate or otherwise. But in the meantime we have a considerable and growing body of general experience upon which those in authority can base their judgements. Actual price-movements must of course provide the most important datum; but the state of employment, the volume of production, the effective demand for credit as felt by the banks, the rate of interest on investments of various types, the volume of new issues, the flow of cash into circulation, the statistics of foreign trade and the level of the exchanges must all be taken into account. The main point is that the objective of the authorities, pursued with such means as are at their command, should be the stability of prices.

II. How can we best combine this primary object with a maximum stability of the exchanges? Can we get the best of both worlds-stability of prices over long periods and stability of exchanges over short periods? It is the great advantage of the gold standard that it overcomes the excessive sensitiveness of the exchanges to temporary influences. Our object must be to secure this advantage, if we can, without committing ourselves to follow big movements in the value of gold itself.

I believe that we can go a long way in this direction if the Bank of England will take over the duty of regulating the price of gold, just as it already regulates the rate of discount. "Regulate," but not "peg." The Bank of England should have a buying and a selling price for gold, just as it did before the war, and this price might remain unchanged for considerable periods, just as bank-rate does. But it would not be fixed or "pegged" once and for all, any more than bank-rate is fixed. The Bank's rate for gold would be announced every Thursday morning at the same time as its rate for discounting bills, with a difference between its buying and selling rates corresponding to the pre-war margin between £3:17:10½ per oz. and £3:17:9 per oz.; except that, in order to obviate too frequent changes in the rate, the difference might be wider than 1½d. per oz.-say,½ to 1 per cent. A willingness on the part of the Bank both to buy and to sell gold at rates fixed for the time being would keep the dollarsterling exchange steady within corresponding limits, so that the exchange rate would not move with every breath of wind but only when the Bank had come to a considered judgement that a change was required for the sake of the stability of sterling prices.

If the bank-rate and the gold-rate in conjunction were leading to an excessive influx or an excessive efflux of gold, the Bank of England would have to decide whether the flow was due to an internal or to an external movement away from stability. To fix our ideas, let us suppose that gold is flowing outwards. If this seemed to be due to a tendency of sterling to depreciate in terms of commodities, the correct remedy would be to raise the bank-rate. If, on the other hand, it was due to a tendency of gold to appreciate in terms of commodities, the correct remedy would be to raise the gold-rate (i.e. the buying price for gold). If, however, the flow could be explained by seasonal, or other passing influences, then it should be allowed to continue (assuming, of course, that the Bank's gold reserves were equal to any probable calls on them) unchecked, to be redressed later on by the corresponding reaction.

It would effect an improvement in the technique of the system here proposed, without altering its fundamental characteristics, if the Bank of England were to quote a daily price, not only for the purchase and sale of gold for immediate delivery, but also for delivery three months forward. The difference, if any, between the cash and forward quotations might represent either a discount or a premium of the latter on the former, according as the bank desired money rates in London to stand below or above those in New York. The existence of the forward quotation of the Bank of England would afford a firm foundation for a free market in forward exchange, and would facilitate the movement of funds between London and New York for short periods, in much the same way as before the war, whilst at the same time keeping down to a minimum the actual movement of gold bullion backwards and forwards.

The reader will observe that I retain for gold an important rôle in our system. As an ultimate safeguard and as a reserve for sudden requirements, no superior medium is yet available. But I urge that it is possible to get the benefit of the advantages of gold without irrevocably binding our legal-tender money to follow blindly all the vagaries of gold and future unforseeable fluctuations in its real purchasing power.

4. THE SPEECHES OF THE BANK CHAIRMEN (1924-1927)

(i) February 1924 We have an admirable custom in this country by which once a year the overlords of the Big Five desist for a day from the thankless task of persuading their customers to accept loans, and, putting on cap and gown, mount the lecturer's rostrum to expound the theory of their practice; --a sort of Saturnalia, during which we are all ephemerally equal with words for weapons. These occasions are of great general interest. But they are more than this. They have a representative significance;--they hold up, as it were, financial fashion-plates. What have they found to say this year about Monetary Policy?

Only one, Mr. Walter Leaf, of the Westminster Bank, has refrained himself entirely. Each of the other four has had something to say. They fall into a pair of couples: one of which, Mr. Beaumont Pease of Lloyds Bank and Sir Harry Goschen of the National Provincial Bank, feel that there is something improper, or at any rate undesirable, in thinking or speaking about these things at all; and the other of which, Mr. Goodenough of Barclays Bank and Mr. McKenna of the Midland Bank, so far from deprecating discussion, join in it boldly.

Mr. Pease, as I have said, deprecates thinking, or--as he prefers to call it--"the expenditure of mental agility." He desires "straightly to face the facts instead of to find a clever way round them," and holds that, in matters arising out of the Quantity Theory of Money, as between brains and character, "certainly the latter does not come second in order of merit." In short, the gold standard falls within the sphere of morals or of religion, where free-thought is out of place. He goes on to say: "As far as any ordinary joint-stock bank is concerned, I do not think it determines its policy consciously on pure monetary grounds. That is to say, its chief concern is to meet the requirements of trade as they arise, regardless of adhesion to any particular theory. Its actions are not the cause of trade movements; they follow after and do not precede them." I think that this, broadly speaking, is a correct account of the matter, and Mr. Pease's emphasis on it is the most valuable part of his speech. It is precisely this automatic element in the reactions of the joint-stock banks which makes the policy of the Bank of England about the volume of the banks' balances and the rate of discount so all-important. In conclusion, Mr. Pease does not propose to take any particular steps at present towards establishing any particular standard. Nevertheless he is "hopeful that we may gradually get back to our gold standard, which, in spite of some defects and difficulties, has, as a matter of fact, worked well in the past."

Sir Harry Goschen goes one better than Mr. Pease in a delightful passage which deserves to be quoted in full:--

I cannot help thinking that there has been lately far too much irresponsible discussion as to the comparative advantages of Inflation and Deflation. Discussions of this kind can only breed suspicion in the minds of our neighbours as to whether we shall adopt either of these courses, and, if so, which. I think we had better let matters take their natural course.

Is it more appropriate to smile or to rage at these artless sentiments? Best of all, perhaps, just to leave Sir Harry to take his natural course.

Leaving, then, these impeccable Spinsters, we come, in the speeches of Mr. Goodenough and Mr. McKenna, to rational, even risqué conversation. In immediate policy there is a large measure of agreement between them. They agree that monetary policy is capable of determining the level of prices, that our destiny is therefore in our own hands, and that the right course to pursue requires much thought and discussion. Mr. Goodenough, however, lays greater stress on the bank-rate, and Mr. McKenna on the amount of the cash resources in the hands of the banks. They are opposed to any revival at the present time of the Cunliffe Committee's policy of Deflation. They both look to internal conditions, and not to the foreign exchanges, as the criterion for expanding or contracting credit; with this difference, however, that Mr. McKenna would look chiefly to the level of employment, whilst Mr. Goodenough would be more influenced by the stability of internal prices. "To sum up my views on the currency question," the latter says, "I feel that our aim should be to maintain as nearly as possible the existing equilibrium between currency and commodities. . . ." Neither of them, however, would be much disturbed by a moderate rise of prices, provided (in the case of Mr. McKenna) that the productive resources of the country had not yet reached the limit of their capacity, and (in the case of Mr. Goodenough) that the rise was due neither to the speculative withholding of commodities nor to British prices rising relatively to American prices. About our ultimate objective, Mr. McKenna does not speak; but there is nothing in his speech to suggest that he would not be in favour of pursuing permanently the policy, which he recommends for the present, of "steering a middle course between Inflation and Deflation," i.e. of aiming, like Mr. Goodenough, at a general stability of prices within certain limits, and of deliberately employing monetary policy to mitigate the evils of the credit cycle: "Ups and downs in trade we are bound to have, but wise monetary policy can always prevent the cyclical movement from going to extremes. The speculative excesses of an inflationary boom and the cruel impoverishment of a prolonged slump can both be avoided. They are not necessary evils to which we must submit as things without understandable or preventable causes." Mr. Goodenough, on the other hand, whilst desisting from the pursuit of the gold standard for the time being, continues the passage from his speech quoted above--". . . although always we should keep in mind our ultimate aim, which is a return

to a gold standard." Meanwhile, he puts his hopes on an inflationary movement in America just sufficient to bring sterling back to
its former parity with gold, without any disturbance to its present
parity with commodities.

What is the net result of these speeches? They strengthen
greatly the hands of the Currency Reformers who believe that the
stability of the internal price level and the damping down of the
credit cycle are desirable and attainable objects. They are also
reassuring, since they show that two of the most influential figures in the City have clearly in mind all the points of immediate
practical importance, and can be relied on to use their influence in
the right direction. Mr. McKenna and Mr. Goodenough are both
in sympathy with the above aims. Nor would it be fair to say that
the Spinsters are definitely opposed to these ideas. (There would
be just as much impropriety for them, just as much mental agility
required, to think one thing as to think another. Their simplicity
is quite impartial.) If they could be led gently by the hand beyond
their copy-book maxims of "looking facts firmly in the face" and
"economy and hard work," it might be found that they, too, had no
objection to a deliberate attempt to keep prices steady and trade on
an even keel, and that, whilst they feel at first the same distaste towards any proposal to "tamper" with "the natural course" of prices
as they might feel towards an attempt to settle the sex of a child
before birth, they are not really prepared to insist on their instinctive preference for having these matters settled by some method of
pure chance.

(ii) February 1925 Once more the Bank chairmen have held up
for our inspection their financial fashion-plates. The captions vary;
but the plates are mostly the same. The first displays marriage
with the gold standard as the most desired, the most urgent, the
most honourable, the most virtuous, the most prosperous, and the
most blessed of all possible states. The other is designed to remind
the intending bridegroom that matrimony means heavy burdens
from which he is now free; that it is for better, for worse; that it will
be for him to honour and obey; that the happy days, when he could
have the prices and the bank-rate which suited the housekeeping
of his bachelor establishment, will be over-though, of course, he
will be asked out more when he is married; that Miss G. happens
to be an American, so that in future the prices of grape-fruit and
pop-corn are likely to be more important to him than those of eggs
and bacon; and, in short, that he had better not be too precipitate.
Some of our chairmen were like him who, being asked whether he

believed that, when he was dead, he would enjoy perfect bliss eternally, replied that of course he did, but would rather not discuss such an unpleasant subject.

Like last year there are two distinct issues,-the abstract merits of the gold standard, and the date and the mode of our return to it. The first is a question about which, as Mr. McKenna justly said, "we are still in the stage of inquiry rather than of positive opinion, and there is no formulated body of doctrine generally regarded as orthodox." The supporters of Monetary Reform, of which I, after further study and reflection, am a more convinced adherent than before, as the most important and significant measure we can take to increase economic welfare, must expound their arguments more fully, more clearly, and more simply, before they can overwhelm the forces of old custom and general ignorance. This is not a battle which can be won or lost in a day. Those who think that it can be finally settled by a sharp hustle back to gold mistake the situation. That will be only the beginning. The issue will be determined, not by the official decisions of the coming year, but by the combined effects of the actual experience of what happens after that and the relative clearness and completeness of the arguments of the opposing parties. Readers of the works, for example, of the great Lord Overstone, will remember how many years it took, and what bitter and disastrous experiences, before the monetary reformers of a hundred years ago established the pre-war policy of bank-rate and bank-reserves (which, in its day, was a great advance), in the teeth of the opposition of the Bank of England.

The other issue is of practical and immediate importance. Last year it was a question of whether it was prudent to hasten matters by deliberate Deflation; this year it is a question of whether it is prudent to hasten matters by a removal of the embargo against the export of gold. This year, like last year, the bankers, faced with the practical problem, are a little nervous. I think that this nervousness is justified for the following reasons.

In common with many others, I have long held the opinion that monetary conditions in the United States were likely, sooner or later, to bring about a rising price level and an incipient boom; and also that it would be our right policy in such circumstances to employ the usual methods to curb our own price level and to prevent credit conditions here from following in the wake of those in America. The result of this policy, if it was successful, would be a gradual improvement of the sterling exchange; and it would not need a very violent boom in America to justify a rise of the sterling exchange at least as high as the pre-war parity. I have, therefore, maintained for two years past that a return of sterling, sooner or later, towards its pre-war parity would be both a desirable and a probable consequence of a sound monetary policy on the part of the Bank of England coupled with a less sound one on the part of the Federal Reserve Board.

What has actually happened? In the spring of 1923 boom conditions in the United States seemed to be developing; but largely through the action of the Federal Reserve Board, the movement was stopped. Since July 1924, however, there has been a strong and sustained upward movement, which--subject always to the policy of the Federal Reserve Board--is expected to go further. The earlier upward movement of American prices was duly followed by an improvement in sterling exchange; and the relapse by a relapse. Similarly, the movement of American prices during the past six months has been accompanied by the improvement in sterling exchange, which has caught the popular attention. As Mr. McKenna pointed out, sterling prices have been a little steadier than dollar prices, and this greater steadiness has involved, as its necessary counterpart, some unsteadiness in the exchange.

The movement of the past six months, however, has been complicated by abnormal factors. The improvement in sterling exchange is more than can be accounted for by our monetary policy. It is true that short-money rates have been maintained at an effective 1/2 per cent above those in New York, and that British prices have risen somewhat less than American prices. But it is generally agreed that these influences have not been strong enough to account for everything. The Board of Trade returns indicate that there has been a movement of funds on capital account in the past year (and most of it, probably, in the second half of the year) from New York to London of the order of magnitude of £100,000,000. This is due (in proportions difficult to calculate) to the return of foreign balances previously held in London, to American investment in Europe resulting from the greater confidence engendered by the Dawes Scheme coming on the top of an investment boom in Wall Street, and to speculative purchases of sterling in the expectation of its improving in value relatively to the dollar. This unprecedented movement introduces a precarious element into the situation;--we cannot expect that it will continue on the same scale, and it may, at any time, be partly reversed. We require an interval, therefore, to readjust our liabilities either by a recovery of exports relatively to imports or by establishing a rate of interest on permanent loans high enough to check the present (in my judgement excessive) flow of new foreign investment outwards. At present we are in danger of lending long (e.g. to Australia) what we have borrowed short from New York. The strength of our pre-war position lay in the fact that (through the bill market) we had lent large sums short, which we could call in. At the present time this position is partly, though perhaps only temporarily, reversed;--which, in itself, is one reason for caution.

What is going to happen next? There are two leading alternatives. It may be that the Federal Reserve Board will come to the conclusion that the incipient boom conditions in the United States are getting dangerous, and will take the position firmly in hand, just as they did two years ago. This, almost certainly, is what the Board ought to do. In this event, the situation would be back again very nearly where it was eighteen months ago, and we should be faced, as we were then, with the alternative of relatively steady sterling prices with the dollar exchange below parity, or of stern Deflation in the effort to keep exchange at parity. A premature announcement of the removal of the embargo on the free export of gold would commit us in advance to the latter alternative,--the alternative which we deliberately rejected two years ago. This is what the fanatics desire. But with our unemployment figures what they still are, it would not be wise.

The other alternative is that the Federal Reserve Board will allow matters to pursue their present course, in which event we may expect that dollar prices will advance a good deal further. During part of 1924 the Board's open-market policy was decidedly inflationary, and has been largely responsible for the sharp rise of prices already experienced. At the present moment their policy is more cautious; but there is no clear indication that they have any steady or considered policy. It may be that misplaced sympathy with our efforts to raise the sterling exchange will be a factor tending to postpone action on their part; and if they delay much longer, boom conditions may become definitely established. In this event we need have no difficulty in raising sterling to pre-war parity. A firm monetary policy, designed to check a sympathetic rise of sterling prices, ought, without any positive Deflation, to do the trick. But it does not follow that the embargo should, therefore, be removed. To link sterling prices to dollar prices at a moment in the credit cycle when the latter were near their peak as the result of a boom which we had not fully shared would ask for trouble. For when the American boom broke we should bear the full force of the slump. The conditions in which we can link sterling prices to dollar prices without immediate risk to our own welfare will only exist when the mean level of dollar prices appears to be stabilised at a somewhat higher level than in recent times.

The removal of the embargo amounts to an announcement that sterling is at parity with the dollar and will remain so. I suggest that the right order of procedure is to establish the fact first and to announce it afterwards, rather than to make the announcement first and to chance the fact. Thus the removal of the embargo should be the last stage in the restoration of pre-war conditions, not the first one. The only prudent announcement on the subject would be to the effect that the embargo will not be removed until after sterling has been at parity for some considerable time, and until all the fundamental adjustments consequent upon this have duly taken place. At the same time--if we want to return to parity--steps should be taken to achieve the fact by raising bank-rate and checking foreign issues. I--without attaching any importance whatever to a return to parity-believe that there is much to be said for these measures in the interests of the stabilisation of our own situation. I do not believe that a somewhat higher bank-rate would do any harm, in view of the present tendencies of the price level, to the volume of trade and employment, and that, in any case, the maintenance of our own equilibrium will soon require the support of a higher rate. Several of the bankers declared that they were in favour of removing the embargo, provided this did not involve a risk of raising the bank-rate. Unless this was merely a polite way of saying that they were not in favour of removing the embargo, I do not follow their analysis of the present situation.

It would be useless for me to attempt in the space at my disposal to give the reasons for wishing to maintain permanently a Managed Currency. The most important of them flow from my belief that fluctuations of trade and employment are at the same time the greatest and the most remediable of the economic diseases of modern society, that they are mainly diseases of our credit and banking system, and that it will be easier to apply the remedies if we retain the control of our currency in our own hands. But whilst avoiding these fundamental questions I may mention, in conclusion, one practical argument which is also connected with what I have said above.

A gold standard means, in practice, nothing but to have the

same price level and the same money rates (broadly speaking) as the United States. The whole object is to link rigidly the City and Wall Street. I beg the Chancellor of the Exchequer and the Governor of the Bank of England and the nameless others who settle our destiny in secret to reflect that this may be a dangerous proceeding.

The United States lives in a vast and unceasing crescendo. Wide fluctuations, which spell unemployment and misery for us, are swamped for them in the general upward movement. A country, the whole of whose economic activities are expanding, year in, year out, by several per cent per annum, cannot avoid, and at the same time can afford, temporary maladjustments. This was our own state during a considerable part of the nineteenth century. Our rate of progress was so great that stability in detail was neither possible nor essential. This is not our state now. Our rate of progress is slow at the best, and faults in our economic structure, which we could afford to overlook whilst we were racing forward and which the United States can still afford to overlook, are now fatal. The slump of 1921 was even more violent in the United States than here, but by the end of 1922 recovery was practically complete. We still, in 1925, drag on with a million unemployed. The United States may suffer industrial and financial tempests in the years to come, and they will scarcely matter to her; but we, if we share them, may almost drown.

And there is a further consideration. Before the war we had lent great sums to the whole world which we could call in at short notice; our American investments made us the creditors of the United States; we had a surplus available for foreign investment far greater than that of any other country; with no Federal Reserve system, American banking was weak and disorganised. We, in fact, were the predominant partner in the Gold Standard Alliance. But those who think that a return to the gold standard means a return to these conditions are fools and blind. We are now the debtors of the United States. Their foreign investments last year were double ours, and their true net balance available for such investment was probably ten times ours. They hold six times as much gold as we do. The mere increase in the deposits of the banks of the Federal Reserve System in the past year has been not far short of half our total deposits. A movement of gold or of short credits either way between London and New York, which is only a ripple for them, will be an Atlantic roller for us. A change of fashion on the part of American bankers and investors towards foreign loans, of but little consequence to them, may shake us. If gold and short credits and foreign bonds can flow without restriction or risk of loss backwards and forwards across the Atlantic, fluctuations of given magnitude will produce on us effects altogether disproportionate to the effects on them. It suits the United States that we should return to gold, and they will be ready to oblige us in the early stages. But it would be a mistake to believe that in the long run they will, or ought to, manage their affairs to suit our convenience.

What solid advantages will there be to set against these risks? I do not know. Our bankers speak of "psychological" advantages. But it will be poor consolation that "nine people out of ten" expected advantages, if none in fact arrive.

That our Bank chairmen should have nothing better to cry than "Back to 1914," and that they should believe that this represents the best attainable, is not satisfactory. The majority of those who are studying the matter are becoming agreed that faults in our credit system are at least partly responsible for the confusions which result in the paradox of unemployment amidst dearth. The "Big Five" have vast responsibilities towards the public. But they are so huge and, in some ways, so vulnerable, that there is a great temptation to them to cling to maxims, conventions, and routine; and when their chairmen debate fundamental economic problems, they are most of them on ground with which they are unfamiliar. It is doubtful, nevertheless, whether too much conservatism on these matters and too little of the spirit of inquiry will redound, in the long run, to their peace or security. Individualistic Capitalism in England has come to the point when it can no longer depend on the momentum of mere expansion; and it must apply itself to the scientific task of improving the structure of its economic machine.

(iii) February 1927   The voices of our old friends the Bank chairmen herald the approach of spring. They have spoken this year--with the exception of Sir Harry Goschen, who sees "no reason to be downhearted," and, as in former years, cannot "remember a time when, throughout the industries of the country, there was such a feeling of expectation and, indeed, optimism"--in somewhat chastened tones. Mr. Beaumont Pease has done a useful service by publishing some important figures analysing the business of Lloyds Bank, which inaugurate a new policy of giving information instead of withholding it. Mr. Walter Leaf made some sound observations on the tendency of business towards amalgamation and, at the same time, of shareholdings towards diffusion, and on the necessity of the State taking some responsibility for guiding this inevitable evolution along the right lines. But none of them except Mr. McKenna--and on one point of detail Mr. Goodenough--had anything to say about the future of monetary policy. So leaving Sir Harry Goschen to chirrup in the bushes, let us join Mr. McKenna in an attempt to dig a few inches below the surface of the soil.

Mr. McKenna reminded us of the overwhelming prosperity of the United States as against our own depression during the past five years. He declared that in the "wide divergence between English and American monetary policy, we have at least a partial explanation of the phenomenon." He found the measure of this divergence of policy in the expansion and contraction respectively of the bank deposits in the two countries, namely, as follows:--

(Volume of Deposits in 1922 = 100)

	United States.	Great Britain.
1922	100	100
1923	107	94
1924	115	94
1925	127	93
1926	131	93

He explained in some detail what is fundamental, yet too little understood, that the volume of bank deposits in Great Britain does not depend, except within narrow limits, on the depositors or on the Big Five, but on the policy of the Bank of England. And he concluded that we can scarcely expect a materially increased scale of production and employment in this country until the Bank of England revises its policy.

Whilst I do not agree with Mr. McKenna in every detail of his argument, I am certain that the broad lines of his diagnosis are correct. He has done a service by his persistent efforts to educate the public and his colleagues to the vital importance of some fundamental principles of monetary policy of which the truth is as certain as the day, but to which the City is blind as night.

Nevertheless, he has on this occasion shirked, in my opinion, half the problem. How far and subject to what conditions is a reversal of the Bank of England's policy consistent with maintaining the gold standard? Is the Bank of England in its new-forged golden fetters as free an agent as Mr. McKenna's policy requires?

What matters is, not some abstraction called the general level of prices, but the relationships between the various price levels which measure the value of our money for different purposes. Prosperity, in so far as it is governed by monetary factors, depends on these various price levels being properly adjusted to one another. Unemployment and trade depression in Great Britain have been due to a rupture of the previous equilibrium between the sterling price level of articles of international commerce and the internal value of sterling for the purposes on which the average Englishman spends his money-income. Moreover, in proportion as we are successful in moving towards the new equilibrium of lower sterling prices all round, we increase the burden of the National Debt and aggravate the problem of the Budget. If the Bank of England and the Treasury were to succeed in reducing the sheltered price level to its former equilibrium with the unsheltered price level, they would ipso facto have increased the real burden of the National Debt by about £1,000,000,000 as compared with two years ago.

Now Mr. McKenna seems to assume that the disequilibrium which admittedly existed two years ago has since disappeared. "Today," he tells us, "such questions have only historic significance." But the evidence does not support this view. So far from having disappeared, the disparity between the price levels is actually greater than it was two years ago.

How, then, have we lived in the meantime? The real ground of the optimism on the lips of the Bank chairmen is to be found, I think, in the fact that there has been no strain on our resources which we have not been able to meet. Is this so great a paradox as it appears? Or so comforting?

We have undoubtedly balanced the difference in our account partly by drawing on the large margin of safety which we used to possess, and partly, during the Coal Strike, by increasing our short-loan indebtedness to the rest of the world. Before the war we probably had a favourable balance on international account, apart from capital transactions, of something like £300,000,000 per annum measured in sterling at its present value. The war and the fall in the value of fixed money payments may have reduced this annual surplus to about £225,000,000; i.e. this is what our surplus would be to-day if our export trades were as flourishing as in 1913. Let us suppose that as the result of our relatively high level of internal prices we have lost £200,000,000 of exports gross, namely, about a quarter of the whole, or (say) £150,000,000 net, i.e. after deducting that part of the lost exports which would have consisted of imported raw material, and that we consequently have unemployed (say) 1,000,000 men who would otherwise, directly or indirectly, have been producing these exports. All these figures are, of course, very rough illustrations of what is reasonably probable, not scientific estimates of statistical facts.

How does our international balance-sheet then stand? We still have a surplus of £75,000,000 per annum. Provided, therefore, we do not invest abroad more than this sum, we are in equilibrium. We can continue permanently with our higher level of sheltered prices, with a quarter of our foreign trade lost, and with a million men unemployed, but also with some surplus still left for the City of London to invest abroad, and, as the crown of all, the gold standard entirely unthreatened. The gold standard may have reduced the national wealth, as compared with an alternative monetary policy, by £150,000,000 a year. Never mind! "Our economic reserves of strength," as Mr. Leaf puts it, "are far greater than any of us supposed.""We are tougher than we thought," in the words of the Chancellor of the Exchequer. In short, we can afford it!The special losses of the Coal Strike period are not allowed for in the above. They seem to have amounted to round £100,000,000, and to have been met by increasing our short-loan indebtedness, partly with the aid of the usual time-lag in the settlement of adverse balances, and partly by a relatively attractive rate of discount drawing foreign balances to London.In determining the future of our National Policy, we have three alternatives before us:--

(1) We can seek at all costs to restore the pre-war equilibrium of large exports and large foreign investments. The return to gold has rendered this impossible without an all-round attack on wages, such as the Prime Minister has repudiated, or a considerable rise of external gold prices which we wait for in vain.

(2) We can continue indefinitely in the pseudoequilibrium described above with trade depressed and a million unemployed. This pseudo-equilibrium has been the result, though probably not the intention, of the Bank of England's policy up to date. I see no convincing reason why it should not be continued for some time yet. Mr. Norman may have an awkward period ahead owing to the delayed results of the Coal Strike. But even if the worst comes, a partial reimposition of the embargo on foreign investments might be enough.

(3) The third course consists in accepting the loss of export trade and a corresponding reduction of foreign investment and in diverting the labour previously employed in the former and the savings previously absorbed in the latter to the task of improving the efficiency of production and the standard of life at home. If the return to gold has the effect in the end of bringing about this result, it may have been a blessing in disguise. For this course has manifold advantages which I must not stop to enumerate at the end of a long article. I believe that a further improvement in the standard of life of the masses is dependent on our taking it.

This brings us back to Mr. McKenna. I assume that his object in advocating an expansion of credit is to absorb the unemployed in a general crescendo of home industry and indirectly to help a little the export industries also by the economies of full-scale production. In short, he favours the third course. For he can hardly hope to lower the sheltered price level or to effect an adequate economy in manufacturing costs by expanding credit. As on some previous occasions, Mr. McKenna has done less than justice to his own ideas by pretending to greater confidence in the effects of the return to gold than he really has.

Now, within the limitations of the gold standard, this is a very difficult policy, and--in view of the £100,000,000 which we may still owe on account of the Coal Strike--possibly a dangerous one. If Mr. McKenna were Governor of the Bank of England with a free hand, I believe it to be probable that he could greatly reduce the numbers of the unemployed whilst maintaining gold parity. But can we expect Mr. Norman to do so, moving within the limitations of his own mentality?

5. THE ECONOMIC CONSEQUENCES OF MR. CHURCHILL (1925)   (i) The Misleading of Mr. Churchill   The policy of improving the foreign-exchange value of sterling up to its pre-war value in gold from being about 10 per cent below it, means that,

whenever we sell anything abroad, either the foreign buyer has to pay 10 per cent more in his money or we have to accept 10 per cent less in our money. That is to say, we have to reduce our sterling prices, for coal or iron or shipping freights or whatever it may be, by 10 per cent in order to be on a competitive level, unless prices rise elsewhere. Thus the policy of improving the exchange by 10 per cent involves a reduction of 10 per cent in the sterling receipts of our export industries.

Now, if these industries found that their expenses for wages and for transport and for rates and for everything else were falling 10 per cent at the same time, they could afford to cut their prices and would be no worse off than before. But, of course, this does not happen. Since they use, and their employees consume, all kinds of articles produced at home, it is impossible for them to cut their prices 10 per cent, unless wages and expenses in home industries generally have fallen 10 per cent. Meanwhile the weaker export industries are reduced to a bankrupt condition. Failing a fall in the value of gold itself, nothing can retrieve their position except a general fall of all internal prices and wages. Thus Mr. Churchill's policy of improving the exchange by 10 per cent was, sooner or later, a policy of reducing every one's wages by 2s. in the £. He who wills the end wills the means. What now faces the Government is the ticklish task of carrying out their own dangerous and unnecessary decision.

The movement away from equilibrium began in October last (1924) and has proceeded, step by step, with the improvement of the exchange --brought about first by the anticipation, and then by the fact, of the restoration of gold, and not by an improvement in the intrinsic value of sterling. The President of the Board of Trade has asserted in the House of Commons that the effect of the restoration of the gold standard upon our export trade has been "all to the good." The Chancellor of the Exchequer has expressed the opinion that the return to the gold standard is no more responsible for the condition of affairs in the coal industry than is the Gulf Stream. These statements are of the feather-brained order. It is open to Ministers to argue that the restoration of gold is worth the sacrifice and that the sacrifice is temporary. They can also say, with truth, that the industries which are feeling the wind most have private troubles of their own. When a general cause operates, those which are weak for other reasons are toppled over. But because an epidemic of influenza carries off only those who have weak hearts, it is not permissible to say that the influenza is "all to the good," or that it has no more to do with the mortality than the Gulf Stream has. The effect has been the more severe because we were not free from trouble a year ago. Whilst, at that date, sterling wages and sterling cost of living were in conformity with values in the United States, they were already too high compared with those in some European countries. It was also probable that certain of our export industries were overstocked both with plant and with labour, and that some transference of capital and of men into home industries was desirable and, in the long run, even inevitable. Thus we already had an awkward problem; and one of the arguments against raising the international value of sterling was the fact that it greatly aggravated, instead of mitigating, an existing disparity between internal and external values, and that, by committing us to a period of Deflation, it necessarily postponed active measures of capital expansion at home, such as might facilitate the transference of labour into the home trades. British wages, measured in gold, are now 15 per cent higher than they were a year ago. The gold cost of living in England is now so high compared with what it is in Belgium, France, Italy, and Germany that the workers in those countries can accept a gold wage 30 per cent lower than what our workers receive without suffering at all in the amount of their real wages. What wonder that our export trades are in trouble!

Our export industries are suffering because they are the first to be asked to accept the 10 per cent reduction. If every one was accepting a similar reduction at the same time, the cost of living would fall, so that the lower money wage would represent nearly the same real wage as before. But, in fact, there is no machinery for effecting a simultaneous reduction. Deliberately to raise the value of sterling money in England means, therefore, engaging in a struggle with each separate group in turn, with no prospect that the final result will be fair, and no guarantee that the stronger groups will not gain at the expense of the weaker.

The working classes cannot be expected to understand, better than Cabinet Ministers, what is happening. Those who are attacked first are faced with a depression of their standard of life, because the cost of living will not fall until all the others have been successfully attacked too; and, therefore, they are justified in defending themselves. Nor can the classes which are first subjected to a reduction of money wages be guaranteed that this will be compensated later by a corresponding fall in the cost of living, and will not accrue to the benefit of some other class. Therefore they are bound to resist so long as they can; and it must be war, until those who are economically weakest are beaten to the ground.

This state of affairs is not an inevitable consequence of a decreased capacity to produce wealth. I see no reason why, with good management, real wages need be reduced on the average. It is the consequence of a misguided monetary policy.

These arguments are not arguments against the gold standard as such. That is a separate discussion which I shall not touch here. They are arguments against having restored gold in conditions which required a substantial readjustment of all our money values. If Mr. Churchill had restored gold by fixing the parity lower than the pre-war figure, or if he had waited until our money values were adjusted to the pre-war parity, then these particular arguments would have no force. But in doing what he did in the actual circumstances of last spring, he was just asking for trouble. For he was committing himself to force down money wages and all money values, without any idea how it was to be done. Why did he do such a silly thing?

Partly, perhaps, because he has no instinctive judgement to prevent him from making mistakes; partly because, lacking this instinctive judgement, he was deafened by the clamorous voices of conventional finance; and, most of all, because he was gravely misled by his experts.

His experts made, I think, two serious mistakes. In the first place, I suspect that they miscalculated the degree of the maladjustment of money values which would result from restoring sterling to its pre-war gold parity, because they attended to index numbers of prices which were irrelevant or inappropriate to the matter in hand. If you want to know whether sterling values are adjusting themselves to an improvement in the exchange, it is useless to consider, for example, the price of raw cotton in Liverpool. This must adjust itself to a movement of the exchange, because, in the case of an imported raw material, the parity of international values is necessarily maintained almost hour by hour. But it is not sensible to argue from this that the money wages of dockers or of charwomen and the cost of postage or of travelling by train also adjust themselves hour by hour in accordance with the foreign exchanges. Yet this, I fancy, is what the Treasury did. They compared the usual wholesale index numbers here and in America, and--since these are made up to the extent of at least two-thirds from the raw materials of international commerce, the prices of which necessarily adjust themselves to the exchanges--the true disparity of internal prices was watered down to a fraction of its true value. This led them to think that the gap to be bridged was perhaps 2 or 3 per cent, instead of the true figure of 10 or 12 per cent, which was the indication given by the index numbers of the cost of living, of the level of wages, and of the prices of our manufactured exports--which indexes are a much better rough-and-ready guide for this purpose, particularly if they agree with one another, than are the index numbers of wholesale prices.

But I think that Mr. Churchill's experts also misunderstood and underrated the technical difficulty of bringing about a general reduction of internal money values. When we raise the value of sterling by 10 per cent we transfer about £1,000,000,000 into the pockets of the rentiers out of the pockets of the rest of us, and we increase the real burden of the National Debt by some £750,000,000 (thus wiping out the benefit of all our laborious contributions to the Sinking Fund since the war). This, which is bad enough, is inevitable. But there would be no other bad consequences if only there was some way of bringing about a simultaneous reduction of 10 per cent in all other money payments; when the process was complete we should each of us have nearly the same real income as before. I think that the minds of his advisers still dwelt in the imaginary academic world, peopled by City editors, members of Cunliffe and Currency Committeeset hoc genusomne omne, where the necessary adjustments follow "automatically" from a "sound" policy by the Bank of England.

The theory is that depression in the export industries, which are admittedly hit first, coupled if necessary with dear money and credit restriction, diffuse themselves evenly and fairly rapidly throughout the whole community. But the professors of this theory do not tell us in plain language how the diffusion takes place.

Mr. Churchill asked the Treasury Committee on the Currency to advise him on these matters. He declared in his Budget speech that their report "contains a reasoned marshalling of the arguments which have convinced His Majesty's Government." Their arguments--if their vague and jejune meditations can be called such--are there for any one to read. What they ought to have said, but did not say, can be expressed as follows:--

"Money wages, the cost of living, and the prices which we are asking for our exports have not adjusted themselves to the improvement in the exchange, which the expectation of your restoring the gold standard, in accordance with your repeated declarations, has already brought about. They are about 10 per cent too high. If, therefore, you fix the exchange at this gold parity, you must either gamble on a rise in gold prices abroad, which will induce foreigners to pay a higher gold price for our exports, or you are committing yourself to a policy of forcing down money wages and the cost of living to the necessary extent.

"We must warn you that this latter policy is not easy. It is certain to involve unemployment and industrial disputes. If, as some people think, real wages were already too high a year ago, that is all the worse, because the amount of the necessary wage reductions in terms of money will be all the greater.

"The gamble on a rise in gold prices abroad may quite likely succeed. But it is by no means certain, and you must be prepared for the other contingency. If you think that the advantages of the gold standard are so significant and so urgent that you are prepared to risk great unpopularity and to take stern administrative action in order to secure them, the course of events will probably be as follows:

"To begin with, there will be great depression in the export industries. This in itself will be helpful, since it will produce an atmosphere favourable to the reduction of wages. The cost of living will fall somewhat. This will be helpful too, because it will give you a good argument in favour of reducing wages. Nevertheless, the cost of living will not fall sufficiently, and, consequently, the export industries will not be able to reduce their prices sufficiently until wages have fallen in the sheltered industries. Now wages will not fall in the sheltered industries merely because there is unemployment in the unsheltered industries, therefore you will have to see to it that there is unemployment in the sheltered industries also. The way to do this will be by credit restriction. By means of the restriction of credit by the Bank of England you can deliberately intensify unemployment to any required degree until wages do fall. When the process is complete the cost of living will have fallen too, and we shall then be, with luck, just where we were before we started.

"We ought to warn you, though perhaps this is going a little outside our proper sphere, that it will not be safe politically to admit that you are intensifying unemployment deliberately in order to reduce wages. Thus you will have to ascribe what is happening to every conceivable cause except the true one. We estimate that about two years may elapse before it will be safe for you to utter in public one single word of truth. By that time you will either be out of office or the adjustment, somehow or other, will have been carried through."

(ii) The Balance of Trade and the Bank of England The effect of a high exchange is to diminish the sterling prices both of imports and of exports. The result is both to encourage imports and to discourage exports, thus turning the balance of trade against us. It is at this stage that the Bank of England becomes interested; for if nothing was done we should have to pay the adverse balance in gold. The Bank of England has applied, accordingly, two effective remedies.

The first remedy is to put obstacles in the way of our usual lending abroad by means of an embargo on foreign loans and, recently, on Colonial loans also; and the second remedy is to encourage the United States to lend us money by maintaining the unprecedented situation of a bill rate 1 per cent higher in London than in New York.

The efficacy of these two methods for balancing our account is beyond doubt--I believe that they might remain efficacious for a considerable length of time. For we start with a wide margin of strength. Before the war our capacity to lend abroad was, according to the Board of Trade, about £181,000,000, equivalent to £280,000,000 at the present price level; and even in 1923 the Board of Trade estimated our net surplus at £102,000,000. Since new foreign investments bring in no immediate return, it follows that we can reduce our exports by £100,000,000 a year, without any risk of insolvency, provided we reduce our foreign investments by the same amount. So far as the maintenance of the gold standard is concerned, it is a matter of indifference whether we have £100,000,000 worth of foreign investment or £100,000,000 worth of unemployment. If those who used to produce exports lose their job, nevertheless, our financial equilibrium remains perfect, and the Governor of the Bank of England runs no risk of losing gold, provided that the loans, which were formerly paid over in the shape of those exports, are curtailed to an equal extent. Moreover, our credit as a borrower is still very good. By paying a sufficiently high rate of interest, we can not only meet any deficit but the Governor can borrow, in addition, whatever quantity of gold it may amuse him to publish in his weekly return.

The President of the Board of Trade calculates that, during the year ended last May, it is probable that there was no actual deficit on our trade account, which was about square. If this is correct, there must be a substantial deficit now. In addition, the embargo on foreign investment is only partially successful. It cannot hold back all types of foreign issues and it cannot prevent British investors from purchasing securities direct from New York. It is here, therefore, that the Bank of England's other remedy comes in. By maintaining discount rates in London at a sufficient margin above discount rates in New York, it can induce the New York money market to lend a sufficient sum to the London money market to balance both our trade deficit and the foreign investments which British investors are still buying in spite of the embargo. Besides, when once we have offered high rates of interest to attract funds from the New York short-loan market, we have to continue them, even though we have no need to increase our borrowings, in order to retain what we have already borrowed.

Nevertheless, the policy of maintaining money rates in London at a level which will attract and retain loans from New York does not really differ in any important respect from the French policy, which we have so much condemned, of supporting the exchange with the help of loans from Messrs. J. P. Morgan. Our policy would only differ from the French policy if the high rate of discount was not only intended to attract American money, but was also part of a policy for restricting credit at home. This is the aspect to which we must now attend.

To pay for unemployment by changing over from being a lending country to being a borrowing country is admittedly a disastrous course, and I do not doubt that the authorities of the Bank of England share this view. They dislike the embargo on foreign issues, and they dislike having to attract short-loan money from New York. They may do these things to gain a breathing space; but, if they are to live up to their own principles, they must use the breathing space to effect what are euphemistically called "the fundamental adjustments." With this object in view there is only one step which lies within their power--namely, to restrict credit. This, in the circumstances, is the orthodox policy of the gold party; the adverse trade balance indicates that our prices are too high, and the way to bring them down is by dear money and the restriction of credit. When this medicine has done its work, there will no longer be any need to restrict foreign loans or to borrow abroad.

Now what does this mean in plain language? Our problem is to reduce money wages and, through them, the cost of living, with the idea that, when the circle is complete, real wages will be as high, or nearly as high, as before. By what modus operandi does credit restriction attain this result?

In no other way than by the deliberate intensification of unemployment. The object of credit restriction, in such a case, is to withdraw from employers the financial means to employ labour at the existing level of prices and wages. The policy can only attain its end by intensifying unemployment without limit, until the workers are ready to accept the necessary reduction of money wages under the pressure of hard facts.

This is the so-called "sound" policy, which is demanded as a result of the rash act of pegging sterling at a gold value, which it did not-measured in its purchasing power over British labour--possess as yet. It is a policy, nevertheless, from which any humane or judicious person must shrink. So far as I can judge, the Governor of the Bank of England shrinks from it. But what is he to do, swimming, with his boat burnt, between the devil and the deep sea? At present, it appears, he compromises. He applies the "sound" policy half-heartedly; he avoids calling things by their right names; and he hopes--this is his best chance--that something will turn up.

The Bank of England works with so much secrecy and so much concealment of important statistics that it is never easy to state with precision what it is doing. The credit restriction already in force has been effected in several ways which are partly independent. First, there is the embargo on new issues which probably retards the normal rate of the circulation of money; then in March the bank-rate was raised; more recently market-rate was worked up nearer to bank-rate; lastly--and far the most important of all--the Bank has manþuvred its assets and liabilities in such a way as to reduce the amount of cash available to the Clearing Banks as a basis for credit. This last is the essential instrument of credit restriction. Failing direct information, the best reflection of the amount of this restriction is to be found in the deposits of the Clearing Banks. The tendency of these to fall indicates some significant degree of restriction. Owing, however, to seasonal fluctuations and to the artificial character of the endJune returns, it is not yet possible to estimate with accuracy how much restriction has taken place in the last three months. So far as one can judge, the amount of direct restriction is not yet considerable. But no one can say how much more restriction may become necessary if we continue on our present lines.

Nevertheless, even these limited measures are responsible, in my opinion, for an important part of the recent intensification of unemployment. Credit restriction is an incredibly powerful instrument, and even a little of it goes a long way--especially in circumstances where the opposite course is called for. The policy of deliberately intensifying unemployment with a view to forcing wage reductions is already partly in force, and the tragedy of our situation lies in the fact that, from the misguided standpoint which has been officially adopted, this course is theoretically justifiable. No section of labour will readily accept lower wages merely in response to sentimental speeches, however genuine, by Mr. Baldwin. We are depending for the reduction of wages on the pressure of unemployment and of strikes and lock-outs; and in order to make sure of this result we are deliberately intensifying the unemployment.

The Bank of England is compelled to curtail credit by all the rules of the gold standard game. It is acting conscientiously and "soundly" in doing so. But this does not alter the fact that to keep a tight hold on credit--and no one will deny that the Bank is doing that--necessarily involves intensifying unemployment in the present circumstances of this country. What we need to restore prosperity to-day is an easy credit policy. We want to encourage business men to enter on new enterprises, not, as we are doing, to discourage them. Deflation does not reduce wages "automatically." It reduces them by causing unemployment. The proper object of dear money is to check an incipient boom. Woe to those whose faith leads them to use it to aggravate a depression!

I should pick out coal as being above all others a victim of our monetary policy. On the other hand, it is certainly true that the reason why the Coal Industry presents so dismal a picture to the eye is because it has other troubles which have weakened its power of resistance and have left it no margin of strength with which to support a new misfortune.

In these circumstances the colliery owners propose that the gap should be bridged by a reduction of wages, irrespective of a reduction in the cost of living--that is to say, by a lowering in the standard of life of the miners. They are to make this sacrifice to meet circumstances for which they are in no way responsible and over which they have no control.

It is a grave criticism of our way of managing our economic affairs that this should seem to any one to be a reasonable proposal; though it is equally unreasonable that the colliery owner should suffer the loss, except on the principle that it is the capitalist who bears the risk. If miners were free to transfer themselves to other industries, if a collier out of work or underpaid could offer himself as a baker, a bricklayer, or a railway porter at a lower wage than is now current in these industries, it would be another matter. But notoriously they are not so free. Like other victims of economic transition in past times, the miners are to be offered the choice between starvation and submission, the fruits of their submission to accrue to the benefit of other classes. But in view of the disappearance of an effective mobility of labour and of a competitive wage level between different industries, I am not sure that they are not worse placed in some ways than their grandfathers were.

Why should coal miners suffer a lower standard of life than other classes of labour? They may be lazy, good-for-nothing fellows who do not work so hard or so long as they should. But is there any evidence that they are more lazy or more good-for-nothing than other people?

On grounds of social justice, no case can be made out for reducing the wages of the miners. They are the victims of the economic Juggernaut. They represent in the flesh the "fundamental adjustments" engineered by the Treasury and the Bank of England to satisfy the impatience of the City fathers to bridge the "moderate gap" between $4.40 and $4.86. They (and others to follow) are the "moderate sacrifice" still necessary to ensure the stability of the gold standard. The plight of the coal miners is the first, but not--unless we are very lucky--the last, of the Economic Consequences of Mr. Churchill.

The truth is that we stand mid-way between two theories of economic society. The one theory maintains that wages should be fixed by reference to what is "fair" and "reasonable" as between classes. The other theory--the theory of the economic Juggernaut--is that wages should be settled by economic pressure, otherwise called "hard facts," and that our vast machine should crash along, with regard only to its equilibrium as a whole, and without attention to the chance consequences of the journey to individual groups.

The gold standard, with its dependence on pure chance, its faith in "automatic adjustments," and its general regardlessness of social detail, is an essential emblem and idol of those who sit in the top tier of the machine. I think that they are immensely rash in their regardlessness, in their vague optimism and comfortable belief that nothing really serious ever happens. Nine times out of ten, nothing really serious does happen--merely a little distress to individuals or to groups. But we run a risk of the tenth time (and are stupid into the bargain) if we continue to apply the principles of an Economics which was worked out on the hypotheses of laissez-faire and free competition to a society which is rapidly abandoning these hypotheses.

(iii) Is there a Remedy? The monetary policy announced in the Budget (of 1925) being the real source of our industrial troubles, it is impossible to recommend any truly satisfactory course except its reversal. Nevertheless, amongst the alternatives still open to this Government, some courses are better than others.

One course is to pursue the so-called "sound" policy vigorously, with the object of bringing about "the fundamental adjustments" in the orthodox way by further restricting credit and raising the bank-rate in the autumn if necessary, thus intensifying unemployment and using every other weapon in our hands to force down money wages, trusting in the belief that, when the process is finally complete, the cost of living will have fallen also, thus restoring average real wages to their former level. If this policy can be carried through it will be, in a sense, successful, though it will leave much injustice behind it on account of the inequality of the changes it will effect, the stronger groups gaining at the expense of the weaker. For the method of economic pressure, since it bears most hardly on the weaker industries, where wages are already relatively low, tends to increase the existing disparities between the wages of different industrial groups.

The question is how far public opinion will allow such a policy to go. It would be politically impossible for the Government to admit that it was deliberately intensifying unemployment, even though the members of the Currency Committee were to supply them with an argument for it. On the other hand, it is possible for Deflation to produce its effects without being recognised. Deflation, once started ever so little, is cumulative in its progress. If pessimism becomes generally prevalent in the business world, the slower circulation of money resulting from this can carry Deflation a long way further, without the Bank having either to raise the bank-rate or to reduce its deposits. And since the public always understands particular causes better than general causes, the depression will be attributed to the industrial disputes which will accompany it, to the Dawes Scheme, to China, to the inevitable consequences of the Great War, to tariffs, to high taxation, to anything in the world except the general monetary policy which has set the whole thing going.

Moreover, this course need not be pursued in a clear-cut way. A furtive restriction of credit by the Bank of England can be coupled with vague cogitations on the part of Mr. Baldwin (who has succeeded to the position in our affections formerly occupied by Queen Victoria) as to whether social benevolence does not require him to neutralise the effects of this by a series of illogical subsidies. Queen Baldwin's good heart will enable us to keep our tempers, whilst the serious work goes on behind the scenes. The Budgetary position will render it impossible for the subsidies to be big enough to make any real difference. And in the end, unless there is a social upheaval, "the fundamental adjustments" will duly take place.

Some people may contemplate this forecast with equanimity. I do not. It involves a great loss of social income whilst it is going on, and will leave behind much social injustice when it is finished. The best, indeed the only, hope lies in the possibility that in this world, where so little can be foreseen, something may turn up --which leads me to my alternative suggestions. Could we not help something to turn up?

There are just two features of the situation which are capable of being turned to our advantage. The first is financial--if the value of gold would fall in the outside world, that would render unnecessary any important change in the level of wages here. The second is industrial-if the cost of living would fall first, our consciences would be clear in asking Labour to accept a lower money wage, since it would then be evident that the reduction was not part of a plot to reduce real wages.

When the return to the gold standard was first announced, many authorities agreed that we were gambling on rising prices in the United States. The rise has not taken place, so far. 1 Moreover, the policy of the Bank of England has been calculated to steady prices in the United States rather than to raise them. The fact that American banks can lend their funds in London at a high rate of interest tends to keep money rates in New York higher than they would be otherwise, and to draw to London, instead of to New York, the oddments of surplus gold in the world markets. Thus our policy has been to relieve New York of the pressure of cheap money and additional gold which would tend otherwise to force their prices upwards. The abnormal difference between money rates in London and New York is preventing the gold standard from working even according to its own principles. According to orthodox doctrine, when prices are too high in A as compared with B, gold flows out from A and into B, thus lowering prices in A and raising them in B, so that an upward movement in B's prices meets half-way the downward movement in A's.

At present the policy of the Bank of England prevents this from happening. I suggest, therefore, that they should reverse this policy. Let them reduce the bank-rate, and cease to restrict credit. If, as a result of this, the "bad" American money, which is now a menace to the London Money Market, begins to flow back again, let us pay it off in gold or, if necessary, by using the dollar credits which the Treasury and the Bank of England have arranged in New York. It would be better to pay in gold, because it would be cheaper and because the flow of actual gold would have more effect on the American price level. If we modified the rules which now render useless three-quarters of our stock of gold, we could see with equanimity a loss of £60,000,000 or £70,000,000 in gold-which would make a great difference to conditions elsewhere. There is no object in paying 4 1/2 per cent interest on floating American balances which can leave us at any moment, in order to use these balances to buy and hold idle and immobilised gold.

Gold could not flow out on this scale, unless at the same time the Bank of England was abandoning the restriction of credit and was replacing the gold by some other asset, e.g.

Treasury Bills. That is to say, the Bank would have to abandon the attempt to bring about the fundamental adjustments by the methods of economic pressure and the deliberate intensification of unemployment. Therefore, taken by itself, this policy might be open to the criticism that it was staking too much on the expectation of higher prices in America.

To meet this, I suggest that Mr. Baldwin should face the facts frankly and sincerely, in collaboration with the Trade Union leaders, on the following lines.

So long as members of the Cabinet continue to pretend that the present movement to reduce wages has nothing to do with the value of money, it is natural that the working classes should take it as a concerted attack on real wages. If the Chancellor of the Exchequer is right in his view that his monetary policy has had no more to do with the case than the Gulf Stream, then it follows that the present agitations to lower wages are simply a campaign against the standard of life of the working classes. It is only when the Government have admitted the truth of the diagnosis set forth in these chapters that they are in a position to invite the collaboration of the Trade Union leaders on fair and reasonable terms.

As soon as the Government admit that the problem is primarily a monetary one, then they can say to Labour: "This is not an attack on real wages. We have raised the value of sterling 10 per cent. This means that money wages must fall 10 per cent. But it also means, when the adjustment is complete, that the cost of living will fall about 10 per cent. In this case there will have been no serious fall in real wages. Now there are two alternative ways of bringing about the reduction of money wages. One way is to apply economic pressure and to intensify unemployment by credit restriction until wages are forced down. This is a hateful and disastrous way, because of its unequal effects on the stronger and on the weaker groups, and because of the economic and social waste whilst it is in progress. The other way is to effect a uniform reduction of wages by agreement, on the understanding that this shall not mean in the long run any fall in average real wages below what they were in the first quarter of this year. The practical difficulty is that money wages and the cost of living are interlocked. The cost of living cannot fall until after money wages have fallen. Money wages must fall first in order to allow the cost of living to fall. Can we not agree, therefore, to have a uniform initial reduction of money wages throughout the whole range of employment, including Government and Municipal employment, of (say) 5 per cent, which reduction shall not hold good unless, after an interval, it has been compensated by a fall in the cost of living?"

If Mr. Baldwin were to make this proposal the Trade Union leaders would probably ask him at once what he intended to do about money payments other than wages--rents, profits, and interest. As regards rents and profits, he can reply that these are not fixed in terms of money, and will therefore fall, when measured in money, step by step with prices. The worst of this reply is that rents and profits, like wages, are sticky and may not fall quick enough to help the transition as much as they should. As regards the interest on bonds, however, and particularly the interest on the National Debt, he has no answer at all. For it is of the essence of any policy to lower prices that it benefits the receivers of interest at the expense of the rest of the community; this consequence of deflation is deeply embedded in our system of money contract. On the whole, I do not see how Labour's objection can be met, except by the rough-and-ready expedient of levying an additional income-tax of 1S. in the £ on all income other than from employments, which should continue until real wages had recovered to their previous level.

If the proposal to effect a voluntary all-round reduction of wages, whilst sound in principle, is felt to be too difficult to achieve in practice, then, for my part, I should be inclined to stake everything on an attempt to raise prices in the outside world--that is on a reversal of the present policy of the Bank of England. This, I understand from their July Monthly Review, is also the recommendation of the high authorities of the Midland Bank.

That there should be grave difficulties in all these suggestions is inevitable. Any plan, such as the Government has adopted, for deliberately altering the value of money, must, in modern economic conditions, come up against objections of justice and expediency. They are suggestions to mitigate the harsh consequences of a mistake; but they cannot undo the mistake. They will not commend themselves to those pessimists who believe that it is the level of real wages, and not merely of money wages, which is the proper object of attack. I mention them because our present policy of deliberately intensifying unemployment by keeping a tight hold on credit, just when on other grounds it ought to be relaxed, so as to force adjustments by using the weapon of economic necessity against individuals and against particular industries, is a policy which the country would never permit if it knew what was being done.

6. MITIGATION BY TARIFF (i) Proposals for a Revenue Tariff (March 7, 1931) Do you think it a paradox that we can continue to increase our capital wealth by adding both to our foreign investments and to our equipment at home, that we can continue to live (most of us) much as usual or better, and support at the same time a vast body of persons in idleness with a dole greater than the income of a man in full employment in most parts of the world--and yet do all this with one quarter of our industrial plant closed down and one quarter of our industrial workers unemployed? It would be not merely a paradox, but an impossibility, if our potential capacity for the creation of wealth were not much greater than it used to be But this greater capacity does exist. It is to be attributed mainly to three factors--the ever-increasing technical efficiency of our indus-

try (I believe that output per head is 10 per cent greater than it was even so recently as 1924), the greater economic output of women, and the larger proportion of the population which is at the working period of life. The fall in the price of our imports compared with that of our exports also helps. The result is that with three-fourths of our industrial capacity we can now produce as much wealth as we could produce with the whole of it a few years ago. But how rich we could be if only we could find some way of employing four-fourths of our capacity to-day!

Our trouble is, then, not that we lack the physical means to support a high standard of life, but that we are suffering a breakdown in organisation and in the machinery by which we buy and sell to one another.

There are two reactions to this breakdown. We experience the one or the other according to our temperaments. The one is inspired by a determination to maintain our standards of life by bringing into use our wasted capacity-that is to say, to expand, casting fear and even prudence away. The other, the instinct to contract, is based on the psychology of fear. How reasonable is it to be afraid?

We live in a society organised in such a way that the activity of production depends on the individual business man hoping for a reasonable profit, or at least, to avoid an actual loss. The margin which he requires as his necessary incentive to produce may be a very small proportion of the total value of the product. But take this away from him and the whole process stops. This, unluckily, is just what has happened. The fall of prices relatively to costs, together with the psychological effect of high taxation, has destroyed the necessary incentive to production. This is at the root of our disorganisation. It may be unwise, therefore, to frighten the business man or torment him further. A forward policy is liable to do this. For reasoning by a false analogy from what is prudent for an individual who finds himself in danger of living beyond his means, he is usually, when his nerves are frayed, a supporter, though to his own ultimate disadvantage, of national contraction.

And there is a further reason for nervousness. We are suffering from international instability. Notoriously the competitive power of our export trades is diminished by our high standard of life. At the same time the lack of profits in home business inclines the investor to place his money abroad, whilst high taxation exercises a sinister influence in the same direction. Above all, the reluctance of other creditor countries to lend (which is the root-cause of this slump) places too heavy a financial burden on London. These, again, are apparent arguments against a forward policy; for greater activity at home due to increased employment will increase our excess of imports, and Government borrowing may (in their present mood) frighten investors.

Thus the direct effect of an expansionist policy must be to cause Government borrowing, to throw some burden on the Budget, and to increase our excess of imports. In every way, therefore--the opponents of such a policy point out--it will aggravate the want of confidence, the burden of taxation, and the international instability which, they believe, are at the bottom of our present troubles.

At this point the opponents of expansion divide into two groups--those who think that we must not only postpone all ideas of expansion, but must positively contract, by which they mean reduce wages and make large economies in the existing expenditure of the Budget, and those who are entirely negative and, like Mr. Snowden, dislike the idea of contraction (interpreted in the above sense) almost as much as they dislike the idea of expansion.

The policy of negation, however, is really the most dangerous of all. For, as time goes by, it becomes increasingly doubtful whether we can support our standard of life. With 1,000,000 unemployed we certainly can; with 2,000,000 unemployed we probably can; with 3,000,000 unemployed we probably cannot. Thus the negative policy, by allowing unemployment steadily to increase, must lead in the end to an unanswerable demand for a reduction in our standard of life. If we do nothing long enough, there will in the end be nothing else that we can do.

Unemployment, I must repeat, exists because employers have been deprived of profit. The loss of profit may be due to all sorts of causes. But, short of going over to Communism, there is no possible means of curing unemployment except by restoring to employers a proper margin of profit. There are two ways of doing this--by increasing the demand for output, which is the expansionist cure, or by decreasing the cost of output, which is the contractionist cure. Both of these try to touch the spot. Which of them is to be preferred?

To decrease the cost of output by reducing wages and curtailing Budget services may indeed increase foreign demand for our goods (unless, which is quite likely, it encourages a similar policy of contraction abroad), but it will probably diminish the domestic demand. The advantages to employers of a general reduction of wages are, therefore, not so great as they look. Each employer sees the advantage to himself of a reduction of the wages which he himself pays, and overlooks both the consequences of the reduction of the incomes of his customers and of the reduction of wages which his competitors will enjoy. Anyway, it would certainly lead to social injustice and violent resistance, since it would greatly benefit some classes of income at the expense of others. For these reasons a policy of contraction sufficiently drastic to do any real good may be quite impracticable.

Yet the objections to the expansionist remedy --the instability of our international position, the state of the Budget, and the want of confidence--cannot be thus disposed of. Two years ago there was no need to be frightened. To-day it is a different matter. It would not be wise to frighten the penguins and arouse these frigid creatures to flap away from our shores with their golden eggs inside them. A policy of expansion sufficiently drastic to be useful might drive us off the gold standard. Moreover, two years ago the problem was mainly a British problem; to-day it is mainly international. No domestic cure to-day can be adequate by itself. An international cure is essential; and I see the best hope of remedying the international slump in the leadership of Great Britain. But if Great Britain is to resume leadership, she must be strong and believed to be strong. It is of paramount importance, therefore, to restore full confidence in London. I do not believe that this is difficult; for the real strength of London is being under-estimated to-day by foreign opinion, and the position is ripe for a sudden reversal of sentiment. For these reasons I, who opposed our return to the gold standard and can claim, unfortunately, that my Cassandra utterances have been partly fulfilled, believe that our exchange position should be relentlessly defended to-day, in order, above all, that we may resume the vacant financial leadership of the world, which no one else has the experience or the public spirit to occupy, speaking out of acknowledged strength and not out of weakness.

An advocate of expansion in the interests of domestic employment has cause, therefore, to think twice. I have thought twice, and the following are my conclusions.

I am of the opinion that a policy of expansion, though desirable, is not safe or practicable today, unless it is accompanied by other measures which would neutralise its dangers. Let me remind the reader what these dangers are. There is the burden on the trade balance, the burden on the Budget, and the effect on confidence. If the policy of expansion were to justify itself eventually by increasing materially the level of profits and the volume of employment, the net effect on the Budget and on confidence would in the end be favourable and perhaps very favourable. But this might not be the initial effect.

What measures are available to neutralise these dangers? A decision to reform the grave abuses of the dole, and a decision to postpone for the present all new charges on the Budget for social services in order to conserve its resources to meet schemes for the expansion of employment, are advisable and should be taken. But the main decision which seems to me to-day to be absolutely forced on any wise Chancellor of the Exchequer, whatever his beliefs about Protection, is the introduction of a substantial revenue tariff. It is certain that there is no other measure all the immediate consequences of which will be favourable and appropriate. The tariff which I have in mind would include no discriminating protective taxes, but would cover as wide a field as possible at a flat rate or perhaps two flat rates, each applicable to wide categories of goods. Rebates would be allowed in respect of imported material entering into exports, but raw materials, which make up an important proportion of the value of exports, such as wool and cotton, would be exempt. The amount of revenue to be aimed at should be substantial, not less than £50,000,000 and, if possible, £75,000,000. Thus, for example, there might be import duties of 15 per cent on all manufactured and semi-manufactured goods without exception, and of 5 per cent on all food stuffs and certain raw materials, whilst other raw materials would be exempt. 1 I am prepared to maintain that the effect of such duties on the cost of living would be insignificant--no greater than the existing fluctuation between one month and another. Moreover, any conceivable remedy for unemployment will have the effect, and, indeed, will be intended, to raise prices. Equally, the effect on the cost of our exports, after allowing for the rebates which should be calculated on broad and simple lines, would be very small. It should be the declared intention of the Free Trade parties acquiescing in this decision to remove the duties in the event of world prices recovering to the level of 1929.

Compared with any alternative which is open to us, this measure is unique in that it would at the same time relieve the pressing problems of the Budget and restore business confidence. I do not believe that a wise and prudent Budget can be framed to-day without recourse to a revenue tariff. But this is not its only advantage. In so far as it leads to the substitution of home-produced goods for goods previously imported, it will increase employment in this country. At the same time, by relieving the pressure on the balance of trade it will provide a much-needed margin to pay for the additional imports which a policy of expansion will require and to finance loans by London to necessitous debtor countries. In these ways, the buying power which we take away from the rest of the world by restricting certain imports we shall restore to it with the other hand. Some fanatical Free Traders might allege that the adverse effect of import duties on our exports would neutralise all this; but it would not be true.

Free Traders may, consistently with their faith, regard a revenue tariff as our iron ration, which can be used once only in emergency. The emergency has arrived. Under cover of the breathing space and the margin of financial strength thus afforded us, we could frame a policy and a plan, both domestic and international, for marching to the assault against the spirit of contractionism and fear.

If, on the other hand, Free Traders reject these counsels of expediency, the certain result will be to break the present Government and to substitute for it, in the confusion of a Crisis of Confidence, a Cabinet pledged to a full protectionist programme.

(ii) On the Eve of Gold Suspension (Sept. 10, 1931)

The moral energies of the nation are being directed into wrong channels, and serious troubles are ahead of us unless we apply our minds with more effect than hitherto to the analysis of the real character of our problems.

The exclusive concentration on the idea of "Economy," national, municipal, and personal-meaning by this the negative act of withholding expenditure which is now stimulating the forces of production into action--may, if under the spur of a sense of supposed duty it is carried far, produce social effects so shocking as to shake the whole system of our national life.

There is scarcely an item in the Economy Programme of the May Report--whether or not it is advisable on general grounds-- which is not certain to increase unemployment, to lower the profits of business, and to diminish the yield of the revenue; so much so that I have calculated that economies of £100,000,000 may quite likely reduce the net Budget deficit by not more than £50,000,000, and we are just hoodwinking ourselves (unless our real object is to pretend to balance the Budget for the benefit of foreign financiers) if we suppose that we can make the economies under discussion without any repercussions on the number of the unemployed to be supported or on the yield of the existing taxes.

Yet if we carry "Economy" of every kind to its logical conclusion, we shall find that we have balanced the Budget at nought on both sides, with all of us flat on our backs starving to death from a refusal, for reasons of economy, to buy one another's services.

The Prime Minister has said that it is like the war over again, and many people believe him. But this is exactly the opposite of the truth. During the war it was useful to refrain from any avoidable expenditure because this would release resources for the insatiable demands of military operations. What are we releasing resources for to-day? To stand at street corners and draw the dole.

When we already have a great amount of unemployment and unused resources of every description, economy is only useful from the national point of view in so far as it diminishes our consumption of imported goods. For the rest, its fruits are entirely wasted in unemployment, business losses, and reduced savings. But it is an extraordinarily indirect and wasteful way of reducing imports.

If we throw men out of work and reduce the incomes of Government employees so that those directly and indirectly affected cannot afford to buy so much imported food, to this extent the country's financial position is eased. But this is not likely to amount to more than 20 per cent of the total economies enforced. The remaining 80 per cent is wasted, and represents either a mere transference of loss or unemployment due to a refusal of British citizens to purchase one another's services.

What I am saying is absolutely certain, yet I doubt if one in a million of those who are crying out for economy have the slightest idea of the real consequences of what they demand.

This is not to deny that there is a Budget problem. Quite the contrary. The point is that the state of the Budget is mainly a symptom and a consequence of other causes, that economy is in itself liable to aggravate rather than to remove these other causes, and that consequently the Budget problem, attacked merely along the lines of economy, is probably insoluble.

What are our troubles fundamentally due to? Very largely to the world depression, immediately to the unbelievable rashness of High Finance in the City, and originally to the policy of returning to the Gold Standard without the slightest appreciation of the nature of the difficulties which this involved. To say that our problem is a Budget problem is like saying that the German problem is a Budget problem, forgetting all about Reparations.

Now as regards the world depression, there is at the moment absolutely nothing that we can do, for we have now lost the power of international initiative which we seemed to be regaining last May. The results of unsound international banking by the City are also, for the time being, irreparable. The choice left to us was whether or not to adhere to the present gold parity of the exchanges.

This was decided in the affirmative for reasons which I understand but with which I do not agree. The decision was taken in a spirit of hysteria and without a calm consideration of the alternative before us. Ministers have given forecasts of what might have been expected if we had taken a different course which could not survive ten minutes' rational discussion.

I believe that we shall come to regret this decision, just as we already regret most of the critical decisions taken during the last ten years by the persons who form the present Cabinet.

But that is not the point at this moment. The decision to maintain the gold standard at all costs has been taken. The point is that the Cabinet and the public seem to have no clear idea as to what has to be done to implement its own decision, apart from the obvious necessity of raising a foreign loan for immediate requirements; which simply has the effect of replacing money which we had previously borrowed in terms of sterling, by money borrowed in terms of francs and dollars. But they cannot suppose that we can depend permanently on foreign loans. The rest of the problem is primarily concerned with improving our current balance of trade on income account. This is what the Cabinet ought to be thinking about.

There are only two possible lines of attack on this. The one (which is the milder measure open to us) consists in direct measures to restrict imports (and, if possible, subsidise exports); the other is a reduction of all money wages within the country. We may have to attempt both in the end, if we refuse to devaluate.

But the immediate question is which to try first. Now the latter course, if it were to be adequate, would involve so drastic a reduction of wages and such appallingly difficult, probably insoluble, problems, both of social justice and practical method, that it would be crazy not to try first the effects of the alternative, and much milder, measure of restricting imports.

It happens that this course also has other important advantages. It will not only relieve the strain on the foreign exchanges. It would also do more than any other single measure to balance the Budget; and it is the only form of taxation open to us which will actually increase profits, improve employment, and raise the spirits and the confidence of the business community.

Finally, it is the only measure for which there is (sensibly enough) an overwhelming support from public opinion. It is credibly reported that the late Cabinet were in favour of a tariff in the proportion of three to one. It looks as if the present Cabinet may favour it in the proportion of four to one. The only third alternative Cabinet is unanimously for it. But sacrifice being the order of the day, we have in the spirit of self-immolation conceived the brilliant contrivance of a "National" Government, the basis of which is that every member of it agrees, so long as it lasts, to sacrifice what he himself believes to be the only sound solution for our misfortunes.

For if we rule out Devaluation, which I personally now believe to be the right remedy, but which is not yet the policy of any organised party in the State, there are three possible lines of procedure.

The first is to take the risks of brisk home development, as being preferable to enforced idleness.

The second is to organise a general reduction of wages, and, in the interests of social justice, of other money-incomes as well, so far as this is feasible.

The third is a drastic restriction of imports.

The "National" Government is pledged, if I understand the position rightly, to avoid all three. Their policy is to reduce the standard of life of as many people as are within their reach in the hope that some small portion of the reductions of standard will be at the expense of imports. Deliberately to prefer this to a direct restriction of imports is to be non compos mentis.

(iii) After the Suspension of Gold (A letter to The Times, Sept. 28, 1931)

Until recently I was urging on Liberals 1 and others the importance of accepting a general tariff as a means of mitigating the effects of the obvious disequilibrium between money-costs at home and abroad. But the events of the last week have made a great difference. At the present gold-value of sterling British producers are probably in many directions among the cheapest in the world. In these circumstances we cannot continue as if nothing had happened. It is impossible to have a rational discussion about tariffs so long as the currency question is altogether unsolved. For until we know more about the probable future level of sterling in relation to gold, and, above all, until we know how many other countries are going to follow our example, it is impossible to say what our competitive position is going to be.

May I urge that the immediate question for attention is not a tariff but the currency question? It is the latter which is urgent and important. It is at present a non-party issue on which none of the political parties has taken up a dogmatic attitude. It is suitable, therefore, for non-party handling. It is most certainly unsuitable for a General Election. It offers immense opportunities for leadership by this country. We are probably in a position to carry the whole of the Empire and more than half of the rest of the world with us, and thus rebuild the financial supremacy of London on a firm basis. Meanwhile, proposals for high protection have ceased to be urgent. To throw the country into a turmoil over them to the neglect of this other more urgent and important problem would be a wrong and foolish thing. Let us give our whole attention and our united energies to devising a sound international currency policy for ourselves and the rest of the world. For it is futile to suppose that we can recover our former prosperity without such a policy, or that tariffs can be any substitute for it. When the currency question has been settled, then we can return to protection and to our other domestic issues with a solid basis to go upon; and that will be the time for a General Election.

7. THE END OF THE GOLD STANDARD (Sept. 27, 1931) 1
There are few Englishmen who do not rejoice at the breaking of our gold fetters. We feel that we have at last a free hand to do what is sensible. The romantic phase is over, and we can begin to discuss realistically what policy is for the best.

It may seem surprising that a move which had been represented as a disastrous catastrophe should have been received with so much enthusiasm. But the great advantages to British trade and industry of our ceasing artificial efforts to maintain our currency above its real value were quickly realised.

The division of inside opinion was largely on a different point. The difficult question to decide was one of honour. The City of London considered that it was under an obligation of honour to make every possible effort to maintain the value of money in terms of which it had accepted large deposits from foreigners, even though the result of this was to place an intolerable strain on British industry. At what point--that was the difficult problem--were we justified in putting our own interests first?

As events have turned out, we have got the relief we needed, and, at the same time, the claims of honour have been, in the judgement of the whole world, satisfied to the utmost. For the step was not taken until it was unavoidable. In the course of a few weeks the Bank of England paid out £200,000,000 in gold or its equivalent, which was about half the total claims of foreigners on London, and did this at a time when the sums which London had re-lent abroad were largely frozen. No banker could do more. Out of the ashes the City of London will rise with undiminished honour. For she has played the game up to the limits of quixotry, even at the risk of driving British trade almost to a standstill.

No wonder, then, that we feel some exuberance at the release, that Stock Exchange prices soar, and that the dry bones of industry are stirred. For if the sterling exchange is depreciated by, say, 25 per cent, this does as much to restrict our imports as a tariff of that amount; but whereas a tariff could not help our exports, and might hurt them, the depreciation of sterling affords them a bounty of the same 25 per cent by which it aids the home producer against imports.

In many lines of trade the British manufacturer to-day must be the cheapest producer in the world in terms of gold. We gain these advantages without a cut of wages and without industrial strife. We gain them in a way which is strictly fair to every section of the community, without any serious effects on the cost of living. For less than a quarter of our total consumption is represented by imports; so that sterling would have to depreciate by much more than 25 per cent before I should expect the cost of living to rise by as much as 10 per cent. This would cause serious hardship to no one, for it would only put things back where they were two years ago. Meanwhile there will be a great stimulus to employment.

I make no forecast as to the figure to which sterling may fall in the next few days, except that it will have to fall for a time appreciably below the figure which cool calculators believe to represent the equilibrium. There will then be speculation and profit-taking in favour of sterling to balance speculation and panic selling on the other side. Our authorities made a great mistake in allowing sterling to open so high, because the inevitable gradual fall towards a truer level must sap confidence and produce on the ignorant the impression of a slide which cannot be stayed. Those who were guilty of undue optimism will quite likely succumb to undue pessimism. But the pessimism will be as unfounded as the optimism was. The equilibrium value of sterling is the same as it was a month ago. There are tremendous forces to support sterling when it begins to fall too far. There is no risk, in my judgement, of a catastrophic fall.

These, in brief, are the consequences in Great Britain. How will the rest of the world be influenced? Not in a uniform way. Let us take first the debtor countries to whom Great Britain has in the past lent large sums in sterling, and from whom interest is due in sterling, such as Australia, Argentina, and India. To these countries the depreciation of sterling represents a great concession. A smaller quantity of their goods will be sufficient to meet their sterling liabilities. The interest due to Great Britain from abroad, which is fixed in sterling, amounts to about £100,000,000 a year. In respect of this sum Great Britain now plays the part of a reasonable creditor who moderates his claim in view of so great a change in the situation as the recent catastrophic fall in commodity prices.

When we try to calculate the effect on other manufacturing countries, whose competition we are now in a better position to meet, the effect is more complex. A large part of the world will, I expect, follow Great Britain in reducing the former gold value of their money. There are already signs in many countries that no great effort will be made to maintain the gold parity. In the last few days Canada, Italy, Scandinavia have moved in our direction. India and the Crown Colonies, including the Straits Settlements, have automatically followed sterling. Australia and the whole of South America had already abandoned the effort to maintain exchange parity. I shall be astonished if Germany delays long before following our example. Will Holland deal final ruin to the rubber and sugar industries of the Dutch Indies by keeping them tied to gold? There will be strong motives driving a large part of the world our way. After all, Great Britain's plight, as the result of the deflation of prices, is far less serious than that of most countries.

Now, in so far as this is the case, we and all the countries following our example will gain the benefits of higher prices. But none of us will secure a competitive advantage at the expense of the others. Thus the competitive disadvantage will be concentrated on those few countries which remain on the gold standard. On these will fall the curse of Midas. As a result of their unwillingness to exchange their exports except for gold their export trade will dry up and disappear until they no longer have either a favourable trade balance or foreign deposits to repatriate. This means in the main France and the United States. Their loss of export trade will be an inevitable, a predictable, outcome of their own action. These countries, largely for reasons resulting from the war and the war settlements, are owed much money by the rest of the world. They erect tariff barriers which prevent the payment of these sums in goods. They are unwilling to lend it. They have already taken nearly all the available surplus gold in the whole world. There remained, in logic, only one way by which the rest of the world could maintain its solvency and self respect; namely, to cease purchasing these countries' exports. So long as the gold standard is preserved--which means that the prices of international commodities must be much the same everywhere--this involved a competitive campaign of deflation, each of us trying to get our prices down faster than the others, a campaign which had intensified unemployment and business losses to an unendurable pitch.

But as soon as the gold exchange is ruptured the problem is solved. For the appreciation of French and American money in terms of the money of other countries makes it impossible for French and American exporters to sell their goods. The recent policy of these countries could not, if it was persistently pursued, end in any other way. They have willed the destruction of their own export industries, and only they can take the steps necessary to restore them. The appreciation of their currencies must also embarrass gravely their banking systems. The United States had, in effect, set the rest of us the problem of finding some way to do without her wheat, her copper, her cotton, and her motor-cars. She set the problem, and, as it had only one solution, that solution we have been compelled to find.

Yet this is quite the opposite of the note on which I wish to end. The solution to which we have been driven, though it gives immediate relief to us and transfers the strain to others, is in truth a solution unsatisfactory for every one. The world will never be prosperous without a trade recovery in the United States. Peace and confidence and a harmonious economic equilibrium for all the closely interrelated countries of the globe is the only goal worth aiming at.

I believe that the great events of the last week may open a new chapter in the world's monetary history. I have a hope that they may break down barriers which have seemed impassable. We need now to take intimate and candid conference together as to the better ordering of our affairs for the future. The President of the United States turned in his sleep last June. Great issues deserve his attention. Yet the magic spell of immobility which has been cast over the White House seems still unbroken. Are the solutions offered us always to be too late? Shall we in Great Britain invite threequarters of the world, including the whole of our Empire, to join with us in evolving a new currency system which shall be stable in terms of commodities? Or would the gold standard countries be interested to learn the terms, which must needs be strict, on which we should be prepared to re-enter the system of a drastically reformed gold standard?

IV

POLITICS

I. A SHORT VIEW OF RUSSIA (1925) (i) What is the Communist Faith? LENINISM is a combination of two things which Europeans have kept for some centuries in different compartments of the soul--religion and business. We are shocked because the religion is new, and contemptuous because the business, being subordinated to the religion instead of the other way round, is highly inefficient.

Like other new religions, Leninism derives its power not from the multitude but from a small minority of enthusiastic converts whose zeal and intolerance make each one the equal in strength of a hundred indifferentists. Like other new religions, it is led by those who can combine the new spirit, perhaps sincerely, with seeing a good deal more than their followers, politicians with at least an average dose of political cynicism, who can smile as well as frown, volatile experimentalists, released by religion from truth and mercy but not blinded to facts and expediency, and open therefore to the charge (superficial and useless though it is where politicians, lay or ecclesiastical, are concerned) of hypocrisy. Like other new religions, it seems to take the colour and gaiety and freedom out of everyday life and to offer a drab substitute in the square wooden faces of its devotees. Like other new religions, it persecutes without justice or pity those who actively resist it. Like other new religions, it is unscrupulous. Like other new religions, it is filled with missionary ardour and oecumenical ambitions. But to say that Leninism is the faith of a persecuting and propagating minority of fanatics led by hypocrites is, after all, to say no more nor less than that it is a religion and not merely a party, and Lenin a Mahomet, not a Bismarck. If we want to frighten ourselves in our capitalist easy-chairs, we can picture the Communists of Russia as though the early Christians led by Attila were using the equipment of the Holy Inquisition and the Jesuit missions to enforce the literal economics of the New Testament; but when we want to comfort ourselves in the same chairs, can we hopefully repeat that these economics are fortunately so contrary to human nature that they cannot finance either missionaries or armies and will surely end in defeat?

There are three questions to answer. Is the new religion partly true, or sympathetic to the souls of modern men? Is it on the material side so inefficient as to render it incapable to survive? Will it, in the course of time, with sufficient dilution and added impurity, catch the multitude?

As for the first question, those who are completely satisfied by Christian capitalism or by egotistic capitalism untempered by subterfuge will not hesitate how to answer it; for they either have a religion or need none. But many, in this age without religion, are bound to feel a strong emotional curiosity towards any religion which is really new, and not merely a recrudescence of old ones, and has proved its motive force; and all the more when the new thing comes out of Russia, the beautiful and foolish youngest son of the European family, with hair on his head, nearer both to the earth and to heaven than his bald brothers in the West-who, having been born two centuries later, has been able to pick up the middle-aged disillusionment of the rest of the family before he has lost the genius of youth or become addicted to comfort and to habits. I sympathise with those who seek for something good in Soviet Russia.

But when we come to the actual thing what is one to say? For me, brought up in a free air undarkened by the horrors of religion, with nothing to be afraid of, Red Russia holds too much which is detestable. Comfort and habits let us be ready to forgo, but I am not ready for a creed which does not care how much it destroys the liberty and security of daily life, which uses deliberately the weapons of persecution, destruction, and international strife. How can I admire a policy which finds a characteristic expression in spending millions to suborn spies in every family and group at home, and to stir up trouble abroad? Perhaps this is no worse and has more purpose than the greedy, warlike, and imperialist propensities of other Governments; but it must be far better than these to shift me out of my rut. How can I accept a doctrine which sets up as its bible, above and beyond criticism, an obsolete economic textbook which I know to be not only scientifically erroneous but without interest or application for the modern world? How can I adopt a creed which, preferring the mud to the fish, exalts the boorish proletariat above the bourgeois and the intelligentsia who, with whatever faults, are the quality in life and surely carry the seeds of all human advancement? Even if we need a religion, how can we find it in the turbid rubbish of the Red bookshops? It is hard for an educated, decent, intelligent son of Western Europe to find his ideals here, unless he has first suffered some strange and horrid process of conversion which has changed all his values.

Yet we shall miss the essence of the new religion if we stop at this point. The Communist may justly reply that all these things belong not to his ultimate Faith but to the tactics of Revolution. For he believes in two things: the introduction of a New Order upon earth, and the method of the Revolution as the only means thereto. 1 The New Order must not be judged either by the horrors of the Revolution or by the privations of the transitionary period. The Revolution is to be a supreme example of the means justified by the end. The soldier of the Revolution must crucify his own human nature, becoming unscrupulous and ruthless, and suffering himself a life without security or joy--but as the means to his purpose and not its end.

What, then, is the essence of the new religion as a New Order upon earth? Looking from outside, I do not clearly know. Sometimes its mouthpieces speak as though it was purely materialistic and technical in just the same sense that modern capitalism is--as though, that is to say, Communism merely claimed to be in the long run a superior technical instrument for obtaining the same materialistic economic benefits as capitalism offers, that in time it will cause the fields to yield more and the forces of Nature to be more straitly harnessed. In this case there is no religion after all, nothing but a bluff to facilitate a change to what may or may not be a better economic technique. But I suspect that, in fact, such talk is largely a reaction against the charges of economic inefficiency which we on our side launch, and that at the heart of Russian Communism there is something else of more concern to mankind.

In one respect Communism but follows other famous religions. It exalts the common man and makes him everything. Here there is nothing new. But there is another factor in it which also is not new but which may, nevertheless, in a changed form and a new setting, contribute something to the true religion of the future, if there be any true religion. Leninism is absolutely, defiantly non-supernatural, and its emotional and ethical essence centres about the individual's and the community's attitude towards the Love of Money.

I do not mean that Russian Communism alters, or even seeks

to alter, human nature, that it makes Jews less avaricious or Russians less extravagant than they were before. I do not merely mean that it sets up a new ideal. I mean that it tries to construct a framework of society in which pecuniary motives as influencing action shall have a changed relative importance, in which social approbations shall be differently distributed, and where behaviour, which previously was normal and respectable, ceases to be either the one or the other.

In England to-day a talented and virtuous youth, about to enter the world, will balance the advantages of entering the Civil Service and of seeking a fortune in business; and public opinion will esteem him not less if he prefers the second. Money-making, as such, on as large a scale as possible, is not less respectable socially, perhaps more so, than a life devoted to the service of the State or of Religion, Education, Learning, or Art. But in the Russia of the future it is intended that the career of money-making, as such, will simply not occur to a respectable young man as a possible opening, any more than the career of a gentleman burglar or acquiring skill in forgery and embezzlement. Even the most admirable aspects of the love of money in our existing society, such as thrift and saving, and the attainment of financial security and independence for one's self and one's family, whilst not deemed morally wrong, will be rendered so difficult and impracticable as to be not worth while. Every one should work for the community--the new creed runs-- and, if he does his duty, the community will uphold him.

This system does not mean a complete levelling down of incomes--at least at the present stage. A clever and successful person in Soviet Russia has a bigger income and a better time than other people. The commissar with £5 a week (plus sundry free services, a motor-car, a flat, a box at the ballet, etc., etc.) lives well enough, but not in the least like a rich man in London. The successful professor or civil servant with £6 or £7 a week (minus sundry impositions) has, perhaps, a real income three times those of the proletarian workers and six times those of the poorer peasants. Some peasants are three or four times richer than others. A man who is out of work receives part pay, not full pay. But no one can afford on these incomes, with high Russian prices and stiff progressive taxes, to save anything worth saving; it is hard enough to live day by day. The progressive taxation and the mode of assessing rents and other charges are such that it is actually disadvantageous to have an acknowledged income exceeding £8 to £10 a week. Nor is there any possibility of large gains except by taking the same sort of risks as attach to bribery and embezzlement elsewhere--not that bribery and embezzlement have disappeared in Russia or are even rare, but any one whose extravagance or whose instincts drive him to such courses runs serious risk of detection and penalties which include death.

Nor, at the present stage, does the system involve the actual prohibition of buying and selling at a profit. The policy is not to forbid these professions, but to render them precarious and disgraceful. The private trader is a sort of permitted outlaw, without privileges or protection, like the Jew in the Middle Ages--an outlet for those who have overwhelming instincts in this direction, but not a natural or agreeable job for the normal man.

The effect of these social changes has been, I think, to make a real change in the predominant attitude towards money, and will probably make a far greater change when a new generation has grown up which has known nothing else. People in Russia, if only because of their poverty, are very greedy for money-at least as greedy as elsewhere. But moneymaking and money-accumulating cannot enter into the life-calculations of a rational man who accepts the Soviet rule in the way in which they enter into ours. A society of which this is even partially true is a tremendous innovation.

Now all this may prove Utopian, or destructive of true welfare, though, perhaps, not so Utopian, pursued in an intense religious spirit, as it would be if it were pursued in a matterof-fact way. But is it appropriate to assume, as most of us have assumed hitherto, that it is insincere or wicked?

After a long debate with Zinovieff, two Communist ironsides who attended him stepped forward to speak to me a last word with the full faith of fanaticism in their eyes. "We make you a prophecy," they said. "Ten years hence the level of life in Russia will be higher than it was before the war, and in the rest of Europe it will be lower than it was before the war." Having regard to the natural wealth of Russia and to the inefficiency of the old régime, having regard also to the problems of Western Europe and our apparent inability to handle them, can we feel confident that the comrades will not prove right?

(ii) Communism's Power to Survive Can Communism in the course of time, with sufficient dilution and added impurity, catch the multitude?

I cannot answer what only time will show. But I feel confident of one conclusion--that if Communism achieves a certain success, it will achieve it, not as an improved economic technique, but as a religion. The tendency of our conventional criticisms is to make two opposed mistakes. We hate Communism so much, regarded as a religion, that we exaggerate its economic inefficiency; and we are so much impressed by its economic inefficiency that we underestimate it as a religion.

On the economic side I cannot perceive that Russian Communism has made any contribution to our economic problems of intellectual interest or scientific value. I do not think that it contains, or is likely to contain, any piece of useful economic technique which we could not apply, if we chose, with equal or greater success in a society which retained all the marks, I will not say of nineteenth-century individualistic capitalism, but of British bourgeois ideals. Theoretically at least, I do not believe that there is any economic improvement for which Revolution is a necessary instrument. On the other hand, we have everything to lose by the methods of violent change. In Western industrial conditions the tactics of Red Revolution would throw the whole population into a pit of poverty and death.

But as a religion what are its forces? Perhaps they are considerable. The exaltation of the common man is a dogma which has caught the multitude before now. Any religion and the bond which unites co-religionists have power against the egotistic atomism of the irreligious.

For modern capitalism is absolutely irreligious, without internal union, without much public spirit, often, though not always, a mere congeries of possessors and pursuers. Such a system has to be immensely, not merely moderately, successful to survive. In the nineteenth century it was in a certain sense idealistic; at any rate it was a united and self-confident system. It was not only immensely successful, but held out hopes of a continuing crescendo of prospective successes. To-day it is only moderately successful. If irreligious Capitalism is ultimately to defeat religious Communism, it is not enough that it should be economically more efficient--it must be many times as efficient.

We used to believe that modern capitalism was capable, not merely of maintaining the existing standards of life, but of leading us gradually into an economic paradise where we should be comparatively free from economic cares. Now we doubt whether the business man is leading us to a destination far better than our present place. Regarded as a means he is tolerable; regarded as an end he is not so satisfactory. One begins to wonder whether the material advantages of keeping business and religion in different compartments are sufficient to balance the moral disadvantages. The Protestant and Puritan could separate them comfortably because the first activity pertained to earth and the second to heaven, which was elsewhere. The believer in progress could separate them comfortably because he regarded the first as the means to the establishment of heaven upon earth hereafter. But there is a third state of mind, in which we do not fully believe either in a heaven which is elsewhere or in progress as a sure means towards a heaven upon earth hereafter; and if heaven is not elsewhere and not hereafter, it must be here and now or not at all. If there is no moral objective in economic progress, then it follows that we must not sacrifice, even for a day, moral to material advantage-in other words, that we may no longer keep business and religion in separate compartments of the soul. In so far as a man's thoughts are capable of straying along these paths, he will be ready to search with curiosity for something at the heart of Communism quite different from the picture of its outward parts which our Press paints.

At any rate to me it seems clearer every day that the moral problem of our age is concerned with the love of money, with the habitual appeal to the money motive in nine-tenths of the activities of life, with the universal striving after individual economic security as the prime object of endeavour, with the social approbation of money as the measure of constructive success, and with the social appeal to the hoarding instinct as the foundation of the necessary provision for the family and for the future. The decaying religions around us, which have less and less interest for most people unless it be as an agreeable form of magical ceremonial or of social observance, have lost their moral significance just because--unlike some of their earlier versions--they do not touch in the least degree on these essential matters. A revolution in our ways of thinking and feeling about money may become the growing purpose of contemporary embodiments of the ideal. Perhaps, therefore, Russian Communism does represent the first confused stirrings of a great religion.

The visitor to Russia from the outside, who tries without prejudice to catch the atmosphere, must alternate, I think, between two moods-oppression and elation. Sir Martin Conway, in his true and sincere volume on Art Treasures in Soviet Russia, writes thus of his departure out of the country:

... After a very long halt the train moved on about half a mile to the Finnish frontier, where passports, visas, and luggage were again examined much less meticulously. The station was new built, a pleasant place, simple, clean, and convenient, and served with much courtesy. It has a charming refreshment room, where simple but nicely cooked food was supplied in an atmosphere of hospitality.

It seems a churlish thing for me to say, after all the kindness shown to me in Russia, but if I am to tell the whole truth I must here put on record that in this frontier station of Finland I experienced a sense as of the removal of a great weight which had been oppressing me. I cannot explain just how this weight had been felt. I did not experience the imposition of it on entering Russia, but as the days passed it seemed slowly to accumulate. The sense of freedom gradually disappeared. Though everyone was kind one felt the presence of an oppression, not on oneself, but allpervading. Never have I felt so completely a stranger in a strange land; with successive days what at first was a dim feeling took more definite shape and condensed into an ever-increasingly conscious oppression.

I imagine one might have passed through the same experience in the Russia of the Tsars. Americans often praise what they call the "air of liberty" which they claim as characteristic of their country. They possess it in common with all the English-speaking dominions. The moral atmosphere of Russia is a very different compound of emotional chemistry.

The part of Finland through which our train now bore us was not different in physical character from the lands across the frontier, but we found ourselves passing "nice little properties" and the signs of comfort and even prosperity. . . .

The mood of oppression could not be better conveyed. In part, no doubt, it is the fruit of Red Revolution--there is much in Russia to make one pray that one's own country may achieve its goal not in that way. In part, perhaps, it is the fruit of some beastliness in the Russian nature--or in the Russian and Jewish natures when, as now, they are allied together. But in part it is one face of the superb earnestness of Red Russia, of the high seriousness, which in its other aspect appears as the Spirit of Elation. There never was any one so serious as the Russian of the Revolution, serious even in his gaiety and abandon of spirit--so serious that sometimes he can forget to-morrow and sometimes he can forget to-day. Often this seriousness is crude and stupid and boring in the extreme. The average Communist is discoloured just as the Methodists of every age have been. The tenseness of the atmosphere is more than one is used to support, and a longing comes for the frivolous ease of London.

Yet the elation, when that is felt, is very great. Here--one feels at moments--in spite of poverty, stupidity, and oppression, is the Laboratory of Life. Here the chemicals are being mixed in new combinations, and stink and explode. Something--there is just a chance--might come out. And even a chance gives to what is happening in Russia more importance than what is happening (let us say) in the United States of America.

I think that it is partly reasonable to be afraid of Russia, like the gentlemen who write to The Times. But if Russia is going to be a force in the outside world, it will not be the result of Mr. Zinovieff's money. Russia will never matter seriously to the rest of us, unless it be as a moral force. So, now the deeds are done and there is no going back, I should like to give Russia her chance; to help and not to hinder. For how much rather, even after allowing for everything, if I were a Russian, would I contribute my quota of activity to Soviet Russia than to Tsarist Russia! I could not subscribe to the new official faith any more than to the old. I should detest the actions of the new tyrants not less than those of the old. But I should feel that my eyes were turned towards, and no longer away from, the possibilities of things; that out of the cruelty and stupidity of Old Russia nothing could ever emerge, but that beneath the cruelty and stupidity of New Russia some speck of the ideal may lie hid.

2. THE END OF LAISSEZ-FAIRE (1926) Let us clear from the ground the metaphysical or general principles upon which, from time to time, laissez-faire has been founded. It is not true that individuals possess a prescriptive "natural liberty" in their economic activities. There is no "compact" conferring perpetual rights on those who Have or on those who Acquire. The world is not so governed from above that private and social interest always coincide. It is not so managed here below that in practice they coincide. It is not a correct deduction from the Principles of Economics that enlightened self-interest always operates in the public interest. Nor is it true that self-interest generally is enlightened; more often individuals acting separately to promote their own ends are too ig-

norant or too weak to attain even these. Experience does not show that individuals, when they make up a social unit, are always less clear-sighted than when they act separately.

We cannot, therefore, settle on abstract grounds, but must handle on its merits in detail, what Burke termed "one of the finest problems in legislation, namely, to determine what the State ought to take upon itself to direct by the public wisdom, and what it ought to leave, with as little interference as possible, to individual exertion." We have to discriminate between what Bentham, in his forgotten but useful nomenclature, used to term Agenda and NonAgenda, and to do this without Bentham's prior presumption that interference is, at the same time, "generally needless" and "generally pernicious." 1 Perhaps the chief task of Economists at this hour is to distinguish afresh the Agenda of Government from the Non-Agenda; and the companion task of Politics is to devise forms of Government within a Democracy which shall be capable of accomplishing the Agenda. I will illustrate what I have in mind by two examples.

(1) I believe that in many cases the ideal size for the unit of control and organisation lies somewhere between the individual and the modern State. I suggest, therefore, that progress lies in the growth and the recognition of semi-autonomous bodies within the State-bodies whose criterion of action within their own field is solely the public good as they understand it, and from whose deliberations motives of private advantage are excluded, though some place it may still be necessary to leave, until the ambit of men's altruism grows wider, to the separate advantage of particular groups, classes, or faculties--bodies which in the ordinary course of affairs are mainly autonomous within their prescribed limitations, but are subject in the last resort to the sovereignty of the democracy expressed through Parliament.

I propose a return, it may be said, towards mediaeval conceptions of separate autonomies. But, in England at any rate, corporations are a mode of government which has never ceased to be important and is sympathetic to our institutions. It is easy to give examples, from what already exists, of separate autonomies which have attained or are approaching the mode I designate--the Universities, the Bank of England, the Port of London Authority, even perhaps the Railway Companies.

But more interesting than these is the trend of Joint Stock Institutions, when they have reached a certain age and size, to approximate to the status of public corporations rather than that of individualistic private enterprise. One of the most interesting and unnoticed developments of recent decades has been the tendency of big enterprise to socialise itself. A point arrives in the growth of a big institution--particularly a big railway or big public utility enterprise, but also a big bank or a big insurance company--at which the owners of the capital, i.e. the shareholders, are almost entirely dissociated from the management, with the result that the direct personal interest of the latter in the making of great profit becomes quite secondary. When this stage is reached, the general stability and reputation of the institution are more considered by the management than the maximum of profit for the shareholders. The shareholders must be satisfied by conventionally adequate dividends; but once this is secured, the direct interest of the management often consists in avoiding criticism from the public and from the customers of the concern. This is particularly the case if their great size or semi-monopolistic position renders them conspicuous in the public eye and vulnerable to public attack. The extreme instance, perhaps, of this tendency in the case of an institution, theoretically the unrestricted property of private persons, is the Bank of England. It is almost true to say that there is no class of persons in the Kingdom of whom the Governor of the Bank of England thinks less when he decides on his policy than of his shareholders. Their rights, in excess of their conventional dividend, have already sunk to the neighbourhood of zero. But the same thing is partly true of many other big institutions. They are, as time goes on, socialising themselves.

Not that this is unmixed gain. The same causes promote conservatism and a waning of enterprise. In fact, we already have in these cases many of the faults as well as the advantages of State Socialism. Nevertheless we see here, I think, a natural line of evolution. The battle of Socialism against unlimited private profit is being won in detail hour by hour. In these particular fields--it remains acute elsewhere--this is no longer the pressing problem.

There is, for instance, no so-called important political question so really unimportant, so irrelevant to the reorganisation of the economic life of Great Britain, as the Nationalisation of the Railways.

It is true that many big undertakings, particularly Public Utility enterprises and other business requiring a large fixed capital, still need to be semi-socialised. But we must keep our minds flexible regarding the forms of this semi-socialism. We must take full advantage of the natural tendencies of the day, and we must probably prefer semi-autonomous corporations to organs of the Central Government for which Ministers of State are directly responsible.

I criticise doctrinaire State Socialism, not because it seeks to engage men's altruistic impulses in the service of Society, or because it departs from laissez-faire, or because it takes away from man's natural liberty to make a million, or because it has courage for bold experiments. All these things I applaud. I criticise it because it misses the significance of what is actually happening; because it is, in fact, little better than a dusty survival of a plan to meet the problems of fifty years ago, based on a misunderstanding of what some one said a hundred years ago. Nineteenth-century State Socialism sprang from Bentham, free competition, etc., and is in some respects a clearer, in some respects a more muddled, version of just the same philosophy as underlies nineteenthcentury individualism. Both equally laid all their stress on freedom, the one negatively to avoid limitations on existing freedom, the other positively to destroy natural or acquired monopolies. They are different reactions to the same intellectual atmosphere.

(2) I come next to a criterion of Agenda which is particularly relevant to what it is urgent and desirable to do in the near future. We must aim at separating those services which are technically social from those which are technically individual. The most important Agenda of the State relate not to those activities which private individuals are already fulfilling, but to those functions which fall outside the sphere of the individual, to those decisions which are made by no one if the State does not make them. The important thing for Government is not to do things which individuals are doing already, and to do them a little better or a little worse; but to do those things which at present are not done at all.

It is not within the scope of my purpose on this occasion to develop practical policies. I limit myself, therefore, to naming some instances of what I mean from amongst those problems about which I happen to have thought most.

Many of the greatest economic evils of our time are the fruits of risk, uncertainty, and ignorance. It is because particular individuals, fortunate in situation or in abilities, are able to take advantage of uncertainty and ignorance, and also because for the same reason big business is often a lottery, that great inequalities of wealth come about; and these same factors are also the cause of the Unemployment of Labour, or the disappointment of reasonable business expectations, and of the impairment of efficiency and production. Yet the cure lies outside the operations of individuals; it may even be to the interest of individuals to aggravate the disease. I believe that the cure for these things is partly to be sought in the deliberate control of the currency and of credit by a central institution, and partly in the collection and dissemination on a great scale of data relating to the business situation, including the full publicity, by law if necessary, of all business facts which it is useful to know. These measures would involve Society in exercising directive intelligence through some appropriate organ of action over many of the inner intricacies of private business, yet it would leave private initiative and enterprise unhindered. Even if these measures prove insufficient, nevertheless they will furnish us with better knowledge than we have now for taking the next step.

My second example relates to Savings and Investment. I believe that some co-ordinated act of intelligent judgement is required as to the scale on which it is desirable that the community as a whole should save, the scale on which these savings should go abroad in the form of foreign investments, and whether the present organisation of the investment market distributes savings along the most nationally productive channels.

I do not think that these matters should be left entirely to the chances of private judgement and private profits, as they are at present.

My third example concerns Population. The time has already come when each country needs a considered national policy about what size of Population, whether larger or smaller than at present or the same, is most expedient. And having settled this policy, we must take steps to carry it into operation. The time may arrive a little later when the community as a whole must pay attention to the innate quality as well as to the mere numbers of its future members.

These reflections have been directed towards possible improvements in the technique of modern Capitalism by the agency of collective action. There is nothing in them which is seriously incompatible with what seems to me to be the essential characteristic of Capitalism, namely the dependence upon an intense appeal to the money-making and money-loving instincts of individuals as the main motive force of the economic machine. Nor must I, so near to my end, stray towards other fields. Nevertheless, I may do well to remind you, in conclusion, that the fiercest contests and the most deeply felt divisions of opinion are likely to be waged in the coming years not round technical questions, where the arguments on either side are mainly economic, but round those which, for want of better words, may be called psychological or, perhaps, moral.

In Europe, or at least in some parts of Europe --but not, I think, in the United States of America--there is a latent reaction, somewhat widespread, against basing Society to the extent that we do upon fostering, encouraging, and protecting the money-motives of individuals. A preference for arranging our affairs in such a way as to appeal to the money-motive as little as possible, rather than as much as possible, need not be entirely a priori, but may be based on the comparison of experiences. Different persons, according to their choice of profession, find the money-motive playing a large or a small part in their daily lives, and historians can tell us about other phases of social organisation in which this motive has played a much smaller part than it does now. Most religions and most philosophies deprecate, to say the least of it, a way of life mainly influenced by considerations of personal money profit. On the other hand, most men to-day reject ascetic notions and do not doubt the real advantages of wealth. Moreover it seems obvious to them that one cannot do without the money-motive, and that, apart from certain admitted abuses, it does its job well. In the result the average man averts his attention from the problem, and has no clear idea what he really thinks and feels about the whole confounded matter.

Confusion of thought and feeling leads to confusion of speech. Many people, who are really objecting to Capitalism as a way of life, argue as though they were objecting to it on the ground of its inefficiency in attaining its own objects. Contrariwise, devotees of Capitalism are often unduly conservative, and reject reforms in its technique, which might really strengthen and preserve it, for fear that they may prove to be first steps away from Capitalism itself. Nevertheless a time may be coming when we shall get clearer than at present as to when we are talking about Capitalism as an efficient or inefficient technique, and when we are talking about it as desirable or objectionable in itself. For my part, I think that Capitalism, wisely managed, can probably be made more efficient for attaining economic ends than any alternative system yet in sight, but that in itself it is in many ways extremely objectionable. Our problem is to work out a social organisation which shall be as efficient as possible without offending our notions of a satisfactory way of life.

The next step forward must come, not from political agitation or premature experiments, but from thought. We need by an effort of the mind to elucidate our own feelings. At present our sympathy and our judgement are liable to be on different sides, which is a painful and paralysing state of mind. In the field of action reformers will not be successful until they can steadily pursue a clear and definite object with their intellects and their feelings in tune. There is no party in the world at present which appears to me to be pursuing right aims by right methods. Material Poverty provides the incentive to change precisely in situations where there is very little margin for experiments. Material Prosperity removes the incentive just when it might be safe to take a chance. Europe lacks the means, America the will, to make a move. We need a new set of convictions which spring naturally from a candid examination of our own inner feelings in relation to the outside facts.

3. AM I A LIBERAL? (1925) I If one is born a political animal, it is most uncomfortable not to belong to a party; cold and lonely and futile it is. If your party is strong, and its programme and its philosophy sympathetic, satisfying the gregarious, practical, and intellectual instincts all at the same time, how very agreeable that must be!--worth a large subscription and all one's spare time;--that is, if you are a political animal.

So the political animal who cannot bring himself to utter the contemptible words, "I am no party man," would almost rather belong to any party than to none. If he cannot find a home by the principle of attraction, he must find one by the principle of repulsion and go to those whom he dislikes least, rather than stay out in the cold.

Now take my own case--where am I landed on this negative test? How could I bring myself to be a Conservative? They offer me neither food nor drink--neither intellectual nor spiritual consolation. I should not be amused or excited or edified. That which is common to the atmosphere, the mentality, the view of life of-- well, I will not mention names--promotes neither my self-interest nor the public good. It leads nowhere; it satisfies no ideal; it conforms to no intellectual standard; it is not even safe, or calculated to preserve from spoilers that degree of civilisation which we have already attained.

Ought I, then, to join the Labour Party? Superficially that is more attractive. But looked at closer, there are great difficulties. To begin with, it is a class party, and the class is not my class. If I am going to pursue sectional interests at all, I shall pursue my own. When it comes to the class struggle as such, my local and personal patriotisms, like those of every one else, except certain unpleasant zealous ones, are attached to my own surroundings. I can be influenced by what seems to me to be Justice and good sense; but the Class war will find me on the side of the educated bourgeoisie.

But, above all, I do not believe that the intellectual elements in the Labour Party will ever exercise adequate control; too much will always be decided by those who do not know at all what they are talking about; and if--which is not unlikely--the control of the party is seized by an autocratic inner ring, this control will be exercised in the interests of the extreme Left Wing--the section of the Labour Party which I shall designate the Party of Catastrophe.

On the negative test, I incline to believe that the Liberal Party is still the best instrument of future progress--if only it had strong leadership and the right programme.

But when we come to consider the problem of party positively--by reference to what attracts rather than to what repels--the aspect is dismal in every party alike, whether we put our hopes in measures or in men. And the reason is the same in each case. The historic party questions of the nineteenth century are as dead as last week's mutton; and whilst the questions of the future are looming up, they have not yet become party questions, and they cut across the old party lines.

Civil and Religious Liberty, the Franchise, the Irish Question, Dominion Self-Government, the Power of the House of Lords, steeply graduated Taxation of Incomes and of Fortunes, the lavish use of the Public Revenues for "Social Reform," that is to say, Social Insurance for Sickness, Unemployment and Old Age, Education, Housing and Public Health--all these causes for which the Liberal Party fought are successfully achieved or are obsolete or are the common ground of all parties alike. What remains? Some will say--the Land Question. Not I--for I believe that this question, in its traditional form, has now become, by reason of a silent change in the facts, of very slight political importance. I see only two planks of the historic Liberal platform still seaworthy-the Drink Question and Free Trade. And of these two Free Trade survives, as a great and living political issue, by an accident. There were always two arguments for Free Trade-the laissez-faire argument which appealed and still appeals to the Liberal individualists, and the economic argument based on the benefits which flow from each country's employing its resources where it has a comparative advantage. I no longer believe in the political philosophy which the Doctrine of Free Trade adorned. I believe in Free Trade because, in the long run and in general, it is the only policy which is technically sound and intellectually tight.

But take it at the best, can the Liberal Party sustain itself on the Land Question, the Drink Question, and Free Trade alone, even if it were to reach a united and clear-cut programme on the two former? The positive argument for being a Liberal is, at present, very weak. How do the other parties survive the positive test?

The Conservative Party will always have its place as a Die-Hard Home. But constructively, it is in just as bad case as the Liberal Party. It is often no more than an accident of temperament or of past associations, and not a real difference of policy or of ideals, which now separates the progressive young Conservative from the average Liberal. The old battlecries are muffled or silent. The Church, the Aristocracy, the Landed Interests, the Rights of Property, the Glories of Empire, the Pride of the Services, even Beer and Whisky, will never again be the guiding forces of British politics.

The Conservative Party ought to be concerning itself with evolving a version of Individualistic Capitalism adapted to the progressive change of circumstances. The difficulty is that the Capitalist leaders in the City and in Parliament are incapable of distinguishing novel measures for safeguarding Capitalism from what they call Bolshevism. If old-fashioned Capitalism was intellectually capable of defending itself, it would not be dislodged for many generations. But, fortunately for Socialists, there is little chance of this.

I believe that the seeds of the intellectual decay of Individualistic Capitalism are to be found in an institution which is not in the least characteristic of itself, but which it took over from the social system of Feudalism which preceded it,--namely, the hereditary principle. The hereditary principle in the transmission of wealth and the control of business is the reason why the leadership of the Capitalist Cause is weak and stupid. It is too much dominated by third-generation men. Nothing will cause a social institution to decay with more certainty than its attachment to the hereditary principle. It is an illustration of this that by far the oldest of our institutions, the Church, is the one which has always kept itself free from the hereditary taint.

Just as the Conservative Party will always have its Die-Hard wing, so the Labour Party will always be flanked by the Party of Catastrophe--Jacobins, Communists, Bolshevists, whatever you choose to call them. This is the party which hates or despises existing institutions and believes that great good will result merely from overthrowing them--or at least that to overthrow them is the necessary preliminary to any great good. This party can only flourish in an atmosphere of social oppression or as a reaction against the Rule of DieHard. In Great Britain it is, in its extreme form, numerically very weak. Nevertheless its philosophy in a diluted form permeates, in my opinion, the whole Labour Party. However moderate its leaders may be at heart, the Labour Party will always depend for electoral success on making some slight appeal to the widespread passions and jealousies which find their full development in the Party of Catastrophe. I believe that this secret sympathy with the Policy of Catastrophe is the worm which gnaws at the seaworthiness of any constructive vessel which the Labour Party may launch. The passions of malignity, jealousy, hatred of those who have wealth and power (even in their own body) ill consort with ideals to build up a true Social Republic. Yet it is necessary for a successful Labour leader to be, or at least to appear, a little savage. It is not enough that he should love his fellow-men; he must hate them too.

What then do I want Liberalism to be? On the one side, Conservatism is a well-defined entity--with a Right of Die-Hards, to give it strength and passion, and a Left of what one may call "the best type" of educated, humane, Conservative Free-Traders, to lend it moral and intellectual respectability. On the other side, Labour is also well-defined--with a Left of Catastrophists, to give it strength and passion, and a Right of what one may call "the best type" of educated, humane, Socialistic Reformers, to lend it moral and intellectual respectability. Is there room for anything between? Should not each of us here decide whether we consider ourselves to be "the best type" of Conservative Free - Traders or "the best type" of Socialistic Reformers, and have done with it?

Perhaps that is how we shall end. But I still think that there is room for a party which shall be disinterested as between classes, and which shall be free in building the future both from the influences of Die-Hardism and from those of Catastrophism, which will spoil the constructions of each of the others. Let me sketch out in the briefest terms what I conceive to be the Philosophy and Practice of such a party.

To begin with, it must emancipate itself from the dead-wood of the past. In my opinion there is now no place, except in the Left Wing of the Conservative Party, for those whose hearts are set on old-fashioned individualism and laissez-faire in all their rigour-- greatly though these contributed to the success of the nineteenth century. I say this, not because I think that these doctrines were wrong in the conditions which gave birth to them (I hope that I should have belonged to this party if I had been born a hundred years earlier), but because they have ceased to be applicable to modern conditions. Our programme must deal not with the historic issues of Liberalism, but with those matters--whether or not they have already become party questions--which are of living interest and urgent importance to-day. We must take risks of unpopularity and derision. Then our meetings will draw crowds and our body be infused with strength.

II. I divide the questions of to-day into five headings:--

1. Peace Questions.

2. Questions of Government.

3. Sex Questions.

4. Drug Questions.

5. Economic Questions.

On Peace Questions let us be Pacifist to the utmost. As regards the Empire, I do not think that there is any important problem except in India. Elsewhere, so far as problems of government are concerned, the process of friendly disintegration is now almost complete--to the great benefit of all. But as regards Pacifism and Armaments we are only just at the beginning. I should like to take risks in the interests of Peace, just as in the past we have taken risks in the interests of War. But I do not want these risks to assume the form of an undertaking to make war in various hypothetical circumstances. I am against Pacts. To pledge the whole of our armed forces to defend disarmed Germany against an attack by France in the plenitude of the latter's military power is foolish; and to assume that we shall take part in every future war in Western Europe is unnecessary. But I am in favour of giving a very good example, even at the risk of being weak, in the direction of Arbitration and of Disarmament.

I turn next to questions of Government--a dull but important matter. I believe that in the future the Government will have to take on many duties which it has avoided in the past. For these purposes Ministers and Parliament will be unserviceable. Our task must be to decentralise and devolve wherever we can, and in particular to establish semi-independent corporations and organs of administration to which duties of government, new and old, will be entrusted;--without, however, impairing the democratic principle or the ultimate sovereignty of Parliament. These questions will be as important and difficult in the future as the Franchise and the relations of the two Houses have been in the past.

The questions which I group together as Sex Questions have not been party questions in the past. But that was because they were never, or seldom, the subject of public discussion. All this is changed now. There are no subjects about which the big general public is more interested; few which are the subject of wider discussion. They are of the utmost social importance; they cannot help but provoke real and sincere differences of opinion. Some of them are deeply involved in the solution of certain economic questions. I cannot doubt that Sex Questions are about to enter the political arena. The very crude beginnings represented by the Suffrage Movement were only symptoms of deeper and more important issues below the surface.

Birth Control and the use of Contraceptives, Marriage Laws, the treatment of sexual offences and abnormalities, the economic position of women, the economic position of the family,-in all these matters the existing state of the Law and of orthodoxy is still mediaeval--altogether out of touch with civilised opinion and civilised practice and with what individuals, educated and uneducated alike, say to one another in private. Let no one deceive himself with the idea that the change of opinion on these matters is one which only affects a small educated class on the crust of the human boiling. Let no one suppose that it is the working women who are going to be shocked by ideas of Birth Control or of Divorce Reform. For them these things suggest new liberty, emancipation from the most intolerable of tyrannies. A party which would discuss these things openly and wisely at its meetings would discover a new and living interest in the electorate--because politics would be dealing once more with matters about which every one wants to know and which deeply affect every one's own life.

These questions also interlock with economic issues which cannot be evaded. Birth Control touches on one side the liberties of women, and on the other side the duty of the State to concern itself with the size of the population just as much as with the size of the army or the amount of the Budget. The position of wage-earning women and the project of the Family Wage affect not only the status of women, the first in the performance of paid work, and the second in the performance of unpaid work, but also raise the whole question whether wages should be fixed by the forces of supply and demand in accordance with the orthodox theories of laissezfaire, or whether we should begin to limit the freedom of those forces by reference to what is "fair" and "reasonable" having regard to all the circumstances.

Drug Questions in this country are practically limited to the Drink Question; though I should like to include gambling under this head. I expect that the Prohibition of alcoholic Spirits and of Bookmakers would do good. But this would not settle the matter. How far is bored and suffering humanity to be allowed, from time to time, an escape, an excitement, a stimulus, a possibility of change?--that is the important problem. Is it possible to allow reasonable licence, permitted Saturnalia, sanctified Carnival, in conditions which need ruin neither the health nor the pockets of the roysterers, and will shelter from irresistible temptation the unhappy class who, in America, are called addicts?

I must not stay for an answer, but must hasten to the largest of all political questions, which are also those on which I am most qualified to speak--the economic questions.

An eminent American economist, Professor Commons, who has been one of the first to recognise the nature of the economic transition amidst the early stages of which we are now living, distinguishes three epochs, three economic orders, upon the third of which we are entering.

The first is the Era of Scarcity, "whether due to inefficiency or to violence, war, custom, or superstition." In such a period "there is the minimum of individual liberty and the maximum of communistic, feudalistic or governmental control through physical coercion." This was, with brief intervals in exceptional cases, the normal economic state of the world up to (say) the fifteenth or sixteenth century.

Next comes the Era of Abundance. "In a period of extreme abundance there is the maximum of individual liberty, the minimum of coercive control through government, and individual bargaining takes the place of rationing." During the seventeenth and eighteenth centuries we fought our way out of the bondage of Scarcity into the free air of Abundance, and in the nineteenth century this epoch culminated gloriously in the victories of laissez-faire and historic Liberalism. It is not surprising or discreditable that the veterans of the party cast backward glances on that easier age.

But we are now entering on a third era, which Professor Commons calls the period of Stabilisation, and truly characterises as "the actual alternative to Marx's communism." In this period, he says, "there is a diminution of individual liberty, enforced in part by governmental sanctions, but mainly by economic sanctions through concerted action, whether secret, semi-open, open, or arbitrational, of associations, corporations, unions, and other collective movements of manufacturers, merchants, labourers, farmers, and bankers."

The abuses of this epoch in the realms of Government are Fascism on the one side and Bolshevism on the other. Socialism offers no middle course, because it also is sprung from the presuppositions of the Era of Abundance, just as much as laissez-faire individualism and the free play of economic forces, before which latter, almost alone amongst men, the City Editors, all bloody and blindfolded, still piteously bow down.

The transition from economic anarchy to a régime which deliberately aims at controlling and directing economic forces in the interests of social justice and social stability, will present enormous difficulties both technical and political. I suggest, nevertheless, that the true destiny of New Liberalism is to seek their solution.

It happens that we have before us, to-day, in the position of the Coal Industry, an objectlesson of the results of the confusion of ideas which now prevails. On the one side the Treasury and the Bank of England are pursuing an orthodox nineteenth-century policy based on the assumption that economic adjustments can and ought to be brought about by the free play of the forces of supply and demand. The Treasury and the Bank of England still believe --or, at any rate, did until a week or two ago-that the things, which would follow on the assumption of free competition and the mobility of capital and labour, actually occur in the economic life of to-day.

On the other side, not only the facts, but public opinion also, have moved a long distance away in the direction of Professor Commons's epoch of Stabilisation. The Trade Unions are strong enough to interfere with the free play of the forces of supply and demand, and Public Opinion, albeit with a grumble and with more than a suspicion that the Trade Unions are growing dangerous, supports the Trade Unions in their main contention that Coalminers ought not to be the victims of cruel economic forces which they never set in motion.

The idea of the old-world party, that you can, for example, alter the value of money and then leave the consequential adjustments to be brought about by the forces of supply and demand, belongs to the days of fifty or a hundred years ago when Trade Unions were powerless, and when the economic Juggernaut was allowed to crash along the highway of Progress without obstruction and even with applause.

Half the copybook wisdom of our statesmen is based on assumptions which were at one time true, or partly true, but are now less and less true day by day. We have to invent new wisdom for a new age. And in the meantime we must, if we are to do any good, appear unorthodox, troublesome, dangerous, disobedient to them that begat us.

In the economic field this means, first of all, that we must find new policies and new instruments to adapt and control the working of economic forces, so that they do not intolerably interfere with contemporary ideas as to what is fit and proper in the interests of social stability and social justice.

It is not an accident that the opening stage of this political struggle, which will last long and take many different forms, should centre about monetary policy. For the most violent interferences with stability and with justice, to which the nineteenth century submitted in due satisfaction of the philosophy of Abundance, were precisely those which were brought about by changes in the price level. But the consequences of these changes, particularly when the Authorities endeavour to impose them on us in a stronger dose than even the nineteenth century ever swallowed, are intolerable to modern ideas and to modern institutions.

We have changed, by insensible degrees, our philosophy of economic life, our notions of what is reasonable and what is tolerable; and we have done this without changing our technique or our copy-book maxims. Hence our tears and troubles.

A party programme must be developed in its details, day by day, under the pressure and the stimulus of actual events; it is useless to define it beforehand, except in the most general terms. But if the Liberal Party is to recover its forces, it must have an attitude, a philosophy, a direction. I have endeavoured to indicate my own attitude to politics, and I leave it to others to answer, in the light of what I have said, the question with which I began--Am I a Liberal?

4. LIBERALISM AND LABOUR (1926)

I do not wish to live under a Conservative Government for the next twenty years. I believe that the progressive forces of the country are hopelessly divided between the Liberal Party and the Labour Party. I do not believe that the Liberal Party will win one-third of the seats in the House of Commons in any probable or foreseeable circumstances. Unless in course of time the mistakes of the Conservative Government produce an economic catastrophe--which is not impossible--I do not believe that the Labour Party will win one-half of the seats in the House of Commons. Yet it is not desirable that the Labour Party should depend for their chances of office on the occurrence of a national misfortune; for this will only strengthen the influence of the party of catastrophe which is al-ready an important element in their ranks. As things are now, we have nothing to look forward to except a continuance of Conserva-tive Governments, not merely until they have made mistakes in the tolerable degree which would have caused a swing of the pen-dulum in former days, but until their mistakes have mounted up to the height of a disaster. I do not like this choice of alternatives.

That is the practical political problem which confronts all those, in whichever party they are ranged, who want to see progressive principles put into effect, and believe that too long a delay in doing so may find the country confronted with extreme alternatives.

The conventional retort by Labour orators is to call upon Liber-als to close down their own Party and to come over. Now it is evi-dent that the virtual extinction of the Liberal Party is a practical possibility to be reckoned with. A time may come when any one in active politics will have only two choices before him and not three. But I believe that it would be bad politics and bad behaviour to promote this end; and that it is good politics and good behaviour to resist it.

Good politics to resist it, because the progressive cause in the constituencies would be weakened, and not strengthened, by the disappearance of the Liberal Party. There are many sections of the country, and many classes of voters, which for many years to come will never vote Labour in numbers, or with enthusiasm, sufficient for victory; but which will readily vote Liberal as soon as the weather changes. Labour leaders who deny this are not looking at the facts of politics with unclouded eyes. Good behaviour to resist it, because most present-day active Liberals, whilst ready on occasion to vote Labour and to act with Labour, would not feel comfortable, or sincere, or in place, as full members of the Labour Party. Take my own case. I am sure that I am less conservative in my inclinations than the average Labour voter; I fancy that I have played in my mind with the possibilities of greater social changes than come within the present philosophies of, let us say, Mr. Sidney Webb, Mr. Thomas, or Mr. Wheatley. The Republic of my imagination lies on the extreme left of celestial space. Yet--all the same--I feel that my true home, so long as they offer a roof and a floor, is still with the Liberals.

Why, though fallen upon such evil days, does the tradition of Liberalism hold so much attraction? The Labour Party contains three elements. There are the Trade-Unionists, once the oppressed, now the tyrants, whose selfish and sectional pretensions need to be bravely opposed. There are the advocates of the methods of violence and sudden change, by an abuse of language called Communists, who are committed by their creed to produce evil that good may come, and, since they dare not concoct disaster openly, are forced to play with plot and subterfuge. There are the Socialists, who believe that the economic foundations of modern society are evil, yet might be good.

The company and conversation of this third element, whom I have called Socialists, many Liberals to-day would not find uncongenial. But we cannot march with them until we know along what path, and towards what goal, they mean to move. I do not believe that their historic creed of State Socialism, and its newer gloss of Guild Socialism, now interest them much more than they interest us. These doctrines no longer inspire any one. Constructive thinkers in the Labour Party, and constructive thinkers in the Liberal Party, are trying to replace them with something better and more serviceable. The notions on both sides are a bit foggy as yet, but there is much sympathy between them, and a similar tendency of ideas. I believe that the two sections will become more and more friends and colleagues in construction as time goes on. But the progressive Liberal has this great advantage. He can work out his policies without having to do lip-service to Trade-Unionist tyrannies, to the beauties of the class war, or to doctrinaire State Socialism-in none of which he believes.

In the realm of practical politics, two things must happen--both of which are likely. There must be one more General Election to disillusion Labour optimists as to the measure of their political strength, standing by themselves. But equally on our side there must be a certain change. The Liberal Party is divided between those who, if the choice be forced upon them, would vote Conservative, and those who, in the same circumstances, would vote Labour. Historically, and on grounds of past service, each section has an equal claim to call itself Liberal. Nevertheless, I think that it would be for the health of the party if all those who believe, with Mr. Winston Churchill and Sir Alfred Mond, that the coming political struggle is best described as Capitalism versus Socialism, and, thinking in these terms, mean to die in the last ditch for Capitalism, were to leave us. The brains and character of the Conservative Party have always been recruited from Liberals, and we must not grudge them the excellent material with which, in accordance with our historic mission, we are now preserving them from intellectual starvation. It is much better that the Conservative Party should be run by honest and intelligent ex-Liberals, who have grown too old and tough for us, than by Die-Hards. Possibly the Liberal Party cannot serve the State in any better way than by supplying Conservative Governments with Cabinets, and Labour Governments with ideas.

At any rate, I sympathise with Labour in rejecting the idea of co-operation with a party which included, until the other day, Mr. Churchill and Sir Alfred Mond, and still contains several of the same kidney. But this difficulty is rapidly solving itself. When it is solved, the relations between Liberalism and Labour, at Westminster and in the constituencies, will, without any compacts, bargains, or formalities, become much more nearly what some of us would like them to be.

It is right and proper that the Conservative Party should be recruited from the Liberals of the previous generation. But there is no place in the world for a Liberal Party which is merely the home of out-of-date or watery Labour men. The Liberal Party should be not less progressive than Labour, not less open to new ideas, not behindhand in constructing the new world. I do not believe that Liberalism will ever again be a great party machine in the way in which Conservatism and Labour are great party machines. But it may play, nevertheless, the predominant part in moulding the future. Great changes will not be carried out except with the active aid of Labour. But they will not be sound or enduring unless they have first satisfied the criticism and precaution of Liberals. A certain coolness of temper, such as Lord Oxford has, seems to me at the same time peculiarly Liberal in flavour, and also a much bolder and more desirable and more valuable political possession and endowment than sentimental ardours.

The political problem of mankind is to combine three things: Economic Efficiency, Social Justice, and Individual Liberty. The first needs criticism, precaution, and technical knowledge; the second, an unselfish and enthusiastic spirit which loves the ordinary man; the third, tolerance, breadth, appreciation of the excellencies of variety and independence, which prefers, above everything, to give unhindered opportunity to the exceptional and to the aspiring. The second ingredient is the best possession of the great party of the Proletariat. But the first and third require the qualities of the party which, by its traditions and ancient sympathies, has been the home of Economic Individualism and Social Liberty.

V

THE FUTURE

1. CLISSOLD (1927) MR. WELLS and his publisher having adopted an ingenious device by which his newest book 1 has been reviewed three times over, perhaps it is too much to write about it again at this late date. But, having read the reviews first and the book afterwards, I am left seriously discontented with what the professional critics have had to say. It is a weakness of modern critics not to distinguish--not to distinguish between one thing and another. Even Mr. Wells's choice of form has confused his review-ers. They fail to see what he is after. They reject the good beef which he has offered the British public, because mutton should never be underdone. Or their delicacies are sharpened against his abundance and omnivorous vitality, the broadness and coarseness of the brush with which he sweeps the great canvas which is to catch the attention of hundreds of thousands of readers and sway their minds onward.

Mr. Wells here presents, not precisely his own mind as it has developed on the basis of his personal experience and way of life, but-shifting his angle--a point of view based on an experience mainly different from his own, that of a successful, emancipated, semi-scientific, not particularly high-brow, English business man. The result is not primarily a work of art. Ideas, not forms, are its substance. It is a piece of educational writing--propaganda, if you like, an attempt to convey to the very big public attitudes of mind already partly familiar to the very small public.

The book is an omnium gatherum. I will select two emergent themes of a quasi-economic character. Apart from these, the main topic is women and some of their possible relationships in the mod-ern world to themselves and to men of the Clissold type. This is treated with great candour, sympathy, and observation. It leaves, and is meant to leave, a bitter taste.

The first of these themes is a violent protest against Conservatism, an insistent emphasis on the necessity and rapidity of change, the folly of looking backwards, the danger of inadaptability. Mr. Wells produces a curious sensation, nearly similar to that of some of his earlier romances, by contemplating vast stretches of time backwards and forwards which give an impression of slowness (no need to hurry in eternity), yet accelerating the Time Machine as he reaches present day, so that now we travel at an enormous pace and no longer have millions of years to turn round in. The Conservative influences in our life are envisaged as Dinosaurs whom literal extinction is awaiting just ahead. The contrast comes from the failure of our ideas, our conventions, our prejudices to keep up with the pace of material change. Our environment moves too much faster than we do. The walls of our travelling compartment are bumping our heads. Unless we hustle, the traffic will run us down. Conservatism is no better than suicide. Woe to our Dinosaurs!

This is one aspect. We stand still at our peril. Time flies. But there is another aspect of the same thing--and this is where Clissold comes in. What a bore for the modern man, whose mind in his active career moves with the times, to stand still in his observances and way of life! What a bore are the feasts and celebrations with which London crowns success! What a bore to go through the social contortions which have lost significance and conventional pleasures which no longer please! The contrast between the exuberant, constructive activity of a prince of modern commerce and the lack of an appropriate environment for him out of office hours is acute. Moreover, there are wide stretches in the career of moneymaking which are entirely barren and nonconstructive. There is a fine passage in the first volume about the profound, ultimate boredom of City men. Clissold's father, the company promoter and speculator, falls first into megalomania and then into fraud, because he is bored. Let us, therefore, mould with both hands the plastic material of social life into our own contemporary image.

We do not merely belong to a latter-day age --we are ourselves in the literal sense older than our ancestors were in the years of our maturity and our power. Mr. Wells brings out strongly a too-much neglected feature of modern life, that we live much longer than formerly, and, what is more important, prolong our health and vigour into a period of life which was formerly one of decay, so that the average man can now look forward to a duration of activity which hitherto only the exceptional could anticipate. I can add, indeed, a further fact which Mr. Wells overlooks (I think), likely to emphasise this yet further in the next fifty years as compared with the last fifty years; --namely, that the average age of a rapidly increasing population is much less than that of a stationary population. For example, in the stable conditions to which we may hope to approximate in the course of the next two generations, we shall somewhat rapidly approach to a position in which, in proportion to population, elderly people (say, sixty-five years of age and above) will be nearly 100 per cent, and middle-aged people (say, forty-five years of age and above), nearly 50 per cent more numerous than in the recent past. In the nineteenth century effective power was in the hands of men probably not less than fifteen years older on the average than in the sixteenth century; and before the twentieth century is out the average may have risen another fifteen years, unless effective means are found, other than obvious physical or mental decay, to make vacancies at the top. Clissold (in his sixtieth year, be it noted) sees more advantage and less disadvantage in this state of affairs than I do. Most men love money and security more, and creation and construction less, as they get older; and this process begins long before their intelligent judgement on detail is apparently impaired. Mr. Wells's preference for an adult world over a juvenile sex-ridden world may be right. But the margin between this and a middle-aged money-ridden world is a narrow one. We are threatened, at the best, with the appalling problem of the able-bodied "retired," of which Mr. Wells himself gives a sufficient example in his desperate account of the regular denizens of the Riviera.

We are living, then, in an unsatisfactory age of immensely rapid transition in which most, but particularly those in the vanguard, find themselves and their environment ill-adapted to one another, and are for this reason far less happy than their less-sophisticated forbears were or their yet more-sophisticated descendants need be. This diagnosis, applied by Mr. Wells to the case of those engaged in the practical life of action, is essentially the same as Mr. Edwin Muir's, in his deeply interesting volume of criticism, "Transition," to the case of those engaged in the life of art and contemplation. Our foremost writers, according to Mr. Muir, are uncomfortable in the world;-they can neither support nor can they oppose anything with a full confidence, with the result that their work is inferior in relation to their talents compared with work produced in happier ages,--jejune, incomplete, starved, anaemic, like their own feelings to the universe.

In short, we cannot stay where we are; we are on the move,--on the move, not necessarily either to better or to worse, but just to an equilibrium. But why not to the better? Why should not we begin to reap spiritual fruits from our material conquests? If so, whence is to come the motive power of desirable change? This brings us to Mr. Wells's second theme.

Mr. Wells describes in the first volume of Clissold his hero's disillusionment with Socialism. In the third volume he inquires if there is an alternative. From whence are we to draw the forces which are "to change the laws, customs, rules, and institutions of the world?""From what classes and types are the revolutionaries to be drawn? How are they to be brought into co-operation? What are to be their methods?" The Labour Movement is represented as an immense and dangerous force of destruction, led by sentimentalists and pseudointellectuals, who have "feelings in the place of ideas." A constructive revolution cannot possibly be contrived by these folk. The creative intellect of mankind is not to be found in these quarters but amongst the scientists and the great modern business men. Unless we can harness to the job this type of mind and character and temperament, it can never be put through--for it is a task of immense practical complexity and intellectual difficulty. We must recruit our revolutionaries, therefore, from the Right, not from the Left. We must persuade the type of man whom it now amuses to create a great business, that there lie waiting for him yet bigger things which will amuse him more. This is Clissold "Open Conspiracy." Clissold's direction is to the Left--far, far to the Left; but he seeks to summon from the Right the creative force and the constructive will which is to carry him there. He describes himself as being temperamentally and fundamentally a Liberal. But political Liberalism must die "to be born again with firmer features and a clearer will."

Clissold is expressing a reaction against the Socialist Party which very many feel, including Socialists. The remoulding of the world needs the touch of the creative Brahma. But at present Brahma is serving Science and Business, not Politics or Government. The extreme danger of the world is, in Clissold's words, lest, "before the creative Brahma can get to work, Siva, in other words the passionate destructiveness of Labour awakening to its now needless limitations and privations, may make Brahma's task impossible." We all feel this, I think. We know that we need urgently to create a milieu in which Brahma can get to work before it is too late. Up to a point, therefore, most active and constructive temperaments in every political camp are ready to join the Open Conspiracy.

What, then, is it that holds them back? It is here, I think, that Clissold is in some way deficient and apparently lacking in insight. Why do practical men find it more amusing to make money than to join the Open Conspiracy? I suggest that it is much the same reason as that which makes them find it more amusing to play bridge on Sundays than to go to church. They lack altogether the kind of motive, the possession of which, if they had it, could be expressed by saying that they had a creed. They have no creed, these potential open conspirators, no creed whatever. That is why, unless they have the luck to be scientists or artists, they fall back on the grand substitute motive, the perfect Ersatz, the anodyne for those who, in fact, want nothing at all--Money. Clissold charges the enthusiasts of Labour that they have "feelings in the place of ideas." But he does not deny that they have feelings. Has not, perhaps, poor Mr. Cook something which Clissold lacks? Clissold and his brother Dickon, the advertising expert, flutter about the world seeking for something to which they can attach their abundant libido. But they have not found it. They would so like to be Apostles. But they cannot. They remain business men.

I have taken two themes from a book which contains dozens. They are not all treated equally well. Knowing the Universities much better than Mr. Wells does, I declare that his account contains no more than the element of truth which is proper to a caricature. He under-estimates altogether their possibilities-how they may yet become temples of Brahma which even Siva will respect. But Clissold, taken altogether, is a great achievement, a huge and meaty egg from a glorious hen, an abundant outpouring of an ingenious, truthful, and generous spirit.

Though we talk about pure art as never before, this is not a good age for pure artists; nor is it a good one for classical perfections. Our most pregnant writers to-day are full of imperfections; they expose themselves to judgement; they do not look to be immortal. For these reasons, perhaps, we, their contemporaries, do them and the debt we owe them less than justice. What a debt every intelligent being owes to Bernard Shaw! What a debt also to H. G. Wells, whose mind seems to have grown up alongside his readers', so that, in successive phases, he has delighted us and guided our imaginations from boyhood to maturity.

2. ECONOMIC POSSIBILITIES FOR OUR GRANDCHILDREN (1930)

I. We are suffering just now from a bad attack of economic

pessimism. It is common to hear people say that the epoch of enormous economic progress which characterised the nineteenth century is over; that the rapid improvement in the standard of life is now going to slow down --at any rate in Great Britain; that a decline in prosperity is more likely than an improvement in the decade which lies ahead of us.

I believe that this is a wildly mistaken interpretation of what is happening to us. We are suffering, not from the rheumatics of old age, but from the growing-pains of over-rapid changes, from the painfulness of readjustment between one economic period and another. The increase of technical efficiency has been taking place faster than we can deal with the problem of labour absorption; the improvement in the standard of life has been a little too quick; the banking and monetary system of the world has been preventing the rate of interest from falling as fast as equilibrium requires. And even so, the waste and confusion which ensue relate to not more than 7½ per cent of the national income; we are muddling away one and sixpence in the £, and have only 18s. 6d., when we might, if we were more sensible, have £1; yet, nevertheless, the 18s. 6d. mounts up to as much as the £1 would have been five or six years ago. We forget that in 1929 the physical output of the industry of Great Britain was greater than ever before, and that the net surplus of our foreign balance available for new foreign investment, after paying for all our imports, was greater last year than that of any other country, being indeed 50 per cent greater than the corresponding surplus of the United States. Or again--if it is to be a matter of comparisons--suppose that we were to reduce our wages by a half, repudiate fourfifths of the national debt, and hoard our surplus wealth in barren gold instead of lending it at 6 per cent or more, we should resemble the now much-envied France. But would it be an improvement?

The prevailing world depression, the enormous anomaly of unemployment in a world full of wants, the disastrous mistakes we have made, blind us to what is going on under the surface-to the true interpretation of the trend of things. For I predict that both of the two opposed errors of pessimism which now make so much noise in the world will be proved wrong in our own time--the pessimism of the revolutionaries who think that things are so bad that nothing can save us but violent change, and the pessimism of the reactionaries who consider the balance of our economic and social life so precarious that we must risk no experiments.

My purpose in this essay, however, is not to examine the present or the near future, but to disembarrass myself of short views and take wings into the future. What can we reasonably expect the level of our economic life to be a hundred years hence? What are the economic possibilities for our grandchildren?

From the earliest times of which we have record--back, say, to two thousand years before Christ--down to the beginning of the eighteenth century, there was no very great change in the standard of life of the average man living in the civilised centres of the earth. Ups and downs certainly. Visitations of plague, famine, and war. Golden intervals. But no progressive, violent change. Some periods perhaps 50 per cent better than others--at the utmost 100 per cent better--in the four thousand years which ended (say) in A.D. 1700.

This slow rate of progress, or lack of progress, was due to two reasons--to the remarkable absence of important technical improvements and to the failure of capital to accumulate.

The absence of important technical inventions between the prehistoric age and comparatively modern times is truly remarkable. Almost everything which really matters and which the world possessed at the commencement of the modern age was already known to man at the dawn of history. Language, fire, the same domestic animals which we have to-day, wheat, barley, the vine and the olive, the plough, the wheel, the oar, the sail, leather, linen and cloth, bricks and pots, gold and silver, copper, tin, and lead--and iron was added to the list before 1000 B.C.--banking, statecraft, mathematics, astronomy, and religion. There is no record of when we first possessed these things.

At some epoch before the dawn of history-perhaps even in one of the comfortable intervals before the last ice age--there must have been an era of progress and invention comparable to that in which we live to-day. But through the greater part of recorded history there was nothing of the kind.

The modern age opened, I think, with the accumulation of capital which began in the sixteenth century. I believe--for reasons with which I must not encumber the present argument--that this was initially due to the rise of prices, and the profits to which that led, which resulted from the treasure of gold and silver which Spain brought from the New World into the Old. From that time until to-day the power of accumulation by compound interest, which seems to have been sleeping for many generations, was re-born and re-newed its strength. And the power of compound interest over two hundred years is such as to stagger the imagination.

Let me give in illustration of this a sum which I have worked out. The value of Great Britain's foreign investments to-day is estimated at about £4,000,000,000. This yields us an income at the rate of about 6½ per cent. Half of this we bring home and enjoy; the other half, namely, 3¼ per cent, we leave to accumulate abroad at compound interest. Something of this sort has now been going on for about 250 years.

For I trace the beginnings of British foreign investment to the treasure which Drake stole from Spain in 1580. In that year he returned to England bringing with him the prodigious spoils of the Golden Hind. Queen Elizabeth was a considerable share-holder in the syndicate which had financed the expedition. Out of her share she paid off the whole of England's foreign debt, balanced her Budget, and found herself with about £40,000 in hand. This she invested in the Levant Company-which prospered. Out of the profits of the Levant Company, the East India Company was founded; and the profits of this great enterprise were the foundation of England's subsequent foreign investment. Now it happens that £40,000 accumulating at 3¼ per cent compound interest approximately corresponds to the actual volume of England's foreign investments at various dates, and would actually amount to-day to the total of £4,000,000,000 which I have already quoted as being what our foreign investments now are. Thus, every £1 which Drake brought home in 1580 has now become £100,000. Such is the power of compound interest!

From the sixteenth century, with a cumulative crescendo after the eighteenth, the great age of science and technical inventions began, which since the beginning of the nineteenth century has been in full flood--coal, steam, electricity, petrol, steel, rubber, cotton, the chemical industries, automatic machinery and the methods of mass production, wireless, printing, Newton, Darwin, and Einstein, and thousands of other things and men too famous and familiar to catalogue.

What is the result? In spite of an enormous growth in the population of the world, which it has been necessary to equip with houses and machines, the average standard of life in Europe and the United States has been raised, I think, about fourfold. The growth of capital has been on a scale which is far beyond a hundredfold of

what any previous age had known. And from now on we need not
expect so great an increase of population.

If capital increases, say, 2 per cent per annum, the capital
equipment of the world will have increased by a half in twenty
years, and seven and a half times in a hundred years. Think of this
in terms of material things--houses, transport, and the like.

At the same time technical improvements in manufacture and
transport have been proceeding at a greater rate in the last ten
years than ever before in history. In the United States factory output per head was 40 per cent greater in 1925 than in 1919. In
Europe we are held back by temporary obstacles, but even so it
is safe to say that technical efficiency is increasing by more than
1 per cent per annum compound. There is evidence that the revolutionary technical changes, which have so far chiefly affected industry, may soon be attacking agriculture. We may be on the eve
of improvements in the efficiency of food production as great as
those which have already taken place in mining, manufacture, and
transport. In quite a few years--in our own lifetimes I mean--we
may be able to perform all the operations of agriculture, mining,
and manufacture with a quarter of the human effort to which we
have been accustomed.

For the moment the very rapidity of these changes is hurting
us and bringing difficult problems to solve. Those countries are suffering relatively which are not in the vanguard of progress. We are
being afflicted with a new disease of which some readers may not
yet have heard the name, but of which they will hear a great deal
in the years to come--namely, technological unemployment. This
means unemployment due to our discovery of means of economis-
ing the use of labour outrunning the pace at which we can find new
uses for labour.

But this is only a temporary phase of maladjustment. All this
means in the long run that mankind is solving its economic problem. I would predict that the standard of life in progressive countries one hundred years hence will be between four and eight times
as high as it is to-day. There would be nothing surprising in this
even in the light of our present knowledge. It would not be foolish
to contemplate the possibility of a far greater progress still.

II. Let us, for the sake of argument, suppose that a hundred
years hence we are all of us, on the average, eight times better off
in the economic sense than we are to-day. Assuredly there need be

nothing here to surprise us.

Now it is true that the needs of human beings may seem to be insatiable. But they fall into two classes--those needs which are absolute in the sense that we feel them whatever the situation of our fellow human beings may be, and those which are relative in the sense that we feel them only if their satisfaction lifts us above, makes us feel superior to, our fellows. Needs of the second class, those which satisfy the desire for superiority, may indeed be insatiable; for the higher the general level, the higher still are they. But this is not so true of the absolute needs--a point may soon be reached, much sooner perhaps than we are all of us aware of, when these needs are satisfied in the sense that we prefer to devote our further energies to non-economic purposes.

Now for my conclusion, which you will find, I think, to become more and more startling to the imagination the longer you think about it.

I draw the conclusion that, assuming no important wars and no important increase in population, the economic problem may be solved, or be at least within sight of solution, within a hundred years. This means that the economic problem is not--if we look into the future--the permanent problem of the human race.

Why, you may ask, is this so startling? It is startling because-- if, instead of looking into the future, we look into the past--we find that the economic problem, the struggle for subsistence, always has been hitherto the primary, most pressing problem of the human race--not only of the human race, but of the whole of the biological kingdom from the beginnings of life in its most primitive forms.

Thus we have been expressly evolved by nature--with all our impulses and deepest instincts--for the purpose of solving the economic problem. If the economic problem is solved, mankind will be deprived of its traditional purpose.

Will this be a benefit? If one believes at all in the real values of life, the prospect at least opens up the possibility of benefit. Yet I think with dread of the readjustment of the habits and instincts of the ordinary man, bred into him for countless generations, which he may be asked to discard within a few decades.

To use the language of to-day--must we not expect a general "nervous breakdown"? We already have a little experience of what I mean --a nervous breakdown of the sort which is already common enough in England and the United States amongst the wives of the wellto-do classes, unfortunate women, many of them, who have been deprived by their wealth of their traditional tasks and occupations--who cannot find it sufficiently amusing, when deprived of the spur of economic necessity, to cook and clean and mend, yet are quite unable to find anything more amusing.

To those who sweat for their daily bread leisure is a longed-for sweet--until they get it.

There is the traditional epitaph written for herself by the old charwoman:--

Don't mourn for me, friends, don't weep for me never, For I'm going to do nothing for ever and ever.

This was her heaven. Like others who look forward to leisure, she conceived how nice it would be to spend her time listening-in-- for there was another couplet which occurred in her poem:--

With psalms and sweet music the heavens'll be ringing, But I shall have nothing to do with the singing.

Yet it will only be for those who have to do with the singing that life will be tolerable-- and how few of us can sing!

Thus for the first time since his creation man will be faced with his real, his permanent problem--how to use his freedom from pressing economic cares, how to occupy the leisure, which science and compound interest will have won for him, to live wisely and agreeably and well.

The strenuous purposeful money-makers may carry all of us along with them into the lap of economic abundance. But it will be those peoples, who can keep alive, and cultivate into a fuller perfection, the art of life itself and do not sell themselves for the means of life, who will be able to enjoy the abundance when it comes.

Yet there is no country and no people, I think, who can look forward to the age of leisure and of abundance without a dread. For we have been trained too long to strive and not to enjoy. It is a fearful problem for the ordinary person, with no special talents, to occupy himself, especially if he no longer has roots in the soil or in custom or in the beloved conventions of a traditional society. To judge from the behaviour and the achievements of the wealthy classes to-day in any quarter of the world, the outlook is very depressing! For these are, so to speak, our advance guard--those who are spying out the promised land for the rest of us and pitching their camp there. For they have most of them failed disastrously, so it seems to me--those who have an independent income but no associations or duties or ties--to solve the problem which has been set them.

I feel sure that with a little more experience we shall use the new-found bounty of nature quite differently from the way in which the rich use it to-day, and will map out for ourselves a plan of life quite otherwise than theirs.

For many ages to come the old Adam will be so strong in us that everybody will need to do some work if he is to be contented. We shall do more things for ourselves than is usual with the rich to-day, only too glad to have small duties and tasks and routines. But beyond this, we shall endeavour to spread the bread thin on the butter--to make what work there is still to be done to be as widely shared as possible. Three-hour shifts or a fifteen-hour week may put off the problem for a great while. For three hours a day is quite enough to satisfy the old Adam in most of us!

There are changes in other spheres too which we must expect to come. When the accumulation of wealth is no longer of high social importance, there will be great changes in the code of morals. We shall be able to rid ourselves of many of the pseudo-moral principles which have hag-ridden us for two hundred years, by which we have exalted some of the most distasteful of human qualities into the position of the highest virtues. We shall be able to afford to dare to assess the money-motive at its true value. The love of money as a possession --as distinguished from the love of money as a means to the enjoyments and realities of life --will be recognised for what it is, a somewhat disgusting morbidity, one of those semicriminal, semi-pathological propensities which one hands over with a shudder to the specialists in mental disease. All kinds of social customs and economic practices, affecting the distribution of wealth and of economic rewards and penalties, which we now maintain at all costs, however distasteful and unjust they may be in themselves, because they are tremendously useful in promoting the accumulation of capital, we shall then be free, at last, to discard.

Of course there will still be many people with intense, unsatisfied purposiveness who will blindly pursue wealth--unless they can find some plausible substitute. But the rest of us will no longer be under any obligation to applaud and encourage them. For we shall inquire more curiously than is safe to-day into the true character of this "purposiveness" with which in varying degrees Nature has endowed almost all of us. For purposiveness means that we are more concerned with the remote future results of our actions than with their own quality or their immediate effects on our own environment. The "purposive" man is always trying to secure a spurious and delusive immortality for his acts by pushing his interest in them forward into time. He does not love his cat, but his cat's kittens; nor, in truth, the kittens, but only the kittens' kittens, and so on forward for ever to the end of cat-dom. For him jam is not jam unless it is a case of jam to-morrow and never jam to-day. Thus by pushing his jam always forward into the future, he strives to secure for his act of boiling it an immortality.

Let me remind you of the Professor in Sylvie and Bruno:--

"Only the tailor, sir, with your little bill," said a meek voice outside the door.

"Ah, well, I can soon settle his business," the Professor said to the children, "if you'll just wait a minute. How much is it, this year, my man?" The tailor had come in while he was speaking.

"Well, it's been a-doubling so many years, you see," the tailor replied, a little gruffly, "and I think I'd like the money now. It's two thousand pound, it is!"

"Oh, that's nothing!" the Professor carelessly remarked, feeling in his pocket, as if he always carried at least that amount about with him. "But wouldn't you like to wait just another year and make it four thousand? Just think how rich you'd be! Why, you might be a king, if you liked!"

"I don't know as I'd care about being a king," the man said thoughtfully. "But it dew sound a powerful sight o' money! Well, I think I'll wait-----"

"Of course you will!" said the Professor. "There's good sense in you, I see. Good-day to you, my man!"

"Will you ever have to pay him that four thousand pounds?" Sylvie asked as the door closed on the departing creditor.

"Never, my child!" the Professor replied emphatically. "He'll go on doubling it till he dies. You see, it's always worth while waiting another year to get twice as much money!"

Perhaps it is not an accident that the race which did most to bring the promise of immortality into the heart and essence of our religions has also done most for the principle of compound interest and particularly loves this most purposive of human institutions.

I see us free, therefore, to return to some of the most sure and certain principles of religion and traditional virtue--that avarice is a vice, that the exaction of usury is a misdemeanour, and the love of money is detestable, that those walk most truly in the paths of virtue and sane wisdom who take least thought for the morrow. We shall once more value ends above means and prefer the good to the useful. We shall honour those who can teach us how to pluck the hour and the day virtuously and well, the delightful people who are capable of taking direct enjoyment in things, the lilies of the field who toil not, neither do they spin.

But beware! The time for all this is not yet. For at least another hundred years we must pretend to ourselves and to every one that fair is foul and foul is fair; for foul is useful and fair is not. Avarice and usury and precaution must be our gods for a little longer still. For only they can lead us out of the tunnel of economic necessity into daylight.

I look forward, therefore, in days not so very remote, to the greatest change which has ever occurred in the material environment of life for human beings in the aggregate. But, of course, it will all happen gradually, not as a catastrophe. Indeed, it has already begun. The course of affairs will simply be that there will be ever larger and larger classes and groups of people from whom problems of economic necessity have been practically removed. The critical difference will be realised when this condition has become so general that the nature of one's duty to one's neighbour is changed. For it will remain reasonable to be economically purposive for others after it has ceased to be reasonable for oneself.

The pace at which we can reach our destination of economic bliss will be governed by four things--our power to control population, our determination to avoid wars and civil dissensions, our willingness to entrust to science the direction of those matters which are properly the concern of science, and the rate of accumulation as fixed by the margin between our production and our consumption; of which the last will easily look after itself, given the first three.

Meanwhile there will be no harm in making mild preparations

for our destiny, in encouraging, and experimenting in, the arts of life as well as the activities of purpose.

But, chiefly, do not let us overestimate the importance of the economic problem, or sacrifice to its supposed necessities other matters of greater and more permanent significance. It should be a matter for specialists--like dentistry. If economists could manage to get themselves thought of as humble, competent people, on a level with dentists, that would be splendid!

44232335R00117

Made in the USA
Middletown, DE
01 June 2017